The Indian
Paradox

Other Books by the Author

Party Politics in India (1957)

Politics of Scarcity: Public Pressure and Political Responses in India (1962)

Political Change in South Asia (1963)

Indian Voting Behavior (editor, with Rajni Kothari, 1965)

Political Parties and Political Development (editor, with Joseph LaPalombara, 1966)

Modernization: The Dynamics of Growth (editor, 1966)

Party Building in a New Nation: The Indian National Congress (1967)

State Politics in India (editor, 1968)

Electoral Politics in the Indian States (co-editor, with John O. Field, 1974–1977)

India at the Polls—The Parliamentary Elections of 1977 (1978)

Sons of the Soil: Migration and Ethnic Conflict in India (1978)

India's Preferential Policies: Migrants, The Middle Classes and Ethnic Equality (with Mary F. Katzenstein, 1981)

India at the Polls, 1980: A Study of the Parliamentary Elections (1983)

The State, Religion and Ethnic Politics: Afghanistan, Iran and Pakistan (co-editor, with Ali Banuazizi, 1986)

Competitive Elections in Developing Countries (co-editor, with Ergun Ozbudun, 1987)

Understanding Political Development (co-editor, with Samuel P. Huntington, 1987)

The Indian Paradox

ESSAYS IN INDIAN POLITICS

WITHDRAWN

Myron Weiner

Edited by Ashutosh Varshney

SAGE PUBLICATIONS
New Delhi/Newbury Park/London

Burgess
DS
480.84
.W39
1989
C-4

Copyright © Myron Weiner, 1989

All rights reserved. No part of this book may be reproduced or utilised in any form or by any means, electronic or mechanical, including photocopying, recording or by any information storage or retrieval system, without permission in writing from the publisher.

First published in 1989 by

Sage Publications India Pvt Ltd
M 32 Greater Kailash Market I
New Delhi 110 048

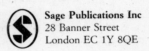

Sage Publications Ltd
2111 West Hillcrest Drive
Newbury Park, California 91320

Sage Publications Inc
28 Banner Street
London EC 1Y 8QE

Published by Tejeshwar Singh for Sage Publications India Pvt Ltd, phototypeset by Aurelec Data Processing Systems and printed at Chaman Offset Printers.

Library of Congress Cataloging-in-Publication Data

Weiner, Myron.
    The Indian paradox: essays in Indian politics / Myron Weiner.
    p. cm.
    includes index.
    1. India—Politics and government—1947– I. Title.

DS480.84.W39   1989   320.954—dc 19   89–4270

ISBN 0–8039–9601–2 (US-hbk.)   81–7036–143–5 (India-hbk.)
      0–8039–9602–0 (US–pbk.)   81–7036–144–3 (India-pbk.)

Contents

9/02/13
cig

IV. STALEMATES, CRISES AND ATTEMPTED REFORMS ·

List of Tables

Preface

The Indian paradox is not the familiar apparent contradiction between India's poverty and India's democracy, but the far more puzzling contradiction between India's high level of political violence and its success at sustaining a democratic political system. How does India sustain competitive elections, changes in government through the ballot-box, a free press and freedom of assembly when the country appears to be torn by conflicts among linguistic, caste and religious communities? Other paradoxes abound in India—such as its apparent process of monarchical succession in a democratic system—and these are also reflected in many of the papers that appear in this volume. These essays, mostly written between 1971 and 1987, record the tumultuous political developments which followed the Nehru era. This period was characterized by four successive political triumphs, in each instance followed by political breakdowns, policy paralysis or loss of popular support:

1. After the Congress party split Mrs. Gandhi had triumphant electoral victories in 1971 and 1972, followed by three years of unstable state governments and growing dissent within the Congress party, culminating in her decision to declare an Emergency.
2. Democracy was restored in the elections of 1977, followed by ruinous factional infighting, the fall of the Janata government and an ignominious electoral defeat.
3. Mrs. Gandhi returned to power in the elections of 1980 with the promise of 'a government that works,' but her government was beseiged by Sikh militants, the armed forces were sent into the Golden Temple and a bloody conflict ensued, and four years after her victory she was dead at the hands of assassins.

4. Finally, Rajiv Gandhi, after winning by the largest electoral margin ever, promised to move India into the twenty-first century with a more competitive economy, a reformed party, better neighborly foreign relations, and a conciliatory policy toward ethnic minorities. Within two years he was beset by one political and policy failure after another.

Beyond providing a running commentary on these events—and the cycle of elation and disillusionment that they have meant for many Indians—the essays in this volume analyze the major issues and trends in Indian politics. The papers are arranged around four themes: how linguistic, religious, caste, and tribal conflicts are managed within India's political institutions; the political controversies over agricultural, industrial and preferential policies; electoral politics from 1971 to the early eighties; and, finally, the metamorphosis of the Congress party under Indira Gandhi and its consequences for governance under Rajiv Gandhi.

I am greatly indebted to Ashutosh Varshney, presently a doctoral candidate in the Department of Political Science at the Massachusetts Institute of Technology, whose editorial efforts have made this book more coherent than it might otherwise have been. He helped me to choose and arrange the papers, edited them to eliminate repetition, dropped out material that diverted from the main arguments, corrected errors, and updated some of the references. I should also like to extend my appreciation to Bashiruddin Ahmed, of the Centre for the Study of Developing Societies, New Delhi, whose thoughtful suggestions for revising an earlier version of this manuscript were exceedingly helpful.

The central theme of the first group of essays is the interplay between the violent struggles among India's linguistic, religious, caste, and tribal communities, and India's political institutions. Here I argue that Indian politics is about both the politics of group identity and the politics of resource allocation. In the politics of group identity, individuals are concerned with the status and honor of and the threats to the group to which they belong. Issues of personal and group loyalty, the emotional ties between leaders and their followers, and the political symbolism of language are central elements in the politics of group identity. In the politics of resource allocation, economic concepts tend to dominate discussions, and the central issues are who gets the economic gains and who loses. Intellectuals often regard the politics of group identity as the politics of the past and the struggle over resources as the politics of the future. They see the politics of group identity as destructive, the politics of resource allocation as potentially trans-formative. They are less concerned with how to resolve the conflicts that arise out of struggles among linguistic, religious, caste, and tribal groups than with persuading those who identify with these communi-ties to turn their attention to the more 'secular' politics of class and to the rationalism implied by conflicts over the allocations of resources and the debates over economic policies.

Ethnic politics is as much a part of modern politics as class-based politics. Chapters 1 and 2 examine some of the determinants of ethnic politics, focusing in particular on the ways in which both policies and politics influence group identities. Paradoxically, government policies intended to ameliorate conflicts among groups and to improve their incomes or status may subsequently intensify group identities and conflicts. By examining these and other factors the essays attempt to explain why India's most violent and politically destructive movement arose not among the impoverished, landless, uneducated, and mis-treated lower castes and classes but among the Sikhs, one of the most prosperous and politically successful communities in the country. In the first several essays I have also tried to explain why Indian democ-racy has thrived in spite of these ethnic conflicts and why conflict-management has become more difficult with the decline of the Cong-ress party organization and the weakening of the federal structure.

The interrelationship of ideas and interests in shaping agricultural, industrial, and preferential policies is a central theme of the section on public policies. Chapter 4 examines the debate in India over whether market-oriented agricultural policies ultimately worsen or improve rural well-being. Chapter 5 explores the debate over whether the deceleration of India's industrial growth during Prime Minister Indira Gandhi's tenure was the result of a decline in public investment or a decline in the efficient use of resources. Behind these policy debates— and largely determining their outcome—lie coalitions of interests: politicians seeking the electoral support of land-owning farmer-culti-vators who preferred remunerative agriculture prices and individual land rights to some form of collectivization and low agricultural prices; and socialist-oriented political leaders with support from sections of the middle class, portions of the business community, and, most importantly, the state bureaucracy who shaped industrial policies. Chapter 6 examines the debate in India (and elsewhere) over whether equality can be achieved through a system of reservations for groups. Again, the policies need to be understood as the result of a combination of ideas (based in part on grafting the conception of equality among *individuals* upon Hindu notions which confer rights and punishments upon *communities* and which devalue competition among individuals as destructive of a social order based upon prescribed norms of conduct for ranked social groups) and interests (those who benefit from reservations). A central theme of this section, particularly with regard to industrial and preferential policies, is that what gives force to the prevailing ideas underlying existing policies are the interests that have been created by these policies.

The third section begins with an analysis of Mrs Gandhi's overwhelming electoral victory in 1971 following the split within her party. It came as a surprise when an Indian Prime Minister, in the fashion of many third world leaders, declared a national Emergency, suspended elections, political parties and freedom of press and assembly, and strengthened paramilitary, police, and intelligence organizations. But even more surprising was that unlike other third world leaders, India's Prime Minister subsequently restored the democratic system, called national elections, and allowed herself to be ousted by an angry electorate. The section on electoral politics traces these developments, focusing on the shifting mood of India's electorate, and examines the consequences for India's party system. Chapter 7 places the electoral process in an historical context. It deals with the determinants of political participation, the social bases of voter alignments, and the emergence of two party systems—one organized around regional and ethnic identities which dominate politics in most of the states, and the other oriented toward national politics.

The transformation of national politics under Indira Gandhi and the efforts of Rajiv Gandhi to undo many of the changes she introduced is the theme of the next two essays. The split in the Congress party in 1969, its subsequent changes under Mrs. Gandhi, and her electoral victories in 1971 and 1972 were followed by a period when the government was neither able to move the economy toward greater equality nor toward growth, while state governments grew increasingly unstable and dependent upon the center. Chapter 10 describes these political changes in the mid-seventies, when it became apparent that the more centralized the governing party became, the more the federal system eroded. Mrs Gandhi demonstrated that a centralized party and an effective federal system are institutionally incompatible. With the decline in India's democratic institutions, the declaration of an emergency, and the poor performance of the economy, Indian modernization in the seventies was stalemated.

Chapter 11 focuses on the efforts at reform initiated by Rajiv Gandhi. The tension that had developed in India between an open society and polity on the one hand and a closed economy on the other was the target of the young Prime Minister. His promise to liberalize imports, de-regulate business, facilitate the development of technology, accelerate industrial growth and, in general, to make the economy more efficient and internationally more competitive excited the imagination of much of the urban middle class. This essay describes Rajiv Gandhi's efforts at 'liberalization'—the Indian equivalent of Gorbachev's *perestroika* or 'restructuring' and Deng Xiaoping's 'four modernizations'. As different as these three countries and their policy reforms are from one another, the leaders of these countries share a concern for what they regard as the restrictive and inefficient character of their economies that result from excessive reliance upon bureaucratic rather than market decisions. In each instance too the constraints upon the leadership are the result of the manner in which previous policies created institutions and interests that gained from the restrictive regime and regarded the new policies as threatening. To bring about change it takes a determined leadership that is capable both of articulating new approaches and of forging a coalition of reformers and of those who will gain from the new policies. By the middle of Rajiv Gandhi's term in office it was clear that that kind of leadership had not emerged and that the margin for innovation had narrowed. Alas, this is the story of a lost opportunity.

The monarchical character of the Indian democratic system—another one of those paradoxes—was revealed not only by the succession process but by the leadership style of both Indira Gandhi and Rajiv Gandhi: the imperial manner associated with the occupancy of a throne or *gaddi* as Indians say, the *durbar*-like audiences, 'to receive Petitions and Presents, to give commands, to see and be seen' as Sir Thomas Roe wrote in the seventeenth century, and, according to several reports, the reluctance of cabinet members and secretaries even to privately take issue with decisions made by the Prime Minister. (On this, as in so many other matters of governance, the contrast with Nehru is striking.) Rajiv Gandhi's experience as Prime Minister also reminds us that in India winning elections (often by an overwhelming margin) has never been as difficult as governing the country and carrying out reforms. Once again, decision-making is narrowly based and authority is simultaneously concentrated and weak.

We conclude in chapter 12 by returning to a central theme of the book—empirical democratic theory and its relevance for India. The durability of India's democratic institutions, in spite of the vast income disparities, the ethnic divisions, the slow economic growth, the hierarchical social order, and the disaffection of many of the intellectuals, leads one to question many of the theories about the conditions for democracy. What has strengthened democratic institutions and what is the potential threat to these institutions is the subject of this concluding essay.

As we write in early 1989, the possibility of a strong opposition and perhaps even an alternative government to the Congress and to Rajiv Gandhi has begun to emerge. Unlike earlier efforts to build an opposition movement, the new one rests on leaders who have a strong political base within several states. But other than a shared interest in winning national power, ending the domination of the Nehru/Gandhi family, and perhaps transferring greater resources from the center to the states, it remains unclear as to what kind of agenda would inform an alternative government and whether it is capable of pursuing the kind of economic liberalization initiated by Rajiv Gandhi. The great danger for India remains deadlock—not disintegration—when neither the government nor the opposition parties can create a coalition for effective governance capable of making and carrying out economic and social reforms.

Cambridge, Massachusetts   MYRON WEINER
March 1989

Editor's Preface

The complexity of Indian politics never ceases to fascinate its students. A democratic system functioning in conditions viewed as inhospitable by existing theories of democracy, ever newer political identities emerging alongside some deeply enduring ones, a vast pool of intellectual expertise in the country co-existing with a political system that after its first round of social, political and economic engineering under Nehru has shown considerable resistance to new ideas, except in the agricultural sector—the list can be made more comprehensive but the basic point is an obvious one. Understanding Indian politics is an endless intellectual challenge. So when Professor Myron Weiner invited me to edit his papers and essays on Indian politics for this book, I viewed the invitation as a two-fold opportunity. First, it gave me a chance to look at Indian politics through the lenses of my teacher who, by emphasizing how some of the basic puzzles of Indian politics cannot be solved except in a *comparative* framework, has often led me to discover elements that I did not know about the politics of my own country, and whose insistence on empirically sound theorization has been a constant source of stimulation. Second, the invitation also gave me considerable discretion in selecting papers from a vast corpus of scholarship produced over two decades, presenting it to a larger body of readers in a manner that captures some of the salient features of Indian polities. The result is a grouping of Professor Weiner's work in four categories.

Section one, dealing with the maintenance of India's democratic system amid conflicts that shook democracies elsewhere in the third world, exemplifies the utility of the comparative method. The existing explanation of the theoretically counter-intuitive persistence of democracy in India was cultural. Recognizing the intellectual puzzle,

Rajni Kothari in his classic *Politics in India* argued that the cultural pluralism and tolerance of Hinduism supported the political pluralism of democracy. Weiner develops a new political explanation, and it is interesting to see how his argument proceeds. Looking comparatively at the third world democracies, he first unearths an intuitively simple but hitherto undiscovered correlation: that democracy in the third world has mostly survived in the former British colonies, not in the Dutch, French, Spanish and Portuguese ex-colonies. Considerable experience with democratic institutions *before* independence, thus, constitutes the first step of the analysis. Another comparative puzzle emerges, however. Most third world democracies were British colonies but not all British colonies stayed democratic. Consider India and Pakistan. This leads to a second step in the explanation—the presence of an institution like the Congress party in India and its absence in Pakistan, and the remarkable skills of political leadership in independent India. The integrative role of the Congress party is long gone, however. Moreover, social conflict has been particularly virulent in the last decade and a half. Why did the democratic system not come apart? A third level of explanation emerges: (a) some abiding peculiarities of India's social structure localize conflict instead of generalizing it, and (b) the existence of a federal system divides up movements between those directed against the state government and those aimed at the central government. An accumulated expression of conflict, potentially insurmountable, is thus precluded by the institutional features of Indian polity and society. As Indians, we are concerned about the deteriorating health of Indian democracy, as indeed we should be. However, looking comparatively, as Weiner does, what is striking is our success in maintaining our democracy. A comparative analysis also leads to some possible solutions for the present political malaise. A revitalized party system appears to be a necessary corrective.

Section two concentrates on the interplay of ideas and interests in the origin and evolution of government policies. Public policy remains a widely understudied field in Indian politics and, partly because of the scholarly preoccupation with the theory of the state in India, even the importance of studying public policy is not often recognized. What for a Marxist would be problems in the theory of the state become in the hands of a liberal puzzles of public policy. The results are revealing. Agricultural and industrial policies are viewed as reflecting different combinations of ideas and interests, not as simply expressing the interests of the same dominant class-coalition. Nehru's death led to a serious restructuring of agricultural policy based on producer *incentives* and new technology instead of land reforms and cooperatives but the industrial policy moved towards further state *control* (partially reversed after Mrs. Gandhi's death). It is not clear how a general theory about the nature of the Indian state, constructed on the lines of Nicos Poulantzas' *Political Power and Social Classes* that influenced a decade of scholarship in India, can even begin to tackle such deep ambivalences in the constitutive principles of economic policy—industrial policy governed by controls and agricultural policy by incentives. Also, with a disaggregation of state policies and their study over time, one can start appreciating how policies are often born in the ideas of state leaders, not in the interests of classes or groups, though the evolution of a policy so born may later get terribly inter-meshed with vested interests. The continuation of Nehru's industrial policy long after it lost its basic utility is attributed by Weiner not to the power of the dominant classes that severely circumscribed the maneouvres of the Indian state but to a lack of re-thinking on policy alternatives by the political leadership. One may support this argument by simply looking at the recurrent features of political behavior in India between 1971 and 1984: instead of debates on how to restructure government policies under changed circumstances, the political agenda was dominated by the numerous acts of toppling state governments, the making and unmaking of Congress party functionaries, dynastic impulses of the political leadership and so on.

Section three provides a commentary on three elections—1971, 1977 and 1980—and a fourth essay presents an overview of electoral politics since independence. The last section of the book documents and analyzes the decay of the Congress party. An institution that performed an integrative role in a vast, diverse and continent-sized polity, and thus steered the democratic process, lay in a shambles by the mid-seventies as Mrs. Gandhi, in an attempt to consolidate her political hold, suspended the electoral principle *inside* the party and centralized its functioning. Myron Weiner was the first scholar to present a systematic empirical investigation of the functioning of the Congress party in the mid-1960s. In the last two essays of the book, he briefly chronicles how today's Congress is a far cry from its resplendent past, and traces the implications of its decay.

In arranging and editing these essays, I have largely kept the original form in which they were published. The main body of editing concerned choosing papers around the organizing themes, clipping duplications and calling Professor Weiner's attention to issues that arose in the light of recent events or scholarship. Instead of letting the book become a collection of discrete essays, my attempt was to turn these essays into a book. It has certainly been a pleasure to go through two decades of Professor Weiner's work. I hope the readers find the book rewarding, too. These essays combine years of acute empirical observation and research with valuable theoretical insights.

Cambridge, Massachusetts ASHUTOSH VARSHNEY
March 1989

I. Nation Building and Political Institutions

1

The Indian Paradox:
Violent Social Conflict and
Democratic Politics

India's Exceptionalism

India is one of a handful of post-colonial countries that could be regarded as having a stable democratic regime. The list is very small and one could quarrel with the inclusion of several of the countries on it: Malaysia, Sri Lanka, Jamaica, Trinidad/Tobago, Papua New Guinea, and a variety of mini-states: Bahama Islands, Barbados, Botswana, Gambia, Mauritius, and Surinam. In the main, post-colonial regimes have been one-party states, military-bureaucratic dictatorships, communist, or personalized autocracies. Though the forms vary, the new regimes typically restrict opposition parties, limit freedom of assembly and freedom of the press, do not permit competitive elections, restrain the judiciary from performing an independent role, and limit the freedoms of their citizens in a variety of ways—to speak out, to travel abroad, to criticize the regime, and to change the government peacefully. In most post-colonial regimes, political participation is restricted and leaders are not held accountable; and, in the worst cases, governments are tyrannical.

India, along with a handful of smaller countries, is a notable exception. It has held eight genuinely competitive parliamentary elections. The governing Congress party has been openly opposed in each of

This paper was presented at the International Colloquium on 'Democracy and Modernity' on the occasion of David Ben Gurion's hundredth birthday, January 4–6, 1987, Jerusalem.

these, and even lost one, in 1977. While the non-Congress parties, with the one exception, have not won national elections, they have often won control of state governments. Today, the Communist party governs West Bengal and Kerala. The Janata party governs Karnataka, and various regional parties control Andhra Pradesh, Tamil Nadu, Sikkim, Haryana and Assam. The press is free and is often critical of the government. The judiciary, though sometimes compliant, has nonetheless taken positions that have constrained both central and state governments. And, most importantly, there is freedom against arbitrary arrest; critics have no fear that they will be picked up by the police for speaking out against the government.

The record is not an unblemished one. India did experience a period of emergency from 1975 to 1977 when democratic rights were suspended, opposition leaders were jailed, the press was censored, and there were no elections. But the Prime Minister chose to end the Emergency in 1977. Elections were held and, in what proved to be an historic occasion, the electorate overthrew Mrs. Gandhi's government in a dramatic demonstration that a largely rural, illiterate population was capable of rejecting a party that it held responsible for acts committed during a period of authoritarian rule.

What is particularly baffling about India's democratic exceptionalism is that for the past forty years the country has been torn by violent social conflict. The country was born in bloodshed: Hindus, Muslims, and Sikhs engaged in brutal killings in 1947, a war not of states but of peoples against one another. In the mid-1950s violent conflicts erupted in several states as a number of linguistic groups demanded states of their own. Though these were not secessionist demands, the call for linguistic states disrupted many state governments and led to conflicts between highly mobilized groups and the central government. The central government responded by redrawing the map of India so that each major linguistic community could have its own state within the federal system. Two border areas, India's northeast and northwest, were excluded from the reorganization, and these two regions soon became the site of political turbulence and violence. Once again the central government interceded, and the states of Punjab and Haryana were formed in the northwest, and Meghalaya, Mizoram, Nagaland and Arunachal Pradesh were formed in the northeast.

Conflicts among religious, caste, tribal, and linguistic communities have shown no signs of abating. In the last half dozen years India has been hit hard by ethnic and religious conflicts: Sikh terrorism in the Punjab and elsewhere in northern India, culminating in the assassination of Prime Minister Indira Gandhi by two Sikh bodyguards; subsequent Hindu pogroms against Sikhs in New Delhi; and, earlier, the Assamese-Bengali carnage, Hindu-Muslim rioting in Moradabad, Meerut, Baroda, Bombay and Hyderabad; the massacre of scheduled caste agricultural laborers by local landlords in Belchi, Bihar; and conflicts between backward and forward castes in Gujarat and Andhra Pradesh.

And yet India's democratic political system continues to function. The central government—the assassination of the Prime Minister notwithstanding—has remained stable. The military shows no sign of assuming political command. Elections have been held with regularity, often even in disturbed areas. What is particularly remarkable is that violence in India has not led to a breakdown of the economic order. In the midst of the violence in Punjab, Assam and elsewhere, peasants continued to plant their crops. Unlike Africa, where a breakdown in political order resulted in famines, in India not a single famine can be attributed to political disorder. Indeed, until fairly recently, the Punjab continued to attract industrial as well as agricultural investment, and its growth rate has been among the highest in India.

Whatever may happen in the future, these questions remain: how does one explain why India's democratic institutional structure persists, and how does one explain the paradox of a democratic system continuing to function in the midst of sharp social cleavages and large-scale violence?

In this and in the subsequent chapter, we shall examine some of the major social cleavages in India, focusing on the ethnic and religious conflicts that have been so destructive of civil order. We shall consider some of the major theoretical explanations for ethnic conflict, the forces that exacerbate these conflicts, and the mechanisms that have existed in India for their management. Elsewhere in this volume we shall re-examine empirical democratic theories to suggest why they are not relevant for India[1] but why, nonetheless, India's democratic institutions have been sustained.

[1] For a discussion on the relevance of these democratic theories to other developing countries, see my 'Empirical Democratic Theory,' in Ergun Ozbudun and Myron Weiner, eds., *Competitive Elections in Developing Countries*, Durham, N.C., Duke University Press, 1987.

Explaining Ethnic and Religious Conflicts

Both the standard Marxist and liberal views of ethnic conflict are inadequate. Marxists have long viewed class consciousness as the 'real consciousness' reflecting the true interests of a collectivity. Despite some reservations, Marxists have continued to view political attachments to language, caste, tribe and religion as forms of 'false consciousness' which will (or should) disappear over time. The capitalist mode of production, it is argued, will lead to the emergence of modern class loyalties, to be eventually superseded by socialism. Andre Beteille, a distinguished Indian sociologist, provides an exposition of the Marxist view:

> The study of class and class conflict is rooted in a sociology of interests of which Marx, more than anybody else, laid the foundation. Marx himself saw not only the conflict of classes but the division of labour itself as being rooted in the structure of interests .... The important step in the study of interests is to go beyond the individual and to see how interests are socially structured .... Interests have a dual role: they unite people into a class and they divide one class from another although this division may be masked by an ideology ... Those who work on the land have similar interests whether they speak Bengali or Santali, or practise Hinduism or Animism.[2]

Thus, to Marxists, it is these common class interests that ultimately bind the proletariat and the peasantry against all forms of oppression by landlords, capitalists, imperialists, clergy, and the state itself. There has been dissatisfaction with this view in some Marxist circles of late,[3]

[2] Andre Beteille, *Six Essays in Comparative Sociology*, Delhi, Oxford University Press, 1974, selections from pp. 103–105.

[3] See, for example, a recent critique by a major Marxist theorist Jon Elster, 'Three Challenges to Class,' in John Roemer, *Analytical Marxism*, Cambridge, Cambridge University Press, 1986. About ethnic and religious conflicts, Elster writes:

> A look at the contemporary world shows that social conflict is far from always about class, in a direct sense. Religious feelings are the mainsprings of struggle in the Middle East, Northern Ireland or Sri Lanka. Racial conflicts shape social life in South Africa and the US. Linguistic differences mobilise the masses in Belgium or Canada. Nationalistic sentiments remain as potent as ever in most of the world. These feelings of cultural identity give rise to non-class collective actors on a vast

but it continues to be the dominant view. At best, ethnic interests, if not an epiphenomenon of class interests, are viewed as *rooted* in the class 'realities.' On their own, they are not 'real.'

There is a version of this view that is widely held by non-Marxist secular liberals. It is the view that the process of modernization, including the expansion of education, the growth of urban centers, the impact of science and technology, and the emergence of industry, will reduce mankind's tribal loyalties, create secular attitudes, and generate more rational materialist and market-oriented behavior. One distinguished American sociologist, Alex Inkeles, argues that what is emerging is a 'modern' modal personality—individuals who are secular in their outlook and nationalist in their identity.[4] Secular liberals share with the Marxists the view that the transformation of the market results in a transformation of identities and attitudes. Where they differ is in their prediction of the outcome: to one the outcome is a new form of class identities; to the other it is a new set of modern attitudes.

Neither the Marxist nor the secular liberal/modernization perspectives

---

scale, and create a serious problem indeed for the Marxist theory of class. Frank Parkin (*Marxism and Class Theory*, London, Tavistock, 1979) argues that 'it becomes increasingly less possible to operate with models of class based predominantly on categories drawn from the division of labor, property ownership, or the productive system, when the political character of collective action is conditioned by the social and cultural make-up of the groups involved.' Is there a plausible Marxist response to this challenge? (p. 159)

'A first line of reply,' Elster continues, 'could be that cultural divisions are never class-neutral . . . . Hence behind the war between Protestants and Catholics, French and Flemish or whites and blacks, there is class conflict between the propertied and the unpropertied. The correlation is not perfect but sufficiently robust to justify the macrosociological view that collective action tends to form around economically defined classes.' Elster then examines this defense:

This response is manifestly implausible. For one thing, there are cases where culture and class are randomly related . . . . For another thing, the response *fails to provide any sense in which class is more basic than culture*, i.e., it fails to provide a mechanism whereby the former generates or otherwise explains the latter. In the absence of such a mechanism, one could equally well turn the argument around and say that class is the imperfect expression of the more fundamental cultural conflicts. (pp. 159–160, emphasis mine.)

[4] The views of Inkeles are available in two co-authored works: Alex Inkeles and David Smith, *Becoming Modern: Individual Change in Six Developing Countries*, Cambridge, Mass., Harvard University Press, 1974, and Inkeles, Smith et al., *Exploring Individual Modernity*, New York, Columbia University Press, 1983.

fit Indian reality. India's most prosperous high growth state is the Punjab. It is the center for the new market-oriented Green Revolution; it has experienced a respectable rate of industrial growth; it has become rapidly urbanized; and educational levels there are among the highest in India. But what has emerged politically is neither class politics nor secular identities. Instead, it is the center of the most powerful fundamentalist and ethnically parochial movement in post-Independence India. Indeed, educated Indians of all political persuasions have found it hard to understand or sympathize with the claims of militant Sikhs for an independent Khalistan, precisely because the demand comes not from an underprivileged and persecuted community but from a prosperous community that has been part of India's political center—as members of the military, the bureaucracy, the modern professions, the business community, and the national political elite.

For those Sikhs who support the cause of an independent Khalistan—and it should be noted that the militants form a minority of the Sikh population—the issue is primarily one of the survival of the community as a distinct cultural identity. Sikh militants, devotees of the traditional Sikh notion of religious piety which combines religious devotion and martial valor, believe that the Sikh religious identity can best be sustained through the exercise of state authority.

It would be equally difficult to explain the other major religious and ethnic conflicts in India either by Marxist or liberal/modernization theories. Briefly consider some of the other recent conflicts in India:

1. In the northeastern state of Assam the local population has reacted vehemently to the growing illegal migration from neighboring Bangladesh.[5] Over the past century, the Assamese-speaking people of the state, now numbering approximately ten million, have been concerned with the influx of Bengali-speaking people, both from what is now Bangladesh (which before 1947 was part of a united India) and from the Indian state of West Bengal. At first the Assamese were concerned over the influx of Bengali-speaking Hindus who moved into the professions and white-collar service jobs. Subsequently the Assamese became alarmed at the immigration of Bengali-speaking Muslim agriculturalists

[5] For a longer discussion, see my 'Political Demography of Assam's Anti-Immigrant Movement,' *Population and Development Review*, June 1983 and my *Sons of the Soil: Migration and Ethnic Conflict in India*, Princeton, NJ, Princeton University Press, 1978.

who occupied land. Much of the concern of the Assamese was economic: outsiders were getting the better jobs in the professions, in the government, and on the land. But beyond that was their concern that Assam itself might be overwhelmed by the Bengalis, that the Bengalis would impose their culture upon the Assamese, and that ultimately the Bengalis would take political control over the state. These concerns became particularly acute in the late 1970s when there was a large increase in the number of people on the electoral rolls. Fearful that Bengalis were now in a position to determine the outcome of the elections, young, urban, educated Assamese organized a campaign to prevent the elections from being held. They demanded that the names of illegal migrants be removed from the electoral registers; they insisted that the central government take steps to seal the borders, prevent a further migration flow, and remove illegal migrants who had entered after 1961. When the central government refused to grant these demands, large-scale violence erupted in the state. The army was sent in to maintain order, and the state was placed under central government control. In 1985 a political settlement between the Assamese and the central government was signed, elections were held, and the regional party that had opposed the central government took control of the state.

2. In the state of Andhra Pradesh, a major conflict emerged in 1986 when the state government controlled by a regional party extended 'reservations' to the backward castes. The Chief Minister, N.T. Rama Rao, a colorful former film actor whose saffron robes and turban have earned him epithets from the educated middle classes but considerable popularity among the peasantry and urban lower classes, sought to win support from the backward castes by announcing that they would be entitled to 44 percent of college admissions and jobs in the state government. These reservations, or quotas, were to be added to the 15 percent currently reserved for scheduled castes, 6 percent for scheduled tribes, and 6 percent for special groups like the handicapped—for a total of 71 percent. The Chief Minister won approval from the backward castes but the upper caste dominated student organizations launched an agitation against the state government. The students demanded that reservations for the backward castes be limited to the 25 percent previously awarded by the state government. The Chief Minister finally

gave in, largely because he was forced to do so by the courts. Thereafter, the backward caste associations launched a statewide protest, setting buses on fire, demonstrating, and clashing with the forward castes and with the police. What was at issue was whether the state should ensure to all economically and socially subordinate groups a position in the modern sector proportionate to their numerical place in society, especially in higher education and in state employment.

3. Another recent example of social conflict arose in 1986 between Hindus and Muslims over the role of the state in regulating the personal law of religious communities. An elder Muslim woman by the name of Shahbano, divorced and left penniless by her husband, filed a case in court demanding alimony. She won the case under a provision of the civil code that provides that a divorced woman must be supported by her husband. Muslim priests informed Shahbano that she had violated Shariat which provides that it is her family, not her former husband, who is financially accountable. The Muslim community was in an uproar, demanding that the civil code be amended so as to enable Muslims to follow Shariat with respect to marriage, divorce, and other personal matters. The Prime Minister, concerned with losing Muslim support, agreed, and a bill was introduced and subsequently passed by parliament. However, there was considerable anguish from the secular middle class, from Hindus, and from the women's movement, which regarded the Prime Minister's move as a concession to Muslim communalism and a break from secularism. What has been and continues to be at issue is whether the same personal law should be equally applicable to all citizens or whether each community is entitled to follow its own religious code, determined not by a legislative body but the interpretation of religious scholars and priests.

The list is by no means complete, but it suggests the variety of ethnic and religious conflicts and the difficulty of explaining all or indeed any of them within the Marxist and liberal/modernization paradigm.

An alternative explanation for these conflicts is that they are simply the consequences of India's heterogeneous social structure. India is, after all, more than a country; it is a civilization divided by many languages and cultures, the home of two major world religions, numerous tribes and a complex hierarchical caste system. In such a heterogeneous society, isn't it inevitable that people organize themselves politically around the communities into which they are born? From this perspective, political cleavages simply reflect social structural differences.

The British colonial rulers explained conflict in this manner. Indeed, one of the arguments for colonial rule was that such a divided society could only be ruled by a strong authority with a national system of administration, an effective police and army, equipped with legal powers to maintain order. For India to remain orderly and united, according to this viewpoint, India requires a strong leader and effective institutions of state authority. Even John Stuart Mill doubted that democracy was possible in a country so sharply divided.[6]

While there is a kernel of truth to this position, it leaves many fundamental questions unanswered. Why, for example, did the Sikhs produce a secessionist movement when they were, and continue to be, part of the central establishment? Why have Hindu-Muslim conflicts grown in the last few years? Why have the Assamese turned against Bengalis, though migration has persisted for decades? Why are the backward castes now pressing for an increase in reservations? And why did these problems become more acute under Mrs. Gandhi, who was widely regarded as a strong leader? In short, that India is an intrinsically divided society is an explanation that does not explain the timing: why now and not earlier, and why have ethnic conflicts become more violent?

Moreover, this explanation appears particularly weak in the light of developments in neighboring Pakistan. There, a militarily-dominated central government proved incapable of holding the country together in 1970–71. How can one argue then that the severity of conflict in India is largely the consequence of the central authority's failure to impose order on an ethnically and religiously divided society?

There is a third explanation to the growth of ethnic and religious conflict in India, one with two parts. One part is that the process of modernization intensifies rather than reduces ethnic attachments. Urbanization, mass communication, the spread of education, and growing social mobility serve to increase political awareness and to heighten identification with the religious, linguistic, caste, and tribal communities to which individuals belong. Precisely because these are forces for cultural homogenization, communities often respond by resisting assimilation and secularization. But this can only be a partial explanation. The other part is that the manner in which people

---

[6] Mill's statement of this view is available in his classic *Representative Government*.

choose to identify themselves is often politically determined by what governments and politicians do. Identities in India are fluid. Each Indian has a religion, a language, generally a caste, and a class and occupation, but politics often influences which identity becomes salient. In the 1940s, for example, the people of East Bengal declared themselves politically as Muslims and supported the creation of the Muslim majority state of Pakistan. In the 1950s, when they became part of a Pakistan whose government pressed for greater centralization, the people of East Pakistan declared themselves Bengalis and demanded political autonomy. And by the late 1960s and certainly by the 1970s, the same people were calling themselves Bangladeshis.

In India a variety of political forces have shaped the political form that identities have taken. The process of identity formation is a complex one with several key elements. One element is the *institutional structure* which shapes the framework within which group identities are maintained and intensified. The federal system, the structure of political parties, the educational system, and the media serve to reinforce some identities while undermining others. A second element can be described as *reactive mechanisms*. Group identities are often formed or reinforced when challenged by others. The challenge may come as a consequence of assimilative pressures, migration, economic competition, or political threats. A third element can be described as *policy feedbacks*. Government policies in the form of entitlements and reservations induce groups to organize for political action, which in turn intensifies group identities. A fourth element is the underlying *cultural conception* of the state's relationship to group identities. Here the issue is whether society is seen as subordinate to the state (as in Confucian and contemporary China), or whether society is viewed as autonomous, as in India. Hindus do not expect the state to inculcate moral behavior in citizens; nor do Hindus believe that the state should remake identities. Individual self-realization through religious rituals, conduct, and thought rather than state-imposed norms of conduct represent the Hindu view. Rather than the state remaking identities, most Indians believe that state structures and policies should be adapted to suit the variegated identities that make up India. The restructuring of state boundaries to coincide with linguistic boundaries; the creation of reservations to give proportional access to government employment; educational policies that require educational institutions to instruct in the mother tongue; and the insistence that official languages of states be those of the local population—all these are examples of state adaptations to social realities rather than efforts by the state to restructure social realities.

If the state is so accommodative, why then has the level of violence increased, especially among religious, caste, and linguistic communities? The emergence of upwardly mobile, educated middle classes has been an element in the politicization of some religious and ethnic communities. Among the Muslims, for example, an alliance has developed between sections of the newly educated middle classes and sections of the clergy, over such matters as the use of Urdu as the language of instruction, the preservation of Islamic personal law, and other matters of concern to the Muslim community. Among other communities too—the backward classes, for example—the most politicized elements are the lower middle classes in urban areas who have recently obtained education, and the recently emerged middle peasantry who are doing well under the new agrarian policies and who seek for their children access to higher education through assured reservations.

Some of the policies adopted in the 1950s and 1960s to accommodate ethnic demands worked then, but do so no longer. Reservations for castes, for example, were widely acceptable to the upper castes so long as they were limited to scheduled castes and tribes. But their extension to other communities now threatens the upper castes. Moreover, there is growing resentment among all groups at the inclusion of individuals who are not 'deserving' of benefits by virtue of their income and class, but who have access to reservations because of their caste.

The offer by the Government of India to the Sikhs that they would be given the capital city of Chandigarh was virtually withdrawn under pressure from Haryana which presently shares the capital. The central government also found it politically difficult to agree to the Assamese demand that illegal Bengali-speaking Muslim migrants from Bangladesh be expelled because of opposition from the government of West Bengal and from India's Muslim leaders. In short, *the claims of one community now rub against another, making it difficult for the government to be accommodative to demands by mobilized groups without taking into account the reactions of other mobilized groups.*

There was also bound to be a conflict between the Government of India's commitment to a secular civil code and its attitude of accommodation toward Islamic personal law. Secularism in India has meant that the state should not patronize any religion and that it should refrain from interfering in the ways in which religious communities conduct themselves. However, some Indians regard secularism in the broader sense that there ought to be a uniform civil code applicable to all, irrespective of religion, based upon a consensus concerning what constitutes justice and equity. These two conceptions of secularism remain in conflict. What gives this conflict a visceral dimension is the recent heightening of Hindu nationalism—a reaction to the claims upon the state by Muslims and Sikhs, reports of conversion by ex-untouchables to Islam, and the growth of Islamic fundamentalism. There is now a conjunction of interests between militant Hindus and the secular middle class that sharpens the conflict with India's Muslims.

Political parties and political leaders mobilize ethnic groups for political support. There are also times when political leaders encourage extremist demands, either to mobilize support for themselves or to undermine support for others. Mrs. Gandhi, it is said, gave indirect support to some of the Sikh militants in an effort to create divisions within the Sikh political party, the Akali Dal. And recently, the Indian Prime Minister expressed sympathy for the demand by Nepalis in the northern districts of West Bengal for a Gorkhaland—that is, for a state to be carved out of West Bengal, a position that undercuts the Communist Party Marxist which now governs the state.

At one level, these various ethnic and group conflicts are an expression of the particular changes at work in each of these communities; at another, they reflect the weakening of political institutions. India's pre-eminent conflict-managing institution in the first two decades after Independence was the Congress party.[7] While Mrs. Gandhi and her son, Rajiv Gandhi, did well in the parliamentary elections of 1980 and 1985, the Congress party itself has become organizationally weak. Intra-party elections for local and state leaders no longer take place, and the heads of the state parties and the Congress chief ministers are now appointed by the Prime Minister. The result is that Congress state government and party leaders hold power by virtue of their

---

[7] For an examination of the de-institutionalization of the Congress party, see James Manor, 'The Dynamics of Political Integration and Disintegration,' in A.J. Wilson and Dennis Dalton, eds., *The States of South Asia: Problems of National Integration*, London, C. Hurst, 1983, and his 'Anomie in Indian Politics,' *Economic and Political Weekly*, Annual Number, 1983. For another view, see Rajni Kothari, 'The Crisis of the Moderate State and the Decline of Democracy,' in Peter Lyon and James Manor, *Transfer and Transformations: Political Institutions in the Commonwealth*, Essays in Honour of W.H. Morris-Jones, Leicester, Leicester University Press, 1983, and his 'India Without Institutions,' *The Hindustan Times*, Sunday magazine, July 4, 1986.

loyalty to the Prime Minister rather than because they have built local support for themselves. The capacity, then, of state leaders to deal with local religious, linguistic, caste, and regional concerns has diminished, with the result that such protest movements have increasingly been channelized into regional and ethnic parties and movements. Moreover, the less able are state governments to manage majority/minority relations, the more likely it is that the central government becomes a party to the dispute. In Assam, for example, an unresponsive Congress party leadership proved incapable of dealing with the demands of the Assamese, who then directed their political attacks against the central government. Similarly, the Punjab conflict became a state/center issue when the Congress leadership in the state proved incapable of dealing with the concerns of the Sikhs. In short, when the state Congress party organization and government fails to politically manage ethnic and religious conflicts, these easily escalate by moving into the bazars and by turning into confrontations between regional interests and the center.

Conflict Management and Indian Democracy

Thus far, the Indian political system has survived the combined assaults of group violence and state repression. What needs to be considered is why that is so. Why has India remained democratic? There is, of course, an historical element: India as an independent country was born democratic. When the British relinquished power they left behind a parliament, a federal structure, an independent judiciary, a nationally recruited bureaucracy, electoral procedures, a free press, and independent political parties. But these assets could easily have been overwhelmed by the country's sharp social cleavages and the violence that accompanied them.

A central thesis of this chapter is that the conflict-managing role of the Congress party has been one of the critical factors in India's capacity to sustain democratic institutions in spite of violent social conflict. I have also argued that while the governing leadership might be tempted to suspend the democratic process to block threats to its power, there has also emerged a large and influential class of professionals who live off the democratic institutions and who thus constitute a vested interest concerned with sustaining democracy. Moreover, I have suggested that the primary reason for the success of India's democracy is political, not economic. I should now like to extend this political argument to suggest that three additional factors have been important in sustaining democratic institutions: the development of political as distinct from state institutions in the post-1947 period; the balance of power between the states and the center; and the hetero-geneous character of the social structure *within* each of the states.

Too often, it is assumed or argued that social divisions and conflicts, or, in Marxist terms, 'social contradictions' will overwhelm democratic institutions, or that electoral democracy tends to aggravate divisions in the society since political parties, in their search for power, exploit these differences. This explanation underestimates the conflict-managing role that democratic institutions and procedures and political parties have played in India.

By now, India has developed two party systems: a national party system and one that dominates the states. The Congress party, till 1967, overwhelmingly dominated the electoral scene at both levels. Since 1967, however, the Congress has lost many state elections, even a national election, and from time to time the non-Congress parties have also banded together to form an electoral front for national elections. The fact that the Congress has never won a national parlia-mentary election with a majority of votes and only occasionally won state assembly elections with a majority has made electoral alliances among the opposition attractive. Only once, in 1977, following the end of a national emergency when democratic procedures and institutions were suspended, did the major non-Congress parties successfully form a coalition capable of winning national elections. In retrospect, the 1977 elections, the formation of a new successful electoral coalition around the Janata party, and the emergence of two national parties, the Janata and the Congress which together won 78 percent of the vote and 83 percent of the seats in parliament, proved to be an aberration. The breakup of the Janata coalition in 1979 and the victory of Mrs. Gandhi's Congress in 1980 restored India to its familiar political state: one national party, and many opposition parties, each confined to a single region or single state or two, with most parties further divided into factions. Faced with a fragmented party structure and factions within every party, including the Congress, Indian politicians spend much of their time trying to build political alliances capable of win-ning elections, undercutting existing coalitions, and forming govern-ments. The political necessity of coalition-building often transcends programs, ideologies, and class and ethnic differences.

In a society of multiple group loyalties, politics plays a critical role in defining group identities and in shaping the kinds of cleavages that emerge. In influencing what kinds of social groups are created, the electoral process has an independent effect. However, electoral politics is not simply an adversarial process. Electoral politics also forces diverse groups to come together, to seek common interests and common identities for the sharing of power. Caste politics may be subsumed under linguistic politics. Tribes may band together to make regional claims. Several castes may come together, redefining themselves as a new multi-caste collectivity, such as backward caste. By bringing diverse groups together for the sharing of power, several state level parties have broadened their base sufficiently to win power, and at the national level, have enabled the Congress party to win seven of the eight parliamentary elections.

That India should have parties organized along the lines of caste and class (the Lok Dal), cultural regionalism (the Dravida parties), religious separatism (the Akali Dal), religious-based nationalism (the Bharatiya Janata party), tribe (the Jharkhand party), caste (the All India Scheduled Caste Federation), and nativism (the Shiv Sena) is hardly surprising in a country of such ethnic heterogeneity and class divisions. What is surprising is that not all parties are so organized, and that a majority of the Indian electorate has voted for parties that have chosen not to make exclusive appeals either to particular ethnic groups or classes. Probably because most of the country's electoral constituencies are heterogeneous, the major national political parties have chosen not to exclusively represent a single ethnic or class group, however defined.

India's federal structure has, moreover, provided a framework within which both heterogeneous national parties and socially more homogeneous state parties can share power. Central authority is not threatened by the control of Punjab by the Akali Dal, Tamil Nadu by the DMK, Assam by the Ahom Ganatantra Parishad, Andhra Pradesh by the Telugu Desam, Jammu and Kashmir by the National Conference, or (in the recent past) by the control of several north Indian states by the Lok Dal. Nor, for that matter, is it threatened by control of some of the states by political parties with national ambitions. The division of powers enables the center to function even when the states are controlled by opposition parties. In turn, state governments dominated by regional parties have developed ways of dealing with the center that protect their own interests.

Federalism, and the highly segmented social system that underlies it, also enables the center to function when some states are in political turmoil. Conflicts that break out in one state rarely spread to neighboring states. Claims are often mutually exclusive, not easily aggregated: the Sikhs want more regional autonomy; the backward classes want reservations; the Muslims want Urdu as a regional language; the Assamese want to eject illegal migrants; the Tamils don't want Hindi imposed upon them. Violent conflicts may erupt over any of these issues, but the conflicts are ordinarily confined to a single state or region of a state. India is thus like a huge lorry with a dozen or more tires; a puncture in one or two tires does not throw the lorry into the ditch. The center can hold even with simultaneous disturbances in a number of states—so long as the divisions within the states do not result in divisions within the central government. The segmented character of Indian society enables the center to intervene in crisis situations in individual states without necessarily creating a national crisis. Constitutionally, the center can declare an emergency in a particular state and through legal powers, known as President's Rule, can take control of a politically disturbed state. *Social structure and constitutional forms thus combine to quarantine violent social conflict and political instability at the state level.*

Moreover, divisions within the states minimize collisions between the states and the center. These divisions are partly factional within each of the parties. More importantly, social divisions reduce the likelihood that states can be unified in their opposition to central authority. Nascent secessionist movements have been unable to rally a people who share a language but are divided by caste and by class. Cultural nationalism, organized around language, has been the basis for political mobilization in India, but in no instance has it led to an enduring popular-based secessionist movement. Secessionism has proven to be a more potent force among religious communities— among the Muslims before 1947, among sections of the Sikh community in recent years, and among some of the tribal people in the northeast. But even among these groups the forces for staying within India have been greater than the forces of secession. In Punjab, the Sikh electorate voted overwhelmingly for the moderate elements within the Akali Dal and repudiated the supporters of Khalistan in 1984. In the Punjab, as elsewhere, a small band of terrorists can terrorize the population; indeed, it is perhaps because the supporters of Khalistan lack majority support that they resort to terrorism.

Conclusion

Can we say that the electoral process, political parties, and the democratic process have been institutionalized in India? Can the center hold in the face of deep social cleavages? That India has done so well with its political institutions over the past forty years is cause for some optimism. Commitment to the maintenance of a single country and to a democratic process is strong where it counts—among the national elite, the military and the bureaucracy, the professional classes, the business community, and the national politicians. However, faced with the choice of exercising coercive authority to maintain a single country or remaining democratic, most of the elite would choose the former over the latter. If need be, the center would exercise all the force at its command to prevent secession even if it meant a suspension of democratic rights. Fortunately, there is no indication that India is faced with such a stark choice.

Short of a threat to the integrity of the national political system, the major threat comes from the possibility of the disintegration of the governing party. That the stability of the central government seems to depend so heavily on a single leader dominating a weak party is a cause for concern. Nor can one be completely confident that a national leader, faced with threats from within his or her own party, might not choose to take coercive measures to maintain power. But memory of the events of 1975 to 1977 when a national emergency was declared, and the subsequent political defeat of Prime Minister Indira Gandhi, will give pause to any leader who is contemplating the suspension of the democratic system. Whatever weaknesses India's democratic process has, the national leadership now knows what the consequences are of its suspension. While Indians fear the consequences of religious and ethnic conflict for the democratic process and for national unity, they also recognize that the democratic process provides the means by which religious and ethnic conflicts can be mitigated.

India's Minorities:
Who are they? What do they Want?

Any assessment of relations between India's minority and majority communities is bound to be colored by the turmoil of the eighties: Sikh terrorism and the Hindu-Sikh conflict escalating after Mrs. Gandhi's assassination, which representative rule in the Punjab has been unable to stem; the Hindu-Muslim conflict over the Babri mosque, the Shahbano controversy and the riots in Meerut, Ahmedabad, and the old walled city of Delhi; the Gorkhaland agitation in West Bengal; the tension between the lower and upper Hindu castes and between scheduled castes and other castes—both lower and upper—in Bihar; and the Assamese-Bengali carnage in Assam

---

This essay first appeared in James R. Roach, ed. *India 2000: The Next Fifteen Years*, Riverdale, MD, The Riverdale Company, Inc., 1986.
Note: According to the 1981 census, published after this essay was written, the population of scheduled tribes increased from 38 million in 1971 to 51.6 million, from 6.9 percent to 7.8 percent of the population. The scheduled caste population increased from 80 million in 1971 to 104.8 million in 1981—that is, from 14.6 percent of India's population to 15.8 percent. In 1981 India's Muslims, Christians, Sikhs, scheduled castes, and scheduled tribes constituted 39.3 percent of the population, compared with 37.2 percent in 1971. See *Census of India, 1981, Paper 2 of 1984, General Population and Population of Scheduled Castes and Scheduled Tribes*; and *Census of India, Paper 3 of 1984, Household Population by Religion of Head of Household.*
Since this essay was written, the Government of India has signed accords with tribal insurgents in Tripura (in 1988) and in Mizoram (in 1986). In 1988, an agreement was also signed between New Delhi and the militant Gurkha movement in West Bengal. Earlier, as noted, an accord was signed with the Assamese. Thus far, only with the Sikh militants and in neighboring Sri Lanka with the Tamil militants have efforts to reduce the violence and confrontation between New Delhi and ethnic groups been unsuccessful

To most observers, these events are by no means transient, but are indications of increased social conflicts among religious, linguistic, and caste communities. If, as some argue, education is increasing aspirations, economic growth is enlarging economic opportunities, and political democracy is increasing politicization, then one can expect more, not less, competition and conflict among India's many social groups. And, it is further argued, if the competition and conflict continue to result in violence, then the central government is likely to increasingly use the army, and suspend civil liberties in disturbed areas. Could the fragile Indian democratic political system survive the combined assaults of group violence and state force?

An alternative view is that violence among caste, linguistic, and religious groups is endemic in India's variegated social structure. There is no reason to believe that the situation is worse now than in the past, or that it is likely to grow significantly worse in the future. One need only recall, it is argued, the communal turmoil at the time of Independence and the linguistic agitations of the 1950s to get a perspective and to appreciate the social order's capacity to generate social conflict in India. All of these recent disturbances have had their precursors. There were Assamese attacks against Marwaris in Guwahati in the late 1960s and against Bengali Hindus in the early 1970s; Hindu-Muslim clashes in Jamshedpur and Ahmedabad; a long history of caste Hindu brutality against ex-untouchables; and the turmoil over the Punjabi Suba movement in the late 1960s. Conditions in the mid-1980s are lamentably bad, but no worse (or better), than those of the 1950s, 1960s, or 1970s—nor are they likely to be worse in the near future. Such is the optimistic view!

This essay also puts forward a third perspective: group conflict is indeed endemic in India and there are forces—some new—that seem likely to worsen minority-majority relations. However, what seems most likely to intensify ethnic conflict is the deterioration of political institutions. The capacity of institutions to manage conflict in the 1980s and 1990s is what is at issue. In a period in which majorities are becoming more self-aware, a sense of territorial nationalism is emerging both among majorities and selected minorities. Moreover, the international ties of some minorities are growing, political coalitions are in a state of flux, and the problems of conflict management are likely to mount.

Who Are India's Minorities?

At a conference several years ago, a prominent Indian journalist referred to India as a 'Hindu island in an Islamic sea.' In the same vein, Theodore Wright quotes a Hindu writer as saying that 'it is taken for granted that the Hindus are a majority . . . but to say so is totally wrong. The vast mass of people that are called Hindus are a vast congeries of sub-caste minorities . . . whereas the Muslims form the actual majority.'[1] These quotes highlight the point that minority and majority status is a matter of self-ascription as well as objective defini-tion. What is a majority from one perspective is a minority from another. Consider the following anomalies:

- Until recently, most Indians did not regard Sikhs as a minority. Today, they are so regarded and they clearly see themselves as a minority. But in the Punjab it is the Hindus who consider themselves a minority.
- The Assamese are among a number of linguistic communities in India with a state of their own, but unlike most of the others they regard themselves as a 'national minority.' They are surrounded, they point out, by 150 million or so Bengalis. In Assam, however, Bengalis regard themselves as a minority.
- Jains are India's oldest religious minority, but the Jains are unobtrusive, politically quietistic, and so intertwined with Hindus that they are often regarded as simply another kind of Hindus rather than a distinctive minority.[2]
- Muslims are India's largest religious minority, but in Jammu and Kashmir it is the Hindus who regard themselves as a minority.
- Bengalis and Tamils are not generally regarded as minorities, but members of these communities living outside their home state often regard themselves, and are regarded by their hosts, as members of a linguistic minority.
- Scheduled castes are regarded as belonging to a disadvantaged and backward minority, a status also sought by other backward

[1] Theodore P. Wright, Jr., 'The Ethnic Numbers Game in India: Hindu-Muslim Conflicts over Conversion, Family Planning, Migration, and the Census,' in William McCrady, ed., *Culture, Ethnicity and Identity*, New York, Academic Press, 1983, p. 412.

[2] R.A. Schermerhorn, *Ethnic Plurality in India*, Tucson, Arizona, University of Arizona Press, 1978, pp. 101–127. Schermerhorn's book on minorities is one of the few comprehensive treatments.

castes, often numbering a quarter or more of the population in some states.

Clearly India contains such a medley of religious, caste, and linguistic groups, that the sense of belonging to a minority depends upon where one lives, how much power and status one has, and one's sense of community threat. Many Indians narrowly use the term 'minority' to refer to those who are not Hindu, a conception which implies that somehow the dominant core of Indian identity is Hinduism—the 'mainstream' (to use a favorite Indian word) with which minorities should identify if they want to be regarded as wholly Indian. Thus, some Hindus speak of the need for the 'Indianization' of minorities, by which they mean that minorities should observe Indian (i.e., Hindu) national holidays, identify with India's historical (i.e., pre-Islamic Hindu and Buddhist) past, its heroes and great events, and be attached to the soil of India (not to Mecca or Rome).[3]

Needless to say, this is not the way India's minorities define the problem. It is not only religious groups who regard themselves as minorities. Caste, tribal, linguistic as well as religious groups can be self-defined minorities for any one of a number of reasons: they have a distinctive group identity that they fear is eroding; they regard themselves as socially and economically subordinate to others; or they believe that they suffer from discrimination, either from others in the society or from the state itself. To regard oneself as part of a minority in India is to suggest that one ought to take group action to remedy one's situation. To declare one's group a minority is, therefore, a political act. In the Indian context, it is a way of calling attention to a situation of self-defined deprivation.

A people who do not share what they regard as the central symbols of the society invariably view themselves as a minority. It is not simply that a community lacks power, but rather that the symbols of authority, the values that are propagated from the center, and the culture that emanates from the center are viewed as not theirs. To members of a minority community, symbol-sharing may be no less important than power-sharing. Members of a minority community may refer to those of its members holding high office as having been 'co-opted' if they share power without the symbols. Moreover, a community may feel

[3] Balraj Madhok, *Indianization? What, Why and How*, New Delhi, S. Chand and Co., 1970.

threatened because its own members are partaking of the symbols, the values, and the culture of the 'center,' even in the absence of explicit repression.

Once we conceive of a minority as a category defined by the observed rather than by observers, a self-definition by a community itself rather than by others, we are faced with a methodological problem of considerable proportion. If we understand the term 'minority' as a socially negotiable concept, then a community that regards itself and is regarded by others as a minority may, under some circumstances, cease to be a minority, while other communities may become minorities. In the United States, for example, Italian-Americans, Irish-Americans, Polish-Americans and Jews once regarded themselves as minorities, but are now seen by others (and sometimes by themselves) as 'ethnics.' The term 'minority' has come to be reserved for those who are 'disadvantaged.' Who belongs to the category 'disadvantaged minority,' as distinct from 'ethnic,' is politically and socially negotiable. In India, Sikhs and Muslims now loom large as minorities. Will other communities join them? In assessing the likely future trends in India, we must consider which new minorities will assert claims, what claims will be put forth by the old minorities, and whether some minorities will cease to think of themselves as minorities.

Since we are the observers and not the observed, we must fall back upon the communities' self-perceptions regarding their minority status. We can then engage in some informed speculation as to which other communities might actively put forth minority claims. It is useful to think of four types of minorities in India: linguistic, religious, caste, and tribal. These can be further divided along three dimensions: whether the minorities have a conception of a territorial homeland; the extent of the sense of cohesion within the community; and whether the community regards itself as a disadvantaged or as an achieving minority.

Linguistic Minorities

Since each of India's states has an official language, those who speak another language as their mother tongue regard themselves as belonging to a linguistic minority. In 1971, in eighteen of India's twenty-two states, plus the union territory of Delhi, 92.8 million people, or 17.1 percent of the population, did not speak the regional language as their mother tongue [see Table 2.1].[4] Urdu was spoken by 28.4 million people; 24.7 million spoke a language not recognized as a regional language of any of the states; and approximately 39.7 million people spoke a regional language other than the official language of their state.[5] A projection of these numbers for 1985 shows 174.5 million people belonging to a linguistic minority.

TABLE 2.1
Linguistic Minorities by State (1971) (in millions)

State	Population	Speakers of Official Language	Linguistic Minority	Linguistic Minority (percent)
Andhra Pradesh	43.5	37.1	6.4	14.7
Assam	14.6	8.9	5.7	39.0
Bihar	56.4	44.9	11.5	20.4
Delhi	4.1	3.1	1.0	33.3
Gujarat	26.7	23.9	2.8	10.5
Haryana	10.0	9.0	1.0	10.0
Himachal Pradesh	3.5	3.0	0.5	14.3
J and K	4.6	2.4	2.2	47.8
Karnataka	29.3	19.3	10.0	34.1
Kerala	21.4	20.5	0.9	4.0
M.P.	41.7	34.7	7.0	16.8
Maharashtra	50.4	38.6	11.8	23.4
Orissa	21.9	18.5	3.4	15.5
Punjab	13.6	10.8	2.8	20.5
Rajasthan	25.8	23.5	2.3	8.9
Tamil Nadu	41.2	34.8	6.4	15.5
Tripura	1.6	1.1	0.5	31.2
U.P.	88.3	78.2	10.1	11.4
West Bengal	44.3	37.8	6.5	14.7
Total	542.9	450.1	92.8	17.1

[4] Throughout this analysis I have used the 1971 census figures on language and caste since statewide figures on religion have been released only for 1981. While the absolute numbers have, of course, substantially changed, the percentages are not likely to have changed a great deal.

[5] For the construction of the tables included here, I have drawn the data from K.P. Ittaman, 'Social Composition of the Population' in *Population in India*, New York, Economic and Social Commission for Asia and the Pacific, United Nations, 1982, pp. 233–254.

The concerns of each of these linguistic minorities are quite different. Urdu speakers, for example, have called for the establishment of Urdu as an official second language of the states in which they live. There are large Urdu-speaking communities in Uttar Pradesh, Bihar, Maharashtra, Andhra Pradesh and Karnataka. In these states, an overwhelming majority of Muslims claims Urdu as its mother tongue.

Some minorities speaking 'unrecognized' languages have demanded statehood. This demand is often made by those linguistic groups concentrated in a particular region of a state, where the group has a strong sense of its own distinctive identity. The largest 'stateless' linguistic minorities (containing more than half a million speakers in 1971), are shown in Table 2.2.

TABLE 2.2
Linguistic Minorities (in millions)

Bhili	3.4	Konkani	1.5
Boro	0.5	Kurukh/Oraon	1.2
Dogri	1.3	Mundari	0.8
Gondi	1.7	Sindhi	1.7
Nepali	1.4	Santali	3.8
Ho	0.8	Tulu	1.2

Except for Dogri, Sindhi, Nepali, and Konkani, the remaining languages are spoken by tribals. Some tribal peoples, though none speaking the languages listed above, already have states of their own. Meghalaya, Nagaland, Arunachal Pradesh, Dadra and Nagar Haveli, Lakshadweep, and Mizoram are predominantly populated by tribals.

The third set of linguistic minority groups comprises those who speak an official language other than the language of the state in which they live. These minorities are concentrated in Assam, Karnataka, Maharashtra, Punjab, Tamil Nadu, and West Bengal. There are nearly nine million Bengalis living outside of West Bengal and Tripura, two million Gujaratis outside of Gujarat, 1.4 million Malayalis outside of Kerala, three million Maharashtrians outside of Maharashtra and Goa, 1.4 million Oriyas not in Orissa, 3.3 million Punjabis not in Punjab, 2.5 million Tamils outside of Tamil Nadu and Pondicherry, 7.7 million Telugus not in Andhra Pradesh, and 11.0 million Hindi speakers living outside of the Hindi belt (including 2.7 million people in Punjab who classify themselves as Hindi speakers) [see Table 2.3].

TABLE 2.3
Linguistic Diasporas (1971) (in millions)

Language	Speakers	Speakers in 'Homeland'[1]	Speakers in Diaspora
Assamese	8.9	8.9	—
Bengali	44.8	38.8	6.0
Gujarati	25.9	23.9	2.0
Hindi	208.5	197.5	11.0
Kannada	21.7	19.3	2.4
Kashmiri	2.5	2.5	—
Malayalam	21.9	20.5	1.4
Marathi	41.8	38.8	3.0
Oriya	19.9	18.5	1.4
Punjabi	14.1	10.8	3.3
Tamil	37.7	35.2	2.5
Telugu	44.8	37.1	7.7
Sub-total	492.5	451.8	40.7
Urdu	28.6	—	28.6
Other languages	27.1	3.4	23.7
Total	548.2	455.2	93.0[2]

[1] For the languages listed in Schedule VIII of the Constitution, the homelands include, in addition to the various states, the union territories of Delhi (Hindi), Goa (Marathi) and Pondicherry (Tamil). For 'other languages' the homelands include Manipur, Meghalaya, Nagaland, Arunachal Pradesh, and Mizoram.

[2] This number is slightly higher than in Table 2.1 since all union territories are included.

Since these minorities, unlike speakers of other 'local' languages or of Urdu, are not regarded as 'sons of the soil,' they are often the target of political groups that demand preferences for 'local' people in employment and in education. In some instances, most notably in Assam, there have been demands that the linguistic minorities leave the state and return to their 'homeland.'

Special note should be taken of the concern by some linguistic majorities that they are in danger of becoming a minority within their own state. The Assamese are particularly fearful, for although they officially account for 61 percent of the state's population, it is generally understood that a substantial portion of the 3.6 million Muslims in the state who claim Assamese as their mother tongue are in fact Bengali speakers. The influx of illegal migrants from Bangladesh has further increased the anxieties of the Assamese.

There are a number of cities in which speakers of the state language are a minority. The Marathi-speaking population constitutes only 42.8 percent of Bombay. Kannada speakers in Bangalore (23.7 percent) are outnumbered by Tamils (31.7 percent). The Assamese lack a majority in Guwahati and in several other towns along the Brahmaputra. It is no surprise, therefore, that these towns have active 'sons of the soil' movements.

Religious Minorities

According to the 1981 census, Muslims constituted 11.4 percent of the Indian population (75.5 million), Christians 2.4 percent (16.2 million), Sikhs 2.0 percent (13.1 million), and Buddhists and Jains 1.2 percent (7.9 million). Hindus constituted 82.6 percent of the population.

Muslims form a majority in the state of Jammu and Kashmir, but otherwise they are widely dispersed. They constitute 21.3 percent of Kerala, 21.5 percent of West Bengal, 15.9 percent of Uttar Pradesh, 14.1 percent of Bihar, and 11 percent of Karnataka. Elsewhere they represent less than 10 percent of the state population. No census was conducted in Assam in 1981, but in 1971 Muslims constituted 24 percent of the population. Two geopolitical features of the Muslims warrant special attention: they are concentrated in selected districts of these states, and, as compared with Hindus and Sikhs, they are disproportionately urban.

Muslims are only 8.5 percent of Andhra's population, but they are concentrated in the Telengana region of the state, with their largest concentration in Hyderabad where they form 26.4 percent of the district. (District figures reported here are from the 1971 census, since district-wise data for 1981 are not yet available.) Muslims are a majority in Malappuram district in Kerala and they form a substantial portion of the adjacent districts to the north and south. They are numerous in the western portions of Uttar Pradesh, especially in Rampur (45.7 percent), Aligarh, Moradabad and Bijnor districts (one third of which are Muslims), and there are substantial concentrations in districts close by—Meerut, Muzaffarnagar and Saharanpur. Similarly, several districts in West Bengal, Maharashtra, and Bihar have well above average concentrations of Muslims.[6] Later, we shall explore the political implications of these concentrations.

In 1971, 19.9 percent of the Indian population lived in urban areas, but 28.8 percent of the Muslim population was urban. Muslims constituted one-fifth or more of the population in Hyderabad (38 percent), Kanpur (20 percent), Lucknow (29 percent), Varanasi (26 percent), and Allahabad (24 percent), and they have more than their national average in Calcutta, Bombay, Bangalore, Ahmedabad, Agra, Jaipur, Indore, and Jabalpur. The 1981 census reported that 34 percent of the Muslim population was urban—a significant increase over the 1971 census [see Table 2.4]. Of special interest is that a number of the urban centers in the north with large numbers of Muslims also have substantial numbers of Hindu refugees who fled from Pakistan at the time of partition. These centers are particularly prone to Hindu-Muslim violence.

TABLE 2.4
Urban Muslim Population (1971) (in percent)

Calcutta	14.2	Lucknow	29.5
Greater Bombay	14.1	Howrah	10.3
Delhi	7.4	Agra	16.3
Madras	8.5	Jaipur	18.7
Hyderabad	38.0	Varanasi	25.9
Bangalore	14.2	Indore	12.4
Ahmedabad	14.6	Madurai	7.6
Kanpur	20.1	Jabalpur	12.5
Nagpur	9.3	Allahabad	23.8
Pune	9.0		

Note: Muslims also have high concentrations in some of the middle-sized cities. They are more than one-third of the population in many of the medium-sized towns in Uttar Pradesh—Bareilly, Meerut, Aligarh, Saharanpur, Firozabad, Shahjahanpur—and they form a majority in Moradabad and Rampur. In addition to the districts of Kashmir, Muslims constitute a majority in the district of Malappuram, Kerala (63.9 percent), Murshidabad, West Bengal (56.3 percent) and in Lakshadweep (94.4 percent). There are 11 other districts in the country, mainly in Assam and in West Bengal, where Muslims constitute 30 percent or more of the population.

[6] Nafis Ahmad Siddique, *Population Geography of Muslims in India*, New Delhi, S. Chand and Co., 1976. According to Siddique, Muslims constitute a majority in nine districts (mainly in Kashmir), 35 to 50 percent of the population in ten more districts, and in 20 more districts they comprise 20 to 35 percent of the population.

India's 13.1 million Sikhs (1981) form a majority of 60.8 percent of the Punjab, but they have been a majority only since 1966. Pre-partition Punjab was 51 percent Muslim, 35 percent Hindu, and 12 percent Sikh. Post-partition Punjab, as of 1961, was 64 percent Hindu, 33 percent Sikh, and two percent Muslim; the 1971 figures are 60 percent Sikh, 38 percent Hindu, and only one percent Muslim. These massive changes are the result of the reorganization of the state boundaries in 1947 and again in 1966, and the movement in 1947 of Muslims out of the Indian Punjab, and of Sikhs and Hindus out of the Pakistani Punjab.[7]

From 1961 to 1971, Sikhs increased more rapidly than did both Hindus and Muslims, and from 1971 to 1981 their growth rate continued to be higher than that of the Hindus. There is no indication of a higher natural population increase among the Sikhs. In fact, Punjab's population growth rates from 1961 to 1971, and from 1971 to 1981, are actually below the national growth rates. This would suggest that there has been a considerable amount of redesignation among Sikhs who had previously declared themselves as Hindus. The growth of self-identification and differentiation among the Sikhs, and among Hindus in the Punjab, has been underway since the turn of the century, but it has accelerated since independence.

One indication of this process is the extent to which Sikhs and Hindus have increasingly distinguished themselves linguistically. After the Sikhs called for the creation of a Punjabi Suba, the Arya Samaj and Jana Sangh urged Punjabi Hindus to repudiate Punjabi as their mother tongue, and to declare themselves Hindi speakers. By 1971 only one-half of the five million Hindus in the state declared Punjabi as their mother tongue, and in neighboring Haryana almost no Hindus declared themselves as Punjabi speakers.

The Sikhs now have a homeland, but they also have a diaspora. Of

---

[7] The demand for a Punjabi Suba was a way of pressing for a Sikh majority state within the framework of a policy that accepted *linguistic* states but rejected statehood on the basis of religion. This view was articulated by Master Tara Singh, leader of the movement for a Punjabi Suba, who was asked by the then Chief Minister of the state in 1955: 'So you want a land wherein the Sikhs should dominate?' To which Tara Singh replied, 'This is exactly what I have in mind,' and continued, 'This cover of a Punjabi-speaking state slogan serves my purpose well, since it does not offend against national-ism. The government should accept our demand under the slogan of a Punjabi-speaking state without a probe. What we want is *azadi* (independence). The Sikhs have no *azadi*. We will fight for our *azadi* with full power, even if we have to revolt.' Baldev Raj Nayar, *Minority Politics in the Punjab*, Princeton, Princeton University Press, 1966, p. 37.

India's 13.1 million Sikhs, 2.8 million—more than one-fifth—live in other parts of India, mostly in Haryana, Rajasthan, Uttar Pradesh, and Delhi. Since the Sikhs in the diaspora are heavily urbanized and are physically distinctive, they are noticeable minorities in cities throughout the country. Moreover, the Sikh diaspora is worldwide. There are substantial numbers of Sikhs in the United States, Canada, the United Kingdom, and West Germany. These diaspora communities are important sources of support for political movements within the Punjab.

India's Christians are more numerous but less politically vocal than the Sikhs. The 1981 census reported 16.2 million Christians—2.4 percent of the population. The bulk of India's Christians live in Kerala, Tamil Nadu, and Andhra, but the concentration is densest in India's northeast. Christians are a majority in Nagaland (80.2 percent) and in Meghalaya (52.6 percent), but since both states are small and Christians lack the cohesion of the Sikhs neither plays the role that the Punjab does for India's Sikhs. The Christians are dispersed, usually speak the language of the region in which they are located, and, in the main, are converts from tribes or low castes.

Jains (3.6 million) are so closely associated with Hindus that they are not usually regarded, by themselves or by Hindus, as a religious minority. Also closely associated with Hinduism are the Buddhists (4.7 million). Many Buddhists, however, regard themselves as distinct from Hindus.

Two features of India's religious minorities warrant special note. The first is their internal divisions and the second is their relationship with Hindus.

None of the three major religious minorities is cohesive. Sikhs are divided between scheduled caste and non-scheduled caste Sikhs, and between Jat Sikhs and other high-caste Sikhs. These divisions enabled the Congress party in the past to win substantial support among the Sikhs in the Punjab and prevented the consolidation of the Sikh vote around the Akali Dal (except, it seems, in the last state elections in 1985).

Muslims are even less cohesive. The Muslims of the southwest have had long-term ties with Arab countries, and they continue to migrate in large numbers to work in the Persian Gulf. They speak Malayalam, and in their diet and dress resemble Hindus in the region. The Muslims of Kashmir form a majority in the state, have a strong Kashmiri identity, and by and large speak Kashmiri rather than Urdu. The Muslims living in the Hindi-speaking region, from the Yamuna in the north through the Gangetic plains, lived in the mainstream of the Turkish, Afghan, Mughal, and Persian invaders, and mostly (64 percent) speak Urdu. It is here that the two-nation theory had its greatest support and where the Muslim League developed. Still further eastward, Bengali Muslims speak Bengali rather than Urdu. Of the nine million Muslims in West Bengal, less than one million speak Urdu. These are mostly migrants from Bihar, eastern Uttar Pradesh, and Orissa. The Muslims of Andhra form still another distinctive group. They lived under a Muslim ruler until 1947; their upper classes (some of Persian origin) formed part of the governing elite. Unlike most Muslims living in the south, they are overwhelmingly (91 percent) Urdu-speaking. It is particularly noteworthy that the Muslims in south India, especially in Andhra and Kerala, have formed their own confessional political parties while north Indian Muslims, perhaps 'tainted' by their association with the League and the two-nation theory, have frequently participated in mainstream political parties.

Finally, as we have noted earlier, the Christians of the northeast, most of whom are tribal people, are culturally distinct from the Christians of the south.

The attitude of Hindus toward religious minorities is guided by one central feature of Hinduism: it is an 'inclusive' religion, unlike Christianity, Judaism, Islam and Sikhism, which are 'exclusive' religions that prescribe rules for membership, insist on adherence to specific dogmas and rules of conduct, and purge the heterodox. Hindus have no clear rules as to what constitutes a Hindu. Hindus view anyone who observes any Hindu rituals, worships any Hindu deities, or philosophically subscribes to any elements of Hinduism, as a Hindu. Hindus have no conception of heterodoxy, no notion of apostasy. Islamic fundamentalists in Pakistan have declared the Ahmadiyas, a heterodox sect, to be non-Muslims. Orthodox Jews attack conversions to Judaism by reformed Jews. Orthodox Sikhs have attacked the heterodox Nirankaris. In contrast, Hindu revivalists have sought to incorporate Indians of various faiths into Hinduism.

Hinduism is inclusive in a second sense as well. Hindus regard religions that originated in south Asia, including Buddhism, Jainism and Sikhism, and variants of Hinduism, such as the Brahmos, Lingayats, and other sects, as Hindu. Article 25 of the Indian Constitution stipulates that Sikhs, Buddhists, and Jains cannot be excluded from Hindu temples—a provision seen by Sikhs as intending to include Sikhs among Hindu communicants. Hindus see no apostasy when members of their religion worship at Sikh Gurdwaras, or at the tombs of saints. It was not unusual for Hindu families to declare one of their male children a Sikh and to give him a Sikh name. Similarly, Hindus incorporate tribal gods into their pantheon as reincarnations of Hindu deities.

Orthodox Hindus do not regard 'heterodox' and 'reformist' Hindu movements as threatening. India has been rife with religious movements during the past century: the Arya Samaj, theosophists, Vedantists, Brahmos, Lingayats, and numerous 'Godheads', or self-proclaimed religious leaders with their own followings. Religious Hindus regard the proliferation of such movements as a sign of religious vitality, not as a threat to any particular orthodoxy. A similar period of religious creativity in sixteenth-century Europe was regarded as a threat to Catholicism.

This tolerance for internal diversity and a readiness to incorporate others is, paradoxically, regarded with distrust by the exclusive religions of Islam, Sikhism, and Christianity. Each has sought, not always successfully, to resist the tendency of their communicants to adopt Hindu customs. Hindus, in turn, regard with equanimity Muslims and Sikhs who succumb to Hindu syncretism. Thus, the Mughal ruler Akbar is regarded highly by Hindus for his efforts to build a composite Indian culture, but by Muslims as an apostate who failed to keep faith. Hindus do, however, regard mass conversion to Islam and Christianity with alarm. The hostility to conversions is largely a reflection of nationalist opposition to religions of foreign origin, but it also reflects the Hindu antipathy towards exclusive religions.

Hindus regard with aversion a philosophical position shared by orthodox Sikhs and Muslims that politics and religion are inseparable.[8] The classical Indian view is that the state preserves order, but it does not impose any particular moral code. Hinduism, unlike Christianity, Islam, Sikhism, and Judaism, has no conception of a universal moral code of conduct, and no notion that rulers should act in moral ways according to some religious code. Politics is viewed as an amoral sphere—a notion partly rooted in the conception that Kshatriyas, not Brahmins, are rulers. Men like Maulana Moududi and Sant Jarnail Singh Bhindranwale are regarded by Hindus as 'fanatics' for their

---

[8] Master Tara Singh, a dominant figure among Sikhs for over a generation, said that 'the Khalsa Panth will either be a ruler or a rebel. It has no third role to play.' (Schermerhorn, *op. cit.*, p. 140). Sikhs share the Muslim view of the inseparability of religion and politics, a position considered anathema by most Hindus.

exclusive attitudes toward their own religion and for their rejection of political secularism.

Tribal Minorities

India's tribals, numbering 38 million or 6.9 percent of the population in 1971, remain her largest, politically slumbering minority. The tribals largely live in areas they regard as their 'homelands,' many of which are designated by the government as reserved or 'scheduled areas.'[9] Some 99,000 square miles are scheduled areas in which legal restrictions are placed on the alienation of land to non-tribals. The six largest tribes are: the Gonds of central India; the Bhils of western India; the Santals of Bihar, West Bengal and Orissa; the Oraons of Bihar and West Bengal; the Minas of Rajasthan; and the Mundas of Bihar, West Bengal, and Orissa. These tribes constitute nearly one-half of India's tribal population. Some tribes, though considerably smaller, constitute a majority of the areas in which they live: the Nagas, Khasis and Garos, for example, in India's northeast.[10]

While tribals are a national minority in India, they constitute a majority of the population in several parts of the country. According to the 1971 census, they are a majority in Nagaland (89 percent), Meghalaya (80 percent), and Arunachal Pradesh (79 percent), and one-fifth or more of the population in Manipur (31 percent), Tripura (29 percent), Orissa (23 percent), and Madhya Pradesh (20 percent). Outside of the northeast, tribes constitute a majority of the population in nineteen districts: three in Orissa, six in Madhya Pradesh, two in Himachal Pradesh, one in Bihar, two in Rajasthan, two in Assam, two in Gujarat, and one in the Lakshadweep [see Tables 2.5 and 2.6].

India's tribes are not wholly isolated, uneducated and poor, but it

[9] Schedule V of the Constitution provides that selected tribal areas should be administered by the state governments, with the Governor of each state given the power to modify central and state laws for the scheduled areas and to frame regulations protecting tribal land rights. Special funds are provided by the central government for the development of scheduled areas. Central government responsibility for the areas is in the hands of the Home Ministry.

[10] For this discussion of the demography of India's tribes I have drawn from Myron Weiner and John Osgood Field, 'How Tribal Constituencies in India Vote,' in Myron Weiner and John Osgood Field, eds., *Electoral Politics in the Indian States,* Vol. II, New Delhi, Manohar Book Service, pp. 78–85.

TABLE 2.5
States in which National, Religious and Tribal Minorities are a Majority or Plurality

Jammu and Kashmir	64.2 percent Muslim
Meghalaya	52.6 percent Christian, 80 percent Tribal
Nagaland	80.2 percent Christian, 89 percent Tribal
Punjab	60.8 percent Sikh
Arunachal Pradesh	79.0 percent Tribal
Mizoram	83.8 percent Christian

TABLE 2.6
Districts with a Scheduled Tribe Majority (percent tribal)

Dangs, Gujarat	92.5
Jhabua, M.P.	84.7
Bastar, M.P.	72.4
Banswara, Rajasthan	71.5
Lahaul and Spiti, H.P.	69.1
Kinnaur, H.P.	62.6
Mandla, M.P.	61.8
Ranchi, Bihar	61.6
Koraput, Orissa	60.9
Mayurbhanj, Orissa	60.6
Dungarpur, Rajasthan	60.1
Sundargarh, Orissa	58.1
Surguja, M.P.	55.6
Shadol, M.P.	51.4
Dhar, M.P.	51.1
Surat, Gujarat	50.0

Note: In nineteen other districts, tribals constitute 30 to 50 percent of the population.

would be accurate to say that they have been less affected by the forces of modernization than have other Indians. Their mortality rates are higher, their literacy rates lower; they are less urbanized than other Indians and with the exception of the Santals, few are employed in the modern industrial sector. As a result of the work of Christian missionaries, some of the tribes in the northeast and to a lesser extent, sections of the Santals, Mundas and Oraons, have above-average levels of literacy. But even among these communities, only a small number have studied in the universities and entered the professions and senior levels of the bureaucracy.

The tribes are concentrated in three principal regions. One is

India's northeast. The second is in middle India, and includes Bihar, the hill areas of inland Orissa, southeastern Madhya Pradesh, and a portion of northern Andhra. The third region is in India's west, and includes parts of eastern Gujarat, western Madhya Pradesh, and southern Rajasthan. There is also a small tribal area in the mountain region of Himachal Pradesh and in the Nilgiri hills in Tamil Nadu.

It is particularly noteworthy that the tribals are not only geographically concentrated, but within their respective regions they are overwhelmingly rural, while the towns are predominantly non-tribal. In southern Bihar, for example, tribals constitute 58 percent of Ranchi district, 46 percent of Singhbhum district, and 36 percent of Santhal Parganas, but not a single large town in any of these districts has a tribal majority. Control over and access to land and forests is, therefore, more a concern among the scheduled tribes than among other minorities.[11]

Caste Minorities

None of India's several thousand castes is in the majority in any region of the country. To speak of a minority caste is to refer not to numbers but to status. Indians generally regard ex-untouchables or scheduled castes as a minority by virtue of their low social status, their economic conditions, and the discrimination to which they have been subjected by caste Hindus. Along with scheduled tribes, they are constitutionally guaranteed rights and benefits not provided to other minorities. These include reserved constituencies for elections to Parliament and to State Assemblies, reservations for admission into colleges and technical schools, and reserved positions in government employment.[12]

Scheduled castes form 14.6 percent of India's population. The largest single statewide concentration is in the Punjab where they form nearly one-fourth of the population. There are major concentrations

[11] *Land Alienation and Restoration in Tribal Communities in India*, S.N. Dubey and Ratna Naidu, eds., Bombay, Himalaya Publishing House, 1977. This is a useful collection of papers on the growing problem of land alienation among tribals in Andhra, Maharashtra, Gujarat, Rajasthan, Madhya Pradesh, West Bengal, Orissa, and Bihar.

[12] See Barbara R. Joshi, *Democracy in Search of Equality: Untouchable Politics and Indian Social Change*, Delhi, Hindustan Publishing Corporation, 1982.

in Uttar Pradesh, West Bengal, Bihar, Tamil Nadu, Andhra, and Madhya Pradesh.

Unlike scheduled tribes, Sikhs, or linguistic groups, scheduled castes do not identify themselves with any homeland or assert territorial demands. Cultural symbols and other measures to enhance group identity have begun to play a role among ex-untouchables as with some other minorities. Efforts to convert ex-untouchables to Buddhism attracted several million in Maharashtra, but the conversion movement has apparently slowed. There have been reports in recent years of conversions to Islam, but while these reports have created anxieties among some Hindus, there is no indication that any large-scale movement is underway.

In recent years, a new self-proclaimed caste minority has appeared— the 'other backward classes.' The 'OBCs,' as they are called, are referred to in provisions of the Constitution [Article 16(4)] which enables the government to make reservations 'of appointments or posts in favour of any backward class of citizens.' Dr. Ambedkar, India's Law Minister at the time, who opposed extending benefits from scheduled castes and scheduled tribes to other backward classes, pointed out that the identity of backward classes was so vague, that ultimately 'a backward community is a community which is backward in the opinion of the government.' T.T. Krishnamachari, another member of the Constituent Assembly, described Article 16(4) as 'a paradise for lawyers.'[13]

While an earlier legislative history settled the identity of scheduled castes and scheduled tribes, Article 16(4) opened up a political debate over the criteria for including particular communities in the category of OBCs. Central government commissions were unable to agree. Some called for the use of objective measures of backwardness, such as average education or income levels, while others emphasized position in the social hierarchy: a caste should be classified as backward on the basis of its low status or the inferior treatment of its members by other communities. There was agreement only on the notion that whatever criteria were chosen they should be applied to groups, not individuals. In the absence of a central government consensus, the matter of deciding who was 'backward' was left to the state governments.

[13] On the backward classes: who they are, how they are statutorily defined, and how they seek preferential status, see Marc Galanter, 'Who Are the Other Backward Classes? An Introduction to a Constitutional Puzzle,' *Economic and Political Weekly*, October 28, 1978, p. 1812.

Thus, there ensued a political battle in a number of states as castes sought to be included on the list of OBCs and politicians vied for their support. Several states placed a substantial number of castes with large populations on their list. It is not unusual for 20 to 25 percent of the population of a state to appear on the list of backward castes, in addition to those classified as scheduled castes and scheduled tribes. The courts have decreed that the total number of reservations for these three groups for admission to colleges and for positions in the administrative services must be below 50 percent. While that has limited the size of the OBC, it has intensified the struggle to be on the list and has increased the debate over precisely what benefits should be provided. In several states, most notably in Bihar, upper castes have violently opposed the extension of reservations to the backward castes.

In early 1985, decisions by the governments of Madhya Pradesh and Gujarat, to extend reservations to the OBCs for engineering, medical, and agricultural colleges—in Madhya Pradesh 80 percent of the seats were in the reserved category and in Gujarat 49 percent—resulted in violent anti-reservation agitation by students. In both states, the reservations were announced on the eve of state government elections and were regarded as measures intended to win electoral support for the governing Congress party from the backward classes.

Conclusion: A Statistical Recapitulation and Projection

India's religious minorities, scheduled castes, and tribes constituted 37.2 percent of the country's population in 1971, while the linguistic minorities were 17.5 percent. These two categories overlap substantially, since virtually all Urdu speakers are Muslims and a majority of speakers of non-regional languages are members of scheduled tribes. Taking these overlaps into account, approximately 45 percent of the population belongs to linguistic, tribal, religious, or caste groups that regard themselves as minorities [see table 2.7]. Since we have categorized 'minority' and 'majority' from an aggregate national rather than a state point of view, an examination of a few states may better demonstrate how majorities and minorities are distributed.

Consider Bihar, a state with a 1971 population of 56.3 million, of whom 7.9 million (14.1 percent) are scheduled castes, 4.9 million (8.6 percent) scheduled tribes, 7.6 million (13.5 percent) Muslims, and 0.6 million (1.2 percent) Christians. The linguistic minorities include 1.9

TABLE 2.7
India's Minorities (1971)

	In Millions	Percent
Religions, tribes, and castes [1]		
Muslims	61.4	11.2
Scheduled castes	80.0	14.6
Scheduled tribes	38.0	6.9
Christians	14.2	2.6
Sikhs	10.3	1.9
	203.9	37.2
Linguistic groups		
Urdu speakers	28.6	5.2
Non-regional languages [2]	27.1	4.9
Minority regional languages [3]	40.7	7.4
	96.4 [4]	17.5

[1] These are not mutually exclusive categories, since some tribals are Christian and some Sikhs are listed as scheduled castes.

[2] This is a somewhat clumsy term to use for those local languages which are not officially listed in Schedule VIII of the Constitution as recognized regional languages. I have, however, included Sindhi in this category, for though it is recognized as a regional language, it is not the official regional language of any state. I have also excluded Urdu.

[3] This refers to those who speak a regional language of a state other than the one in which they live.

[4] The number is slightly higher than given in the text, since I have included union territories in these calculations.

million Bengalis and 300,000 Oriyas, some of whom are Muslim, Christian, or belong to scheduled castes. If we add one-half of these to our list of minorities, we have 22.1 million minorities (39 percent), and a caste Hindu, Hindi-speaking 'majority' of 34.2 million (61 percent).

West Bengal has a population of 44.3 million (1971), with a scheduled tribe population of 2.5 million, 9.1 million Muslims, 250,000 Christians and 8.8 million scheduled castes. These minorities total 20.6 million, or 46.5 percent of the population. There are approximately three million people in West Bengal speaking Hindi, Oriya, Telugu, and other regional languages. If one-half of these do not overlap with the other minority categories, then as many as 22.1 million people in the state regard themselves as members of 'minorities,' a bare majority being Bengali-speaking caste Hindus!

Finally, let us take two states in the south. Kerala's Muslim population is 19.5 percent, its Christian population 21.1 percent, scheduled caste population 8.3 percent, and tribal population 1.3 percent. The caste Hindu population, therefore, is only 49.8 percent, some of whom (3.1 percent) are not Malayalee speakers. In Tamil Nadu, 5.1 percent is Muslim, 5.8 percent Christian, 17.8 percent scheduled caste, 0.8 percent scheduled tribe—these groups together comprising 29.5 percent of the total population. A regional language other than Tamil or Urdu is spoken by 13.5 percent of the population. Assuming some overlap among the categories, minorities form 35 to 40 percent of the state population.

A projection of these figures for the year 2000, extrapolating from current growth rates, gives us 172.0 million Muslims, Christians, and Sikhs, 255 million scheduled castes and tribes, approximately 42.3 million linguistically 'stateless' people (without a state of their own), and another 73.7 million people living outside of their 'home' state (some of whom, of course, are members of religious minorities or scheduled castes) [see Table 2.8]. The number of minorities for the year 2000 thus ranges from 472 to 545 million, the difference including many who are 'double' minorities. In short, if we think of the dominant majority as those who speak the official regional language as their mother tongue and are caste Hindus, then perhaps only 45 to 52 percent of the population can be regarded as part of this 'majority' in the year 2000 (as compared with 51 to 58 percent in 1971). It is likely that the 'majority' will fall below 50 percent in several states. Assam, with its Assamese-speaking caste Hindu population already below 50 percent, may foreshadow the anxieties that other 'majorities' may feel, as their majority status becomes precarious.

India's Emerging Majorities

To be part of the 'majority' is no less a matter of self-identification than to be part of a 'minority.' The growing articulation of minority claims in India is matched by an assertion of 'majority' claims as well. What remains problematic, however, is what constitutes this self-conscious 'majority.' Two overlapping identities have been competing for majority status: one is Hinduism; the other is determined by various regional languages.

The much noted 'revivalism' of Hinduism in recent years is hardly a

TABLE 2.8
India's Minorities (1971): Projections for the Year 2000[1]

	In Millions	Percent
Hindus	806.8	81.2
Muslims	128.8	12.9
Christians	22.1	2.2
Sikhs	20.8	2.1
Other religions	15.5	1.6
Total population	994.0	100.0
Scheduled castes	170.0	17.1
Scheduled tribes	85.0	8.5
Urdu speakers	51.8	5.2
Non-regional languages	49.0[2]	4.9
Minority regional languages	73.7	7.4

[1] I have used World Bank projections for India's population. The World Bank projects that India's population will grow by 45 percent from 1981 to the year 2000. According to the 1981 census, all tribal, caste, and religious minorities, with the exception of Christians, have increased more rapidly than the population as a whole. In making projections, I have assumed that these differences in growth rates continue. Should the population growth rates of the scheduled tribes, scheduled castes, and the various religious minorities decline more rapidly than for the population as a whole over the next 15 years, then these projected increases would, of course, be lower. For the languages, I have simply used the projected all-India population growth rates. These projections are to be taken as rough orders of magnitude.

[2] Of whom 6.7 million live in 'homelands' in the northeast, leaving 42.3 million 'stateless.'

Source: The World Bank, *World Development Report 1984*, New York, Oxford University Press, 1984

reassertion of religious piety. On that score, there is no evidence that there had been any decline in the performance of rituals, devotion to deities, participation in religious festivals, religious observance or whatever else one chooses as an indicator of religiosity in a religion that defies easy categorization. Hindu revivalism, or what some Hindus prefer to call a 'renaissance,' is a political statement, a reassertion less of religion than of nationalism.

It takes many forms: the militant stance of the RSS toward Christian institutions; the establishment of the Virat Hindu Samaj as an institution both for social reform and for the assertion of Hindu solidarity; the call to treat Bharat Mata as a kind of 'national' deity; the call for the establishment of compulsory national Hindu holidays; and Hindu movements for the reconversion of Muslims and Christians and for the Hinduization of tribals.

The reassertion of Hinduism sometimes takes a defensive form. 'How can you expect,' asks Karan Singh, Member of Parliament and President of the Virat Hindu Samaj, 'millions of people who are called Hindus to continue to accept a second class position in Hindu society?'[14] The sense that India, its secularism notwithstanding, is the heir to Hindu civilization, informs the growing assertiveness of India in its relations with its neighbors and in its commitment to greater military (and nuclear) power. This combined defensiveness and assertiveness of contemporary Hindus is a sentiment that can be tapped by political leaders. It was tapped by Mrs. Gandhi—some say her policies helped create it—and it has been tapped by Rajiv Gandhi. It was manifest by the support for Congress by the RSS in the December 1984 parliamentary elections, and it was manifest in the fact that for the first time in post-independence elections the Congress party won a clear majority of votes among caste Hindus in northern India.

Among educated Hindus one often heard the view that the government's use of military force in the Golden Temple complex was not only necessary as an anti-terrorist measure, but was also a necessary reassertion of Hindu authority against those who would destroy India. Indeed, the private expression of pride at times seemed to outweigh the government's official expressions of regret. So too, the reactions to the pogroms against Sikhs after Mrs. Gandhi's assassination. Rajiv Gandhi captured the mood, coming close to justifying the Hindu mobs, when he said during the election campaign that 'when a great tree falls, the ground will quake.'

Linguistic regionalism (a form of linguistic 'nationalism' as distinct from an all-India nationalism) is the other claimant for majority status. Its perception of the majority-minority distinction is, however, at the regional rather than at the national level. It takes the form of 'sons of the soil' sentiments, protection in education and employment against 'alien' migrants, the insertion of regional histories, regional symbols, and regional pride into school textbooks, and above all, the demand for greater regional autonomy in relation to the central government. If Hindu revivalism stirs anxieties among Sikhs, Muslims and Christians, then linguistic regionalism stirs anxieties among linguistic minorities in each of the states and among elites in the center who see regionalism as undermining the creation of an all-Indian nationalism. These latter

[14] Karan Singh, 'Hindu Renaissance', *Seminar*, April 1983, p. 17.

anxieties are most deeply felt by Hindi-speaking Hindus of the north, who see themselves as the center of the center, so to speak.

If the emphasis on group claims and rights for minorities has served to strengthen group assertiveness on the part of various majorities, this new assertiveness has also further intensified the anxieties of the minorities. To religious minorities, the embrace of Hindu tolerance, its eagerness to absorb others, is psychologically threatening. To linguistic minorities, the protective, assimilative, and exclusionary stance of linguistic majorities is a cultural threat and a barrier to educational, occupational, and spatial mobility. It is in this context of the new majorities that one must understand the demands of India's minorities.

What Do India's Minorities Want?

In the midst of the black power movement in the United States in the 1960s, a black activist was asked, 'What do you people want?' His recorded answer was: 'What is it that you have?'

The Demand for a Homeland

The comparable answer of many members of India's minorities is: 'We want a *homeland*.' Consider the following:

1. The demand by India's Muslims before 1947 for a homeland was the driving force among Muslims living in Hindu-majority areas of northern and western India. The demand, fundamentally ethnic, not religious, was for a Muslim-majority state, not an Islamic state. Islamic fundamentalists recognized the Muslim League demand for what it was—a nationalist demand—and therefore rejected it as antithetical to Islamic ideals. The League rejected Indian nationalism, but it was nationalist nonetheless. The demand was also initially rejected by Muslim leaders in Muslim majority states, since they had a homeland. However, they were ultimately persuaded by the Muslims from the Hindu-majority areas that their homeland would not be secure unless they had a nation-state of their own.

2. The demand for linguistic homelands or states was the driving force in Indian politics in the 1950s. Minority linguistic groups wanted states of their own where they could become a majority.

The movement resulted in the massive reorganization of India's states so as to give almost all the linguistic groups listed in Schedule VIII of the Constitution (the exceptions were Sindhi and Urdu speakers) linguistic states of their own. The achievement of statehood was, thus, the means by which some minority groups became a majority.

3. Prior to independence, a demand for a Sikh homeland was made by some Sikh leaders who conceived of India as having three 'nations:' the nations of Islam, Hinduism, and Sikhism. The demand became the driving force among virtually all Sikh leaders after 1947, when the possibility of a Sikh-majority state was within their grasp. The achievement of a separate state with a Sikh majority in 1966 left Sikh nationalists unsatisfied largely because divisions within the Sikh community frustrated their efforts to seize power.[15]

4. The movement in India's northeast among the various tribes was also for a homeland. The initial rejection of these demands by the Indian government led to India's longest insurrectionary movement, which dissipated (but did not wholly disappear) only after the center agreed to provide the various peoples of the northeast with states of their own.

5. The unsatisfied demand for a homeland persists in several of India's tribal areas, most notably in the Munda-Oraon-Ho-Santhal region of Bihar, Orissa, Madhya Pradesh, and West Bengal. The movement in part is frustrated by the fact that except in a handful of districts the tribals lack a majority. Nonetheless, the movement for a homeland persists and is unlikely to disappear. There are other areas with sufficiently large concentrations of tribals (though the areas themselves are sometimes small) that have developed homeland movements.

[15] After the Punjab was reorganized on a linguistic basis in November 1966, the Akalis were able to form a government for the first time, but their hold on political power was tenuous. It was not simply because the Sikhs constituted only 60 percent of the population, but, because a substantial portion of the Sikh community—the scheduled caste Sikhs—in their antagonism to Sikh Jats, voted for the Congress party. For a time, the Akalis were in coalition with the Congress, then with the Jana Sangh, and then with the Janata party. Thrust out of power in Mrs. Gandhi's Congress victory of 1980, the Akalis adopted a more radical posture, articulating an earlier demand for more autonomy for the Punjab, but also explicitly articulating Sikh religious concerns as well.

For an informative analysis of the Sikh issue, see *Seminar*, February 1984, devoted to 'The Punjab Tangle.' The issue contains articles by I.K. Gujral ('The Sequence'), Rajendra Sareen ('Source of Trouble'), Attar Singh ('What Went Wrong'),

The sense of attachment to 'place' in India is as powerful as attachment to group, and the two are closely intertwined. Groups often regard the territory in which they live as the site of their exclusive history—a place in which great events have occurred and sacred shrines are located. Tribal and linguistic groups often regard a homeland as exclusively their own. They would, if they could, exclude others, or deny them the right to enjoy the fruits of the land or find employment within the territory. Hence, India's linguistic majorities define themselves as 'sons of the soil,' with group rights to employment, land, and political power not granted to those who come from 'outside.' It is not sufficient that the group occupy the territory that is their homeland; they also seek to exercise political control.

For this reason, many minority groups with a territorial base have pressed for statehood. Statehood converts minority status into majority status. It enables minorities to resist assimilation (linguistic or religious) by the majority. And in more practical terms it gives them control over the resources of the government, employment, patronage, and education. In India, where the state exercises so much control over the market, ethnic groups believe that it is essential to hold political power to enable their members to redistribute public goods into their own hands.[16]

It is in this context that we may be able to forecast which groups, now minorities, will seek to turn themselves into majorities by demanding statehood. *Any group that has a territorial base but does not now have a state is a likely candidate, particularly if the group has its own political leadership and political organizations to articulate ethnic group interests.* Over the next decade or so, a number of minority groups will seek majority status by demanding their own states. If I had to predict the areas, I would focus on districts with tribal concentrations. Resentment over the intrusion of non-tribals into these rural communities is

T.V. Sathyamurthy ('Crisis Within the Crisis'), Prakash Tandon ('Another Angle'), Sajjan Singh Murgin Puri ('Sanctuary'), and K.R. Bombwall ('Ethnonationism'). The issue also contains an excellent bibliography.

[16] The American liberal view, to quote Arthur M. Schlesinger, that 'politics, after all, is in the art of solving problems' and that 'political tendencies rise or fall depending on the results they produce' ('The Elections and After', *New York Review of Books*, August 16, 1984, p. 35), hardly fits the Indian view of politics. For Indians politics means acquiring power over others, maintaining or elevating one's status, and using power to provide patronage to one's supporters. Policies and issues have little to do with politics. While dozens of governments have fallen, I can think of none where a split in the government party on an issue of public policy led to a legislative defeat in the assembly.

particularly great, while the inability of the tribals to compete for industrial and professional jobs in the urban centers and to gain access to senior administrative positions is a source of considerable anger on the part of educated tribals. The government's policy of fostering the industrial development of districts without industries, many of which are tribal-populated districts, could serve to increase migration into these localities and further widen the gap between the tribal and non-tribal populations.

The achievement of statehood by the tribals of the northeast stands as a model for others. There have already been demands that a Bodo state be carved out of Assam and a Jharkhand state out of Bihar. One could imagine these demands becoming more articulate. Tribals in other parts of the country will seek statehood or greater autonomy within their states not only to gain control over state resources but to place restrictions on the entry of non-tribals into the local labor market.

In addition to the tribal areas, there are indications that a distinctive identity exists among some linguistic groups not listed as official languages in the eighth schedule of the Constitution. There are indications of a territorial-cum-cultural identity in the hill regions of Uttar Pradesh, and in sub-regions of Andhra and Maharashtra. There could be a demand for statehood among any of these people.

Some ethnic groups do not have a sufficiently large population in any single district or region to seek statehood, but many of them would substantially increase their political power were they in smaller states. Indeed, a Jharkhand state would not have a tribal majority, but tribal power would be substantially greater than it now is in Bihar. Similarly, were West Bengal, Maharashtra, Uttar Pradesh, and Bihar reorganized into smaller units, as some have proposed, the proportion of Muslims in several of the resulting smaller states would be substantially higher than in the present states. A decision to reorganize these states would result in the mobilization of Muslims (along with tribals and the Nepalis) to seek gerrymandered borders that would concentrate and maximize their numbers in the newly formed states.

The close association between group identity and political power has been put forth by every group in India seeking statehood. One scholar quotes a Sikh leader as saying, 'No nation can maintain itself without political power.'[17] He quotes another Sikh politician as saying,

[17] M.S. Dhami, *Minority Leaders' Image of the Indian Political System: An Exploratory Study of the Attitudes of Akali Leaders*, New Delhi, Sterling Publishers, 1975, p. 34.

'Akalis seek some sort of cultural and religious freedom by which they could keep the cultural identity of the Sikhs intact. Furthermore, they also feel that without political power in the hands of the Sikhs, this may not be possible.'[18] The same statement could easily have been made by Mizo, Naga, Munda, Oraon, Ho, Assamese, Nepali, Telugu, and other tribal and linguistic leaders.

Linguistic Recognition

A major demand of a number of linguistic groups is that their language be included in the eighth schedule of the Constitution. Inclusion in the list enables a linguistic group to take all-India examinations in their own language. Similarly, recognition as an official language of a state enables a people to compete for positions in the state services without having to take examinations in another language. Official recognition, linguistic minorities argue, reduces the pressures for linguistic assimilation and enables the group to strengthen its identity and solidarity.

It should be noted that linguistic minorities are allowed to have primary and secondary school classes in their mother tongue when there is a sufficient number of children to form a class. But the question of whether linguistic minorities have classes in their own language at the university level and whether examinations for state employment can be taken in their own language have been bitter political issues in several states. The issue has been pressed, among others, by Nepalis living in Darjeeling and Dehra Dun, by Marathi speakers in Karnataka, by Bengalis in Assam, and by Urdu speakers in almost any state in which they are numerous.

Reservations

The alternative to statehood for dispersed minorities is to have reserved seats in legislative bodies and in the administrative services. The Indian Constitution, as we have already noted, legitimizes claims for groups' rights. The Constitution provides for group benefits for scheduled castes, scheduled tribes, and other backward classes. In addition to group representation through reserved constituencies in elected bodies, the government-can provide for quotas for appointments in the administrative services and admissions into colleges, universities, and medical and technical schools.

[18] *Ibid.*, p. 35.

The system of reservations has a long history in India. Under the Morley-Minto reforms of 1909, separate electorates were established for Muslims. The British subsequently provided separate electorates for Sikhs, scheduled castes, Anglo-Indians, and other minority groups. With partition and a new constitution, all separate electorates were abolished except those for scheduled castes and tribes.

While the Government of India has steadfastly held the position that only these groups are entitled to reserved constituencies, reservations have been extended to others in education and employment.[19] They were first extended, as we have discussed earlier, to 'other backward classes.' In recent years, legislation has extended group rights to 'sons of the soil,' that is, people who speak the recognized regional language of the state or, in at least one case (Telengana), to the 'native' people of a sub-region of the state. The principle of reservations has thereby been extended to a majority that wants to be protected against competition from a successful minority.

State and central governments in India have moved toward the principle that membership in educational institutions, in state and central administrative services, in the military, and in public sector employment should ultimately reflect the demographic division of the country. While that policy is welcomed by some minorities (and some majorities!), it leaves two groups unhappy: those who are left out and those who lose.

Muslims, once the primary beneficiaries of reservations, are now excluded from reservations, although Muslim leaders have called for reservations on the grounds that they too are backward in employment and education. The Government of India has, however, consistently refused to extend reservations to religious groups on the grounds that it would be divisive. The government's opposition to reservations along religious lines strikes many Muslims as discriminatory, given the government's willingness to grant benefits to caste, tribal, and linguistic groups.

Sikhs have reacted against the government's reservation policies. This is not only because they are excluded from the system of reservations, but because they view the government's policy to achieve a greater ethnic balance in the military by proportional recruitment in the states as effectively reducing the number of Sikhs in the armed

[19] For an analysis of the ways in which preferential policies, once restricted to scheduled castes and scheduled tribes, have been extended to other groups, including the majority communities, see Chapter 6.

forces. It has been estimated that Sikhs have comprised as much as 15 percent of the military, though they constitute less than two percent of the population; proportional recruitment would thus very substantially undermine the opportunities of young Sikhs to seek military careers.

Among higher caste Hindus there has developed resistance to reservations, most recently in Madhya Pradesh, Gujarat and Bihar. The backlash is not only against the demand of the other backward classes, but in some instances even against reservations for scheduled castes and tribes. The more successful reservations become at improving the capacity of scheduled castes and tribes to compete for jobs in the administrative services, the less willing are others to support a system of employment based on group membership. Reservations in India, as elsewhere, has left all communities dissatisfied—beneficiaries because they believe that the reservations are not satisfactorily administered, and those who are excluded because they view the system as discriminatory.

Security

Minorities in India, as elsewhere, are particularly concerned over their security. Poor and dispersed minorities, most especially members of the scheduled castes, are particularly vulnerable to attacks from the majority. In recent years, there have been repeated charges from minorities that they can no longer rely upon the police to assure them of protection and that the police themselves have attacked minorities or supported attackers. There is considerable evidence from media reports that the police in India have become increasingly politicized and that factions of the governing party and their supporters within local communities have used the police to their own advantage. The collusion of sections of the police with sections of the Congress party against minorities was particularly evident in the attacks against Sikhs in the capital following Mrs. Gandhi's assassination. Not until the army was called in did the attacks subside.

In other recent ethnic conflicts in Punjab, Gujarat, West Bengal and UP, the police have been ineffective. Acknowledging their weakness, the central government has often turned to the military. In the Punjab, for example, the central government charged the state government—even when it was run by its own party in the early eighties—of failing to deal with Sikh terrorism, failing to provide adequate intelligence to its own police, and having its civil services and police take a partisan position towards the various groups.

The use of the military to deal with ethnic conflict entails very substantial risks for the military itself, as the mutiny by Sikhs in the army after the assault on the Golden Temple demonstrated. Moreover, as the government contemplates the use of the army to deal with ethnic conflicts and consults with army personnel, the army itself may become politicized.

Even if the military remains non-political, the frequent use of armed forces (including the Central Reserve Police and the Border Security Forces), usually accompanied by the suspension of the state government and the imposition of restrictions upon the press and upon the opposition, involves a suspension of democratic procedures. This represents a significant erosion of the democratic process and democratic institutions.

While opposition leaders have not disagreed with the government's decision to deploy the army in Punjab, Assam, and other regions of ethnic conflict and violence, critics have argued that Mrs. Gandhi often failed to take political measures prior to the outburst of violence. Indeed, many went further in arguing that actions by the government often precipitated the violence, which was then used by the government to justify the use of force and thereby win popular credit for restoring law and order. Thus, say the critics, the decision to hold elections in Assam prior to an agreement over disputed electoral rolls made violence more likely. In the Punjab, the exclusion of the Akali Dal from political power in the state, and steps taken by Congress leaders to encourage Bhindranwale's attacks against the moderates in the Akali Dal, served to strengthen the radical terrorist elements. It has been noted that Hindu-Muslim clashes grew in Hyderabad at the very moment when Mrs. Gandhi's supporters were seeking to bring down the state government, charging it with a weak handling of communal disturbances. These are persuasive criticisms, highlighting the inability of a weakened governing party to share power with minorities, and the temptation on the part of some government supporters to encourage ethnic strife so as to justify central government intervention and to win support from majority communities. There is in India a deep and justifiable fear of uncontrollable violence among religious, caste, and linguistic groups. This fear serves to legitimize armed intervention by the state and can easily be played upon by a government. A government whose leaders and supporters deliberately, or through inaction, enable such conflicts to grow, however, is in danger of unleashing uncontrollable forces that could ultimately lead to its own undermining.

Politics: The Problem or the Solution?

Indians have two views of the impact of politics on ethnic group conflict: that it worsens group relations, and that politics is the way to reduce group conflict. Both views are correct.

The distribution of education, employment, and wealth in India is largely determined by the political process. This central feature of political life means that each ethnic group can best improve its share of education and employment by increasing its political power. The twin objectives of all ethnic groups in India—to strengthen their group identity and to improve both the social status and economic well-being of the group—can best be achieved through the route of politics. It is this central fact that induces politicians to appeal to their ethnic group for votes.

In this sense, politics can intensify and sometimes even create group consciousness, but it is by no means the only determinant. How group consciousness develops has been a subject of considerable scholarly inquiry.[20] A review of that literature is not called for here, except to say that most scholars give considerable importance to such matters as the impact of external threats, the influence of cultural and intellectual elites, the effects of government policies and programs, and the growth in mass communications, education, and urbanization. Often of critical importance are increase in social mobility, rise in education, and gains in employment that exceed the traditional status held by a social group. This tension between aspirations (and sometimes material achievement) and status often arouses group consciousness. The reverse—a decline in income which threatens to lower social status—can also arouse group consciousness. In India, it is the former rather than the latter that has more often been the stimulus to political action.

It is not necessary that we know which of these factors will strengthen

[20] For an analysis of the impact of politics on shaping linguistic and religious group consciousness in India, see Paul Brass, *Language, Religion and Politics in North India*, Berkeley, University of California Press, 1974.

group consciousness in India over the next fifteen years. It is sufficient to know that group consciousness has been growing and that it shows no signs of withering under the forces of modernization.[21] It is important to note that it is in the perceived interests of caste, tribal, religious, and ethnic groups to seek political power to improve their status and economic well-being.[22] Ethnic groups have interests no less than do classes. In India, as in other multi-ethnic societies, individuals are members both of a class and an ethnic group. In a society without ethnic divisions, class consciousness develops more easily. However, in a society divided along ethnic lines historical and comparative evidence overwhelmingly suggests that ethnic group consciousness is likely to prevail. The fictive ties of kinship that characterize ethnic groups provide a more effective sense of attachment than do the appeals to interests made on the behalf of classes. Class has its

---

[21] An elderly Indian socialist, Achyut Patwardhan, reflecting on the ways in which Marxism affected his own capacity to understand the determinants and durability of religious and ethnic group consciousness in India, had this to say:

> There is another error which is now equally apparent in retrospect which must be confessed frankly. Pt. Jawaharlal Nehru and the younger section of Congressmen (among these must be counted the present writer and his other socialist colleagues) sincerely believed that regional and parochial loyalties would be defeated logically and inevitably by more basic 'class' loyalties. Our generation was under the spell of Marx and Lenin and economic factors seemed to us far more decisive in determining the direction of world history. We felt, therefore, that Indian Muslim masses would be weaned away from the reactionary sectarian domination of the Mullahs.

Achyut Patwardhan, foreword to M.A. Karandhikar, *Islam in India's Transition to Modernity*, Westport, Connecticut, Greenwood Publishers Corporation 1969, pp. vii–viii.

[22] Since Marxists see 'interests' only in class terms they are unable to see religion, tribe, language, and caste as rational bases for social action or political conflict. When they analyze such behavior it is either seen as derivative of economic differences or as a false consciousness. For a statement of the Marxist view of interests, see André Beteille, *Six Essays in Comparative Sociology*, Delhi, Oxford University Press, 1974. Beteille, a leading Indian sociologist, writes that 'the task of sociology, as I see it, is to study the dialectical relationship between ideas and interests' (p. 98) . . . . Those who work on the land have similar interests whether they speak Bengali or Santali, or practice Hinduism or Animism' (pp. 104–105). This notion that people in the same occupation 'have similar interests' precludes an understanding of how individuals and groups define their 'interests,' and it fails to recognize that people in the same class but in different ethnic groups (Bengali and Santali peasants, for example, or Hindu and tribal middle class) may, in fact, have competing interests in land or employment.

effective appeals, but the sense of class comradeship often has a lesser pull than the attractions of blood ties, real or imagined.

Class appeals are of growing importance in India. Punjabi farmers have sought to influence government policies on agricultural prices and access to irrigation and electric power. The middle classes in Assam have called for more job-producing central government public sector investments. And Maharashtrian factory workers have demanded higher wages. But these same interests organized to make class demands have assumed quite a different garb with other claims when they act as Sikhs, Assamese, and Muslims.

Heightened group consciousness does not necessarily result in intergroup conflict. Group consciousness may lead to a sense of pride, may result in a more strict observance of cultural and religious practices, may lead members of a group to help one another. Conflicts arise when a group asserts its identity by attacking the identity of other groups and, above all, when a claim for group rights and group power is perceived by others as threatening.

Conflicts among ethnic groups and between ethnic groups and the government are unlikely to abate in the near future. In India it is particularly important to note that governmental instability and perceived governmental weakness exacerbate social conflict. At one level, Hindu-Muslim conflicts in various parts of India, Hindu-Sikh conflicts in Punjab, and Bengali-Assamese conflicts in Assam can be understood in terms of particular social changes at work in each of these states and among each of these communities; but at another level, they can be explained by the weakening of the governing Congress party. The loosening of the bonds between the Congress party and ex-untouchables and Muslims has created new conditions for caste and communal conflict. The failure of state Congress parties and their governments to be responsive to local religious, linguistic, caste, and regional concerns has sometimes led to the channelization of protests into regional and ethnic parties and movements. Weak political institutions are more often a cause than a consequence of growing social conflict.

Conflict Management in the 1980s and 1990s

The organizational decline of the Congress party at the state and local level, and the politicization of the police and the lower levels of administration, do not augur well for conflict management by government. Moreover, a number of public policies which had mitigated group conflict in the past have now themselves become sources of conflict. Reservations ameliorated the plight of scheduled castes and scheduled tribes, but the pressure for their extension to other groups has now made reservations a divisive issue. Federalism and the rearrangements of state boundaries to provide statehood for linguistic, tribal, and (in the case of Punjab), religious minorities worked well for reducing conflict in the 1950s and 1960s, but it is not working well in the 1980s, as many of the states now seek a rearrangement of center-state powers and resources. The earlier government policy of seeking to reduce foreign influence (particularly with respect to foreign missionaries) is less effective when India's Muslims employed in the Gulf are sending remittances home, Sikhs are living in Western Europe and North America, Bangladeshis are moving into Assam, and Tamil-Sinhalese conflicts in Sri Lanka arouse south Indian Tamil sentiments.[23] Even the language formulas of the 1960s are questioned, as Urdu-speaking Muslims, Nepalis, and other linguistic minorities press for official recognition. Nor do strategies of sitting it out, waiting for ethnic feelings to dissipate, or of incorporating leaders of ethnic groups, seem to work as well as they did earlier.

In the coming years the demands of ethnic groups—majorities or minorities—are bound to force a rethinking of many of India's hitherto successful policies to manage conflict.

One major policy thrust in the coming years is likely to be a growing concern for what can *loosely* be defined as 'majority' interests. There is concern that some minorities, through their control over critical resources or critical institutions, could coerce the national government. The threat by Sikh militants to block the sale of grains to the central government constituted one such attempt, though the attempt itself

---

[23] The movement of Bangladeshis, Tamils from Sri Lanka, Nepalis into India, and of Indians into Nepal, the Gulf states, West Europe, and the United States has created new issues of internal and international relations for India (some of which led Mrs. Gandhi to speak of a 'foreign hand'), that cry out for a full-scale analysis.

did not succeed. Another example was the effort by the Assamese to prevent the movement of oil from Assam to the refineries.

The issue of control over some critical institutions has been more important. Military officials are concerned that military units be ethnically diversified and Muslims, Sikhs and other self-conscious ethnic groups not be in a position to undermine the use of military power in domestic crises. The government's policy of diversifying military recruitment geographically has been vindicated by recent developments. So too has been the government's policy of having statewide quotas for recruitment into the national administrative service, even at the cost of purely 'merit' considerations. Similarly, some regard for geographical distribution—since geography is a surrogate for linguistic and religious affiliation—is an important consideration in the selection of students by the central universities and the national institutes of engineering, management, and medicine. Wide geographic representation assures that the next generation of the country's scientific, engineering, management, and medical personnel is ethnically diversified.

The state governments are no less likely to protect their interests than is the central government. Even as the states make claims upon the center for more resources and greater autonomy, so too will tribal and linguistic minorities make claims upon the states. And just as the central government will resist demands made by the states, so too will state governments resist demands made by the minorities. Under such circumstances, local minorities turn to the center for political support; indeed, by generating violence and creating disturbances that the state government cannot handle, local groups (notably opponents of the government) hope to force central government intervention.

The less able state governments are to manage majority-minority relations, the more likely is central government intervention. Of critical importance, therefore, in the future of majority-minority relations in India, is the viability of the state governments. Rajiv Gandhi's overwhelming victory in the national parliamentary elections will be of little avail in the peaceful management of ethnic conflict, if state governments are weak. Should minorities become more assertive and conflict prove to be unmanageable by state government authorities, then the powers of the central government will increase.

A pessimistic scenario is one in which majority-minority conflicts increase, state governments do not demonstrably increase their capacity to deal with these conflicts, the center by its actions provokes opposition to central authority, and the growth of violent conflict leads to greater coercion and the use of the armed forces.

An optimistic scenario is one in which leaders at both the national and the state levels demonstrate their skill at accommodating the demands for substantial administrative decentralization and prove skillful at reassuring minorities without threatening the cultural identity and interests of majorities. We can make no predictions about which scenario is more likely.

3

Institution Building in India

Of the imperial powers, only the Soviet Union and the United Kingdom have an impressive record of leaving behind their distinctive political institutions in the countries they once occupied. From one point of view, the Soviet record of institutional transfer is perfect. In every country of Eastern Europe once occupied by the Soviet army, the basic institutions of governance put in place by the Soviets have remained: the communist party, the secret police, the military, state-run public corporations, and collective agricultural institutions. Some older institutions of the pre-communist period have persisted, and some new institutions have emerged—the Catholic Church and Solidarity come to mind—but thus far they have not significantly transformed the Soviet-modeled institutional structure. However, how legitimate these state institutions are is a matter of doubt: would they continue in their present form in Poland, for example, were they not sustained by the threat of Soviet intervention, or would they have remained in Czechoslovakia and Hungary if the Soviet army had not intervened?

The British imprint on its former colonies is less all-inclusive than the Soviet's, but considerably more legitimate in the sense that these institutions are not sustained by the prospect of British intervention. To be sure, many former British colonies have long since given up the Westminster system: Tanzania, Kenya and Uganda have abandoned democratic elections, competitive parties and a freely elected parliament.

This paper first appeared in Seizabura Sato, Robert Scalapino and Jusuf Wanandi, eds., *Asian Political Institutionalization*, Berkeley, University of California, Institute of Asian Studies, 1985.

Pakistan and Bangladesh have mostly been under military rule, as have Ghana and several other countries in Africa. Nonetheless, an impressive number of erstwhile British colonies have maintained British-style democratic institutions for all or most of their post-independence history. Among them, India, Malaysia, Nigeria (until December 1983), Sri Lanka (until recent violent ethnic strife), Jamaica, Papua New Guinea, Botswana, Gambia, Mauritius, Nauru, Belize and Fiji (except in the current turbulent period). In some of these countries, the democratic parliamentary model has been fragile and erratic; nor can one speak with great confidence about the future of democratic institutions in all of them. Still, what is striking is that among the newly independent countries of the Caribbean, Asia, Africa, the Middle East, and the Pacific, competitive democracies have existed only among the former British colonies. Not a single former Dutch, Belgian, or French colony currently has democratic institutions, and the Philippines, a former American colony, has acquired them only recently after a long authoritarian phase. In Indonesia, Zaire and Vietnam, the political institutions introduced by their former rulers have not survived.

Why the British have had more success in institutional transfer than other imperial powers, and why these institutions have remained intact in some of the former British colonies, is an important issue in comparative political analysis. It is the purpose of this essay to deal with the second question, focusing attention on institutional developments in South Asia, with the hope that such an analysis may illuminate the larger question of the conditions under which institutions, especially democratic institutions, are transferred, sustained, modified, or eroded.

Viceregal and Westminster Models

Of the three successor states to British India, only India has successfully sustained a British democratic model, with competitive political parties, eight national parliamentary elections, an independent judiciary, a non-political military, the police and paramilitary institutions controlled by elected representatives, a free press, and associations (including trade unions, peasant organizations, and caste associations) more or less free from state domination. True enough, the Indian experience has been flawed: for twenty-one months from June 26,

1975 to March 1977 India lived under emergency rule when the electoral process was suspended, leading opposition figures were jailed, a number of political parties banned, the press censored, and the power of the judiciary circumscribed. But the elections of March 1977 (called by an authoritarian government) brought about the defeat of Mrs. Indira Gandhi and her governing Congress party, and the restoration of democratic institutions, a process not reversed by Mrs. Gandhi's return to power in the parliamentary elections of 1980. The durability of India's democratic institutions was further demonstrated by the orderly transition of Rajiv Gandhi to power following the assassination of Prime Minister Indira Gandhi by Sikh extremists. This transition was legitimized through parliamentary elections several months after the assassination.

In Pakistan, British parliamentary institutions formally came to an end on October 7, 1958. President Iskander Mirza dissolved the national parliament and the provincial assemblies, dismissed the central and provincial governments, banned all political parties, abrogated the 1956 constitution, and declared martial law. He appointed General Mohammad Ayub Khan, the commander-in-chief of the Pakistan army, as chief martial law administrator, placing all armed forces of Pakistan under his command. In a national radio broadcast the next day, General Ayub Khan explained that the decision had been taken 'with great reluctance, but with the fullest conviction that there was no alternative to it except the disintegration and complete ruination of the country.' Thus, Pakistan abruptly ended a decade of Westminster parliamentary government characterized by competitive political parties, elections, a free press, an independent judiciary, and freedom of association. In its place emerged an administrative state controlled by a civil and military bureaucracy, a viceregal system of authority based upon a patrimonial process of decision making.

Efforts to create a competitive parliamentary system in Bangladesh proved to be abortive. The founders of Bangladesh, Mujibur Rahman and his Awami League party, assured their supporters that once East Pakistan became an independent country it would (in contrast to Pakistan), be an open, competitive, democratic system run by freely elected political parties. But it was Mujib himself who on December 28, 1974, barely three years after Bangladesh became independent, proclaimed a state of emergency, suspended all fundamental rights, abolished all opposition parties, closed down most of the country's daily newspapers, and created a one-party dictatorship. Eight months later, on August 15, 1975—the anniversary of the British withdrawal from South Asia—in a lightning and bloody coup, the military over-threw Sheikh Mujib, killing him and almost every member of his family, and established an administrative state under the civil and military bureaucracy.

Both Pakistan and Bangladesh have experienced institutional changes since their first coup. Pakistan had a competitive national parliamentary election in 1971, but it proved to be a catalyst for civil war when the military refused to turn power over to an East Pakistani Awami League majority. Civilian government was restored in 1972 when the army stepped down and the leader of the Pakistan People's Party, Zulfikar Ali Bhutto (whose party had a majority), was invited to form a government. The new government, however, was nearly as autocratic as its military predecessors, and it ended in 1978 with a military coup that had considerable support from the opposition parties.

The attempt to move Bangladesh out of military government proved no more successful. In 1978, three years after he took power, General Ziaur Rahman held Bangladesh's first general elections with some measure of open, competitive politics. But only three years later, in May 1981, President Ziaur Rahman was killed by an assassin. Once again elections were held, with candidates put up by the Bangladesh Nationalist Party that Zia had founded in 1978, and the Bangladesh Awami League, the party of the late Sheikh Mujibur Rahman. Abdus Sattar, leader of the BNP, easily won with 66 percent of the vote, but the following year Lieutenant General Hossain Mohammad Ershad seized power on behalf of the army and appointed himself chief martial law administrator. Some 200 persons were arrested including former ministers, and parliament was dissolved. A martial law order was issued, enabling Ershad to act in place of the parliament, and the martial law administrator assumed the authority to appoint civilian judges. Once again, the military and civil administrations were in complete control.

It would be incorrect to conclude from this brief account that the Indians inherited the British institutional legacy, while Pakistan and Bangladesh did not. Each in its own way has built upon the institu-tional foundations initially created by the British: Pakistan and Bangladesh on those institutions that sustained the imperial state, and India on the electoral institutions, parliament, state assemblies, and political parties that the British either nurtured or tolerated. Indeed, it is commonplace in much of the scholarly writings about Pakistan and Bangladesh to point out the similarities between these governments and the *spirit* as well as *institutions* of British viceregal rule. The viceroys and governors-general were, after all, not democratic rulers, and British authority rested upon the coercive powers of the military, the police, and civil administration. The commander-in-chief of the military shared authority with civilian administrators, reporting directly to the British government, and neither military nor civilian authorities were held accountable to elected officials for their actions. There was a division of powers between the executive and judicial branches of government at the higher levels, but at the district level the senior officers combined both judicial and administrative functions. Administrators had a paternalistic view of their own authority and little regard for the elected politicians permitted by the British to exercise some authority at the local and provincial level.

The viceregal model is thus just as much a part of the British tradition as the Westminster model.

Why the Institutional Divergences in South Asia?

How, then, does one explain the divergent institutional paths taken by India, Pakistan and Bangladesh? Many conventional explanations about why some countries in the third world have taken an authoritarian path while others have remained democratic do not apply to India. For instance, the 'socio-economic determinants' theory of democracy holds that democracy is unsuited to countries having widespread illiteracy, poverty, unemployment, and population growth. A specifically economic variant of this theory was that without high rates of economic growth democracy would not survive in the third world. To this was later added the qualification by some that not only a high rate of economic growth but an equitable distribution of income was required for the sustenance of democracy.[1]

Inequities and impoverishment are, however, commonplace in India, and of roughly the same magnitude as in Pakistan and Bangladesh.

---

[1] A review of various theories of democracy and their applicability (or inapplicability) to contemporary developing countries can be found in Myron Weiner, 'Empirical Democratic Theory,' in Myron Weiner and Ergun Ozbudun, eds., *Competitive Elections in Developing Countries*, Durham, N.C., Duke University Press, 1987.

Growth rates have been different in different phases, and neither the level nor the rate of change in national income has had any distinctive impact on the form of government. Few observers would argue that Mrs. Gandhi's decision to declare a national emergency in 1975 was a consequence of economic deterioration. Most of the key economic indicators in the two or three years preceding the Emergency were not significantly different from those for the entire preceding decade. (In fact, some critical economic indicators, such as the food supply, were not as constraining as in the mid-sixties.)

It is true, on the other hand, that the military coup in Pakistan in 1958 followed a period of economic decline. The cost-of-living index had risen from 98 to 120 between 1949 and 1958 in West Pakistan, and from 103 to 117 in East Pakistan. Pakistan also had problems in its balance of payments. On almost any economic measure, however, India's economic performance during this period was hardly better. The cost-of-living index rose from 96 to 124 in the five years 1953 to 1958, and the balance-of-payments deficit was substantial. 'In all cases,' wrote Wayne Wilcox, 'an objective comparison would favor Pakistan . . . [but] no one seriously advocated martial law for India.'[2]

According to another theory, social heterogeneity is a threat both to democratic institutions and to the state itself. On the scale of social heterogeneity, post-independence Pakistan ranked among the most diversified countries in the world. Pakistan's cleavages were made worse by two factors: the division of the country into two parts, and the overlapping of ethnic groups across international borders. Pakistan shared its Pathan population with Afghanistan, a country that asserted a claim over the Pushtun-speaking regions, and it shared its Baluch population with both Iran and Afghanistan. It controlled a small part of Kashmir and claimed the entire province of Kashmir from India. Both the Punjab and Bengali-speaking East Pakistan shared the same linguistic/ethnic identity with neighboring populations in India, although they diverged on matters of religious identity.

It is, therefore, plausible to conclude that ethnic strains must have played a role in the demise of democracy in Pakistan. Moreover, it also appeared as if religious, caste, and linguistic cleavages would tear India apart, leaving either a weak, truncated center with powerful provincial rulers, or, alternatively, an authoritarian state that would hold the

[2] Wayne Ayres Wilcox, 'The Pakistan Coup d'Etat of 1958,' *Pacific Affairs*, Vol. 38, No. 2, Summer, 1965, p. 149.

country together by coercion. Heterogeneity, however, has not destroyed Indian democracy, nor that of Malaysia and Mauritius, nor that of Canada, Belgium, Switzerland, the Netherlands or the United States. Moreover, though Bangladesh is a remarkably homogeneous country—almost the entire population speaks Bengali and there are few sharp cultural-cum-economic cleavages, the well-to-do Hindus having left the country in 1947 and the West Pakistani capitalists having left in 1971—the country has not sustained democratic institutions.[3]

Instead of looking for socio-economic determinants, one might wish to account for the divergent post-independence institutional developments of South Asian countries in terms of their institutional legacies. One can begin with comparing the state institutions. In August 1947, the Indian army was divided: fifteen infantry regiments were given to India, eight to Pakistan. A similar division took place in the armored corps and artillery regiments. But ordnance factories were located primarily in India, and in the division of equipment Pakistan actually received less than the one-third initially proposed. Among commissioned officers, Pakistan received disproportionately fewer than India, since only 23.7 percent of the officers were Muslims as compared with 56 percent Hindus.[4]

Nor did Pakistan fare better in administrative services. At the time of independence there were 549 Indians in the Indian Civil Service and Indian Political Service, of whom 101 were Muslims. Ninety-five opted for service in Pakistan. Moreover, the penetration of the administrative services into the North West Frontier Province and into Baluchistan was less than in most provinces of India or the other provinces of Pakistan.[5]

In short, the administrative services and the military were initially weaker in Pakistan than in India. Moreover, within Pakistan both the administration and military were less developed in East Pakistan than in the West: only two members of the Indian Civil Service were from

[3] The classic statement concerning the inappropriateness of democracy in a heterogeneous society is John Stuart Mill's *Representative Government*. For an alternative view of the way in which representative government and cultural pluralism can be and have been made compatible, see Arend Lijphart, *Democracy in Plural Societies: A Comparative Exploration*, New Haven, Conn., Yale University Press, 1977.

[4] Hasan Askari Rizvi, *The Military and Politics in Pakistan*, Lahore, Progressive Publishers, 1974, p. 39.

[5] Muneer Ahmad, *The Civil Servant in Pakistan*, Karachi, Oxford University Press, 1964, p. 53.

East Pakistan and there were few military officers from the lower ranks who came from Bengal. Even on the eve of the civil war, the Bengalis were disproportionately under-represented within both the Pakistan military and the civil bureaucracy—an important element in Bengali resentment of what they viewed as Pakistani domination. But the breakdown of civilian rule in Pakistan in 1958, as we shall explore later, can hardly be attributed to the weakness of the military or civil bureaucracy. The military grew quickly in size, and its political position was enhanced as the politicians proved unable to resolve the major institutional issues of governance. For an explanation of why political developments in India and Pakistan diverged as they did, we need to examine the way in which the *political* as distinct from *state* institutions developed within the pre-1947 areas that ultimately went to Pakistan.

Electoral and Party Politics in British India

The political party system that developed in British India not only reflected the divisions between Hindus and Muslims, but it was substantially conditioned by the electoral process created by the British authorities. The electoral principle was first introduced in India in 1884 for local bodies and in 1892 for provincial councils. The Gladstone Liberals looked upon the introduction of elected governments as a first step toward national self-government. In contrast, the British Conservatives were of the opinion that an electoral system along British lines—one person/one vote, territorial representation, and majority rule—would be disastrous for India's Muslims. Their concern for the Muslims was based less on an abstract notion of justice than on their awareness of the need to sustain Muslim support for British rule in India. Once the Liberals had won on the question of whether the elective principle should be introduced into India, the Conservatives turned their attention to the question of how best to ensure representation for the Muslim minority. The issue was resolved with the appointment of a commission co-chaired by John Morley, the Liberal Secretary of State for India, and Lord Minto, the Conservative viceroy.[6]

Minto successfully argued for 'communal' electorates in which

[6] Stanley Wolpert, *Morley and India, 1906–1910*, Berkeley, University of California Press, 1967, p. 189.

Muslims could vote for their own candidates. In 1909 the Morley-Minto Reforms were introduced. They provided for a further extension of the elective principle to the legislative councils in the states, an extension of the suffrage, and the establishment of a system of communal electorates into all elected bodies. Communal electorates freed both Hindu and Muslim politicians from needing to win the support of the other community. Communal electorates assured Muslim politicians that they could win elections solely by appealing to the interests and loyalties of Muslims. Communal electorates guaranteed that two party systems—not a two-party system—would develop, one for the Muslims and the other for the Hindus. Social cleavages were thus institutionalized into a system of political dualism.

The major institutions of state in South Asia were created by the British—the military, the bureaucracy, the courts, the legal system, and elections themselves—but the political parties, though shaped by these institutions, were wholly an outgrowth of an indigenous process, not a foreign transplant. There are, however, two separate stories to be told: the story of the development of parties primarily among Hindus in the areas that subsequently became part of India, and the story of the growth of the parties among the Muslims, both in the areas that became part of Pakistan and within those that remained in India. Both histories have been told at great length elsewhere and need not be repeated here. What does need to be emphasized, however, are those features of the pre-independence party development that significantly influenced the role played by parties after partition and independence.

Among the Hindus, the great social division at the turn of the century was between the newly emerging urban middle classes and the older elites, the landlords and members of the ruling families. Initially, the Indian National Congress primarily reflected the interests of the urban middle classes, but in the 1920s, Gandhi turned the Congress into a mass movement, appealing to the peasantry and industrial labor as well as to the middle classes. The party functioned at the level of a mass protest movement, but at the same time it also took on characteristics of a political party with provincial and district offices, dues-paying members, internal elections, and fund raising, all made necessary by the need to contest elections to legislative bodies. The Indian National Congress was not the only political party that won support among India's Hindus. There were a variety of regional parties and countless local political agitations of limited duration. But in the elections of 1936–37 for the provincial assemblies, the regional parties among the non-Muslim population were virtually wiped out: the

Congress formed ministries in seven of the eleven provinces, six with a clear majority of seats.

The Muslim League, organized in 1906, was the first major national Muslim organization, but unlike the Congress its roots were primarily among the landholding aristocracy and only later did it attract the urban Muslim middle classes. Not until the late thirties and early forties did it acquire mass support among Muslims. Indeed, in the 1936–37 elections the League failed to win a majority of the reserved Muslim seats. The League won only 109 out of 485 seats, and these were primarily in the Hindu majority provinces, not in the areas that subsequently became Pakistan. In the Muslim-majority provinces the League did poorly, winning forty out of 117 seats in Bengal, two out of eighty-six seats in Punjab, and none in the North West Frontier Province and in Sind. In each case it was a regional party that won the Muslim vote: the Krishak Praja Party in Bengal, the Unionist Party in the Punjab, the Khudai Kidmatgar in the North West Frontier Province—parties that opposed the League and its proposal for a Muslim-majority Pakistan state.[7] The League subsequently won popular support, and its popularity increased as the prospect of British withdrawal grew. Fear of Congress (and Hindu) domination became a driving force behind the movement for a Pakistan state. Many provincial leaders, though distrustful of Jinnah and his associates in the Muslim League, rallied behind the League as the one political force capable of representing India's Muslims in negotiations with the British over the future of the Indian state.

The commitment to the *idea* of a Pakistan state, however, was historically rooted in the Muslim-minority areas of India, mainly in Uttar Pradesh, Bihar, and Bombay, and not in the areas that subsequently became part of Pakistan. Thus, when Pakistan was founded in 1947, its strongest supporters—those who cherished a Pakistani as opposed to a regional identity—were the migrants from the Muslim-minority areas that remained in India. Pakistan's governing party after independence had its roots, both historically and socially, in areas outside of Pakistan. League leaders saw themselves not only as the founders of Pakistan but as the only political group sufficiently identified with the state to legitimately take part in the country's political life. Said Prime Minister Liaquat Ali Khan in 1950: 'The formation of

[7] Khalid B. Sayeed, 'The Historical Origins of Some of Pakistan's Persistent Political Problems,' in A.J. Wilson and Dennis Dalton, eds., *The States of South Asia: Problems of National Integration*, London, C. Hurst, 1983, p. 30.

new political parties in opposition to the Muslim League is against the best interests of Pakistan. If the Muslim League is not made strong and powerful and the mushroom growth of parties is not checked immediately, I assure you that Pakistan which was achieved after great sacrifices, will not survive.'[8]

League leaders did not trust the recent converts to the cause of Pakistan, and many of the provincial leaders were hostile to the centralizing, nationalizing instincts of *muhajirs*, the immigrants from India. From the moment of its birth, Pakistani elites and their supporters were divided over what should be the institutional structure of the new nation.[9]

India's Fragile Democratic Structure

The institutional structure of a political system determines who can participate in the political arena. The political struggles over institutions in much of the third world is thus a struggle among various groups about how much power each should have and who should be excluded from power sharing. The victory of one group or coalition in determining the institutional structure does not end the struggle, unless the new institutional arrangements are perceived as legitimate by all significant politically articulate forces. In the absence of that legitimacy, the struggle to reshape the country's institutional structures will continue. The political problem in much of the third world is demonstrated by the frequent need of many military regimes to promise a return to civil government (an admission of their own illegitimacy); by the head of one-party dictatorships to promise more competitiveness and openness within the party; and by the efforts of many dictators to create ideologies ('Nasserism,' 'Mujibism,' 'Islamic socialism,' 'Guided Democracy,' 'The Burmese Way to Socialism,') that might serve to legitimize governing institutions.

In post-independence Pakistan the central questions were over the very institutional structures of the country—the authority of the president in relation to parliament; bureaucratic-military rule versus elected representative government; and a federalized West Pakistan or a single

---

[8] Rizvi, *The Military*, p. 61.

[9] 'The defence of the state is our foremost consideration. It dominates all other governmental activities.' Liaquat Ali Khan, 1948. Quoted by Rizvi, *ibid.*, p. 52.

province. In India, on the other hand, there has been remarkable agreement on the need for a democratically elected parliamentary government, a federal system, and competitive political parties.

Nonetheless, the political system has been fragile, as demonstrated in 1975 when Mrs. Gandhi declared a national emergency and suspended many of India's democratic institutions and procedures. The threat came not from a revolt of the masses, nor disillusioned intellectuals or the middle class, but from a coup within the government itself. While modern mass movements have sought to overthrow governments, they have rarely attempted to overthrow democratic structures. It is individuals and groups within the state that undermine democracy, not the masses. These individuals and groups do so to prevent themselves from being overthrown by their party, by parliament, or by the electorate, or to establish themselves in power when they find it difficult to do so by democratic means.

India's experience in this respect is not unique. The political histories of Bangladesh, Pakistan, Ghana, Indonesia, and other developing countries tell a similar story. Threats to the political survival of a single ruler, the ruling party, or of some groups within the government have led a ruling group to argue that the state itself is in danger and that the democratic process must therefore be suspended. That just one person or a small group can take such measures shows not only how powerful is the state, but also how easily it can be dominated by a small group and how weak are the democratic institutions in these countries. Democracy has returned to India, but her brief authoritarian interlude is an indicator of how fragile her democratic system had become and what this institutional fragility means for India's political evolution.

The Decline of the Congress Party Organization

It is the weakness of India's political parties that makes her democratic institutions vulnerable. It was the growing centralization of power within the Congress party from 1972 to 1975, and a corresponding decline in the organization and popularity of the party within the state that set the stage for Mrs. Gandhi's decision to declare an emergency. And it was the breakup of the Janata Party in 1979 that led to the fall of the Morarji Desai government, new parliamentary elections, and the subsequent re-election of Mrs. Gandhi. Though Mrs. Gandhi's party won an overwhelming majority of seats in parliament in 1980 and in subsequent state assembly elections, the party remained organization-ally weak. Prime Minister Gandhi was reluctant to allow Congress political leaders with an independent popular support to emerge in the states or in the center.

Mrs. Gandhi had a patrimonial view of Indian politics. She saw the political system as a kind of estate she inherited from her father, which she believed should be transmitted to her heirs. The 1980 elections placed her youngest son, Sanjay Gandhi, in a strong position to become her successor. As many as half of the 354 Congress members of parliament, and a quarter of the 2300 Congress state-legislative assembly members, reportedly received their nominations through Sanjay's intervention. Many of the chief ministers appointed by Mrs. Gandhi in Maharashtra, Rajasthan, Bihar, Orissa, and Karnataka were Sanjay's men. These politicians (A.R. Antulay, Jagannath Pahadia, Jagannath Misra, J.B. Patnaik, and Gundu Rao) did not command support from any significant social force. Nor were they chosen be-cause of support from the rank and file of Congress party workers in their states. Their power and position rested solely upon Sanjay Gandhi's influence over his mother.

With Sanjay's death, Mrs. Gandhi turned to her eldest son to assume the mantle of succession. An airplane pilot for Indian Airlines, Rajiv had no experience in public life and was initially reluctant to stand for parliament in the seat previously held by his brother. But he did, and he was quickly recognized as heir presumptive. Appointed by his mother as general secretary of the Congress party, he was placed in charge of preparing the party for the forthcoming parliamentary elec-tions. When Mrs. Gandhi was assassinated, a handful of party leaders, all members of Mrs. Gandhi's cabinet, immediately chose Rajiv as Prime Minister. He was duly sworn in by the President of India, and the choice was subsequently ratified by the Congress parliamentary delegation.

The politics of dynastic succession at first seems incongruous for a democracy, but it demonstrated not only Mrs. Gandhi's personal commitment to dynastic rule, but the importance of patrimonialism as a consequence of the de-institutionalization of the Congress party. The de-institutionalization of the party is by now a familiar story.[10] Its

[10] The de-institutionalization of the Congress is described by James Manor, 'The Dynamics of Political Integration and Disintegration,' in Wilson and Dalton, *The States of South Asia*, pp. 89–110.

organizational weakness—which can be dated back to the party's initial split in 1969—has been disguised by its electoral victories in 1971, 1972, and again in 1980 and 1984.[11] And yet signs of a weak Congress party are unmistakable:

1. A large number of the *taluka* and district Congress committees do not function. Out of 365 district Congress committees, it is reported that as many as 143 are not functioning. Of the remainder, most consist of a few appointed members.

2. There have been no organizational elections at the *taluka*, district, or *pradesh* (state) levels. Nor have there been elections to the All India Congress Committee. Historically, the principle of internal elections was central to the Congress organization, for these elections enabled it to nurture political leadership and to endow its leadership with popular legitimacy. As internal elections within the Congress disappeared, the party lost its ability to respond to grievances both within and outside the party.

3. In the absence of organizational elections, office-bearers to various committees were appointed by Mrs. Gandhi or by her appointees. Many of these committees, including the All India Congress Committee, were only rarely convened.

4. The result of this organizational weakness was that the chief ministers of the states were not chosen by the party, but by the Prime Minister. They had no roots, therefore, within the party, the state legislative assemblies, or the electorate. In many states dissension was open, factional struggles had become acute, and cabinets and state assemblies were barely able to function. Mrs. Gandhi dismissed several chief ministers, and much of her time was spent patching up state governments. Congress state leaders have been uniformly weak—even weaker than the chief ministers who held power between 1972 and 1975, when by all accounts, the Congress party was losing its capacity to govern and its electoral support was declining.

5. Though the Congress easily won the 1980 parliamentary elections, the party did badly in the subsequent state assembly elections. In the Kerala, West Bengal, Haryana, and Himachal

[11] For analyses of the 1977 and 1980 parliamentary elections, see Myron Weiner, *India at the Polls: The Parliamentary Elections of 1977*, Washington, D.C., American Enterprise Institute, 1978, and Myron Weiner, *India at the Polls, 1980: A Study of the Parliamentary Elections*, Washington, D.C., American Enterprise Institute, 1983.

Pradesh elections of mid-1982, the Congress was able to win only 135 out of the 443 seats it contested. In the state assembly elections of 1983, the Congress was defeated in Andhra Pradesh and Karnataka. Both states had been strongholds for the Congress party and Mrs. Gandhi had won both states even in the 1977 elections.

This combination of the de-institutionalization of the Congress party and the growth of patrimonial politics at the national level, has facilitated the emergence of new forms of both party and non-party mass politics in India.

Regional Parties and Protest Movements

India has had an increase in regionalism. In Assam, a fragmented and weak state government failed to find a political solution to popular local protest over the infiltration of large numbers of illegal migrants from Bangladesh. The outcome was violent clashes between Bengalis, Assamese and local tribals, resulting in the brutal massacre of thousands of people and the creation of an estimated quarter of a million refugees.

In the Punjab, a minority of Sikhs demonstrated an unexpected capacity to disrupt the state and the country by demanding a Khalistan—an enlarged autonomous and virtually independent state for the Sikhs. In Goa, a 'sons of the soil' movement erupted, leading to the forceful ejection of substantial numbers of Kannada-speaking workers. In Andhra, a film star organized the Telugu Desam, a regional party that won the state elections and cut into Rajiv Gandhi's parliamentary victory. In some areas, especially in the north, Hindu-Muslim tensions grew, stimulated by the flow of Gulf money to Islamic schools and mosques, by the increasing migration of Indian Muslims to the Gulf, and by the growth of a Muslim middle class increasingly conscious of its Islamic ties and resentful of the limited opportunities for social mobility. Finally, the conversion of some former untouchables to Islam stirred anxieties among caste Hindus.

Class-oriented politics has also increased. The farm lobby has grown as farmers have been pressing for higher procurement prices, subsidized inputs, and an improvement in the terms of trade between the city and the countryside. One striking feature of the farmers' agitations—they assumed mass proportions in Maharashtra and Karnataka—is that they have been organized outside the framework of existing political parties.

Similarly, the number of strikes among India's industrial workers has grown especially in Bombay where a forty-nine year old Bombay doctor, D.N. Samant, emerged as a popular organizer. In Maharashtra alone, Samant organized 159 work stoppages in 1981, and he has negotiated more settlements than any other trade union leader. Neither the Congress-affiliated Indian National Trade Union Congress nor the Communist Party of India's All India Trade Union Congress has been able to prevent its workers from rallying to Samant's non-political, militant demand for high wages. Samant's success in winning substantial wage increases has won for him a large following within the industrial labor force. While he may yet prove to be a short-lived public figure, Samant's success is another indication of the failure of existing institutions to retain the loyalty of their supporters.

Political violence continues to rise. The incidence of rioting per unit of population has doubled from 6.9 per 100,000 in 1965 to 12.6 in 1977. There were nearly 33,000 riots (defined as violence by five or more people) in 1965 and 76,000 in 1977. Rioting declined during the Emergency, but increased between 1978 and the summer of 1980.[12] Communal violence grew in the early eighties, reaching an acute level in the killing of Sikhs by Hindus in Delhi following the assassination of Mrs. Gandhi.

Protest and demand-making is most advanced among the more modern sectors of Indian society: farmers who have gained from the Green Revolution, the urban middle classes, and the most advanced, upwardly mobile sectors of the Muslim, former untouchable, and tribal communities. There are no indications thus far that the lower social classes are in the forefront of agitation. Earlier arguments that the Green Revolution would turn red as immiseration among the lower classes grew do not appear to be valid. The workers' movements in Bombay, the farmers' movements in Andhra, Karnataka, and Tamil Nadu, and the regional movements in the Punjab, Andhra, Goa, Assam, and elsewhere are all within the more developed regions and among the more advanced social strata.

[12] David H. Bayley, 'The Police and Political Order in India', *Asian Survey*, Vol. 23, No. 4, April 1983, p. 492.

Protest movements are a persistent phenomenon in India's demo-cratic politics, and one should not presume that their presence neces-sarily represents a threat to India's political stability or national unity. Compartmentalization is characteristic of India's social structure and its politics. What happens in one region does not necessarily spread to another, nor does it necessarily present a threat to the central govern-ment. The Assam disturbances persisted for several years. The Khalistan agitation is limited to the Punjab. The increasing importance of national economic links has stirred issues that have transcended regions, but no political party has successfully identified itself with the cause of the newly militant classes. Parties are ambivalent about supporting the demands of farmers at the cost of the urban population; even the left parties are not sure whether they should appeal to a united peasantry against the city, or seek to distinguish between *kulaks* and marginal farmers and agricultural laborers. Similarly, the Congress was ambiv-alent about how to respond to the efforts of Muslims to convert former untouchables—a phenomenon that involved two groups that make up the Congress party's electoral coalition.

The opposition parties have had little success in breaking out of their regional boundaries. The Marxist left parties remain tied to the Bengali- and Malayalam-speaking regions. The Bharatiya Janata Party has tried to break out of the Hindi-speaking region to which its predecessor, the Jana Sangh, was tied, but its energetic forays into Karnataka, Andhra, and Gujarat have yet to yield major electoral benefits.

Thus, India's opposition parties were poorly poised to take advan-tage of the weaknesses within the Congress party. The Janata leadership that held power from 1977 to 1980 is old and politically discredited, and none of the younger opposition leaders has succeeded in building a national constituency. Several popular opposition figures have emerged in the states—N.T. Rama Rao, the Chief Minister of Andhra, is one, and Ramakrishna Hegde in Karnataka is another—but none has made the leap thus far into national leadership. In the absence of a national leader or a 'cause,' it has been difficult for the opposition to create an enduring national party or effective coalition. India's many social divisions—religious, caste. linguistic, regional—continue to be mirrored in its party system.

The organizational weakness of the Congress party, the emergence of extra-parliamentary movements, and the fragmentation and region-alization of the opposition parties created opportunities for a variety of electoral alignments in the 1984 parliamentary elections. But Mrs. Gandhi's assassination and a wave of national sympathy for Rajiv Gandhi enabled the Congress party to win some 80 percent of the parliamentary seats and, for the first time, a majority of the electoral vote. One should not, however, confuse Rajiv Gandhi's personal triumph with that of the vitality of the Congress party itself. Indeed, Mrs. Gandhi's electoral triumphs in the elections of 1971 and 1980 were both followed by the center's loss of control over the various states, increased conflict within the Congress party, a growth of regionalism, and a recurrence of violence. India's central political problems of how to manage state/center relations and how to accommodate the claims of ethnic groups, have become more difficult with the de-institutionalization of the Congress party. In the absence of a strong governing party at the center, government has become highly personalized and the danger exists that personalized rule will not remain benign. For as conflict grows, the pressure on government to exercise force will increase, all at the cost of the country's parliamentary institutions. That conflicts will grow in India's extraordinarily variegated social system with its mobilized caste, class, tribal, religious, and linguistic groups is as sure as anything can be. Whether they are managed by national and state political leaders organizationally linked in an institutionalized national party or by national and state leaders of different parties capable of bargaining, or whether national leaders must rely upon bureaucratic and coercive institutions is what is now at issue. India's parties, parliamentary institutions, and press continue to have extraordinary vitality, but they can be easily eroded by a central and personalized leadership too weak to deal with conflicts except through coercion. If conflicts are managed through coercion, then the *institutions* of coercion will become more powerful, and they in turn will have a larger voice in the way future conflicts are managed. The weaker the governing party is organizationally, and the more personalized rule becomes in India, the more likely it is that a prime minister will look within the state apparatus for the authority and means to deal with societal demands and conflicts. Thus, the issue in India is which institutions will prevail: those of the state or those of society.

An equally fundamental question is: what will be the character of India's state institutions? The extent to which many of these institutions were weakened under Mrs. Gandhi was revealed by the extraordinary breakdown of the governmental machinery after her death.

Mrs. Gandhi's assassination by two members of her own security guard demonstrated the incompetence of officials responsible for the protection of the Prime Minister's life. The subsequent large-scale killings of Sikhs in Delhi by gangs, some led by local Congress politicians, demonstrated the inability of the politicized police to maintain law and order. And the revelation that more than a dozen officers in the Prime Minister's secretariat, the cabinet, and key ministries had for years been selling secret documents to an Indian businessman who in turn sold them to French and Eastern European agents demonstrated how pervasive corruption had become. To many Indians, these developments confirmed the widely held view that the civil administration, the police, and the intelligence services have become politicized and criminalized.

The major concerns of any Indian government—the maintenance of order and the management of the economy—depend on the character of governmental administration. A complex system of governmental regulation that now provides government officials with an opportunity for acquiring a second income has pushed up the cost of doing business and slowed the pace of industrial expansion, while the corruption and politicization of the police have weakened the ability of government to manage civil conflict without recourse to the military.

In the early months of his administration, Prime Minister Rajiv Gandhi took steps to weed out some of the most corrupt figures within the Congress party and within the government bureaucracy, and he indicated his intent to begin a process of governmental deregulation. But he will surely encounter deeply entrenched interests in any effort to reform either the Congress party or the administration. Rajiv Gandhi will soon learn that it is easier to build an electoral coalition that can provide him with overwhelming victories in parliamentary elections, than it is to build a coalition to carry out institutional reforms.[13]

[13] These lines were originally written in mid-1985.

II. Changing Public Policies and their Consequences

4

Capitalist Agriculture and Rural Well-Being

India's agricultural growth of the past two decades has been heralded by some as an example of what can be done when modern agricultural technology is combined with the market incentives of capitalist agriculture. But, say the critics, India's experience demonstrates the defects of agrarian capitalism: it increases inequality in the countryside, decreases the well-being of the rural poor, and is unable to provide for *continuous* agricultural growth.

For over a decade and a half after the Green Revolution, Indian intellectuals debated the dynamics of their peasant society—whether it is semi-feudal or capitalist, whether immiseration and inequality are growing, whether there are 'contradictions' between agricultural workers, tenants and the near landless and those who own land and provide credit, whether there are 'contradictions' between the countryside and the city, and whether (or to what degree) the government should extract resources from the countryside to provide capital for industrial growth.

There are few policy issues that are not affected by these broader conceptual questions. How much grain, for example, should government

This paper originally appeared in Volume 6 of *Research in Domestic and International Agribusiness Management*, Boston, Harvard University Graduate School of Business Administration, 1986. For suggestions and comments on this paper, I am grateful to Paul Brass, Morris David Morris, Abraham Weisblat, Pranab Bardhan, Robert Lucas, the late Raj Krishna, Francine Frankel, George Rosen, Norman Uphoff, John Mellor, Joshua Cohen, Paul Streeten, Philip Oldenburg, Richard Eckaus, Ronald Herring, Ashutosh Varshney, and Catherine Boone, none of whom, of course, have any responsibility for what is written here, and some of whom, I know, take exception to some of my views.

procure for its reserves and for fair price ration shops, and what should the procurement price be? Should government subsidise fertilizers, seeds and pesticides? Should government provide credit and if so, should it make a special effort to aid small farmers and tenants? Should farmers be allowed to import tractors, harvestors and diesel pumps? Should trade in foodgrains be controlled by private traders or by government? Should government permit food exports? What, if anything, should the government do about the terms of trade between the countryside and the city? How these questions are answered depends largely upon whether one believes that capitalist farmers, operating in an open market, will grow rich at the expense of the rest of rural and urban India, or whether capitalist farming can be both productive and beneficial to ever larger numbers of people.

These issues are reminiscent of one of the greatest intellectual debates of the twentieth century—the nature of peasant society in Russia at the beginning of this century. Teodor Shanin writes:

> The conception of the basic dynamics of a peasant society accepted by Russain policy-makers and, indeed, by the majority of educated Russians at the beginning of this century can be outlined in a few sentences. It was believed that, in the process of inevitable economic advance, every human society necessarily headed toward an increasing division of labor, the establishment of market relations, the accumulation of capital, and social diversification. It was believed that these processes were centered in towns but inevitably spread into the countryside. Rich peasant farms, which were larger and better equipped and had a higher capital/worker ratio, found themselves in an advantageous position as far as the optimal use of the factors of production and their further accumulation were concerned. For precisely opposite reasons, poor peasant farms were at a disadvantage in any attempt to improve their economic position. Continuing cumulation of economic advantages and disadvantages led to a polarization of peasant society into rich farmers, who increasingly acquired the characteristics of capitalist entrepreneurs, and poor farmers, who lost their farms and became landless wage labourers in the employ of rich farmers, estate owners, or urban entrepreneurs. Some of the typical characteristics of a traditional peasant family farm could still be seen in the middle strata of the peasantry, but these would disintegrate or change in the inevitable process of economic advance. With them would disappear the survivals of the traditional peasant society. A new social structure

based on capitalist farming would finally come to be established in the countryside.[1]

This picture, writes Shanin, became so much a part of the prevailing ideology that it shaped the rural policies of Russia for a quarter of a century. This image of immiseration leading to polarization was the basis for Stolypin's policies from 1906 onward, Lenin's New Economic Policy (1921–28) and Stalin's policy of liquidating the *kulaks* and collectivizing the land.

No significant political group in India today openly advocates 'liquidating' the '*kulaks*' or rich farmers or collectivizing the land, but the question of whether one should encourage the growth of capitalist agriculture has been and continues to be a significant issue. One question is whether it can continue to provide increases in agricultural productivity. And the second is whether capitalist agriculture is, or is not, equitable—that is, how it affects the well-being of the landless, the near landless, small farmers and agricultural laborers.

To do full justice to these questions one needs to review a large and controversial literature, describe the significant variations from one region to another and from one crop to another, and to explore the complex and contentious questions of what data are appropriate and reliable for assessing growth rates, regional variations, the relative contribution of small and large holdings to increased productivity, and a host of related questions. In this brief essay I can only deal with two issues. One is whether, on balance, the evidence suggests that capitalist agriculture has improved well-being in rural India, as well as increased productivity. And the second is the question of how Indian beliefs as to what the distributive effects are, have shaped Indian agricultural policies. A central argument will be that the *belief* that capitalist agriculture will have inequitable effects has at times led to policies which slow the rate of agricultural growth and, thereby, in my judgment, slow the improvement in the well-being of the rural poor.

Agricultural Productivity in India: An Overview

The expansion of grain production in India is rightly considered one of the country's major accomplishments. Foodgrain production rose

---

[1] Teodor Shanin, *The Awkward Class: Political Sociology of Peasantry in a Developing Society: Russia 1910–1925*, Oxford, Clarendon Press, 1972, p. 1.

from 55 million tons in 1950–51 to 82 million tons in 1960–61, 108 million tons in the early seventies, and 150 million tons per year in the mid-eighties. The growth rate compares favorably to that of other developing countries and is higher (though not on a per capita basis) than that achieved by Japan before World War II.

The growth rates were greatest in the 1950s (49 percent in a decade) when the amount of arable land used for cultivating foodgrains increased from 97 to 115 million hectares. In the 1960s and 1970s, the annual increases in production were smaller (32 percent and 21 percent per decade respectively), but they reflected increasing *yields* on existing acreage. The largest increases were in wheat which rose from 6.8 million tons in 1950 to 45 million tons in 1985, whereas rice production increased from 22 million tons to 58 million tons. From 1950 to 1980, productivity per acre doubled in a country whose agriculture had been more or less stagnant for the previous fifty years. Without these increases in food production, India would have had to import vast quantities of food simply to keep pace with population growth. Instead, by 1980 India was self-sufficient in foodgrains and was even exporting some of its production to pay back earlier loans. In 1979 India exported grain to the Soviet Union (1.5 million tons of wheat), Vietnam and Mauritius, and loaned grain (1.5 millions tons of rice) to Bangladesh.

Though almost all states in India have registered some growth, the greatest increases in foodgrain production were in Punjab (8.1 percent per annum), Haryana (5.3 percent), Gujarat (3.6 percent) and Rajasthan (3.0 percent) in the northwest, and Karnataka (3.4 percent) in the south, compared with an average national growth rate of 2.8 percent per annum for 1960 to 1978.

Increases in productivity were made possible by extending the irrigation system, introducing high yielding variety (HYV) seeds, an expansion of rural credit, and by price policies which increased the profitability of agriculture, both enabling peasants to acquire new seeds, fertilizers, pesticides and water to expand production and giving them incentives to do so.

Increases in foodgrain production had in fact slowed down in the early seventies, but they picked up again in the late seventies and early eighties. By now, relative to the purchasing power in the economy, India has a large food surplus. However, since a portion—and from the viewpoint of marketable surplus, a critical portion—of agriculture is now price and input responsive, the availability and price of fertilizers and diesel fuel readily affects productivity. A sharp increase in fertilizer prices and, in some years, actual shortages were perhaps the main reason for the relative deceleration between 1972 and 1975. Besides, differences in productivity as between wheat and rice have led some observers to conclude that the high yielding varieties of wheat have been more adaptive to Indian conditions than high yielding rice, that the limited availability of irrigation is a more serious constraint upon rice production, and that, for some years, there were greater price incentives for wheat than for rice.[2] As of the early eighties, only about 28 per cent of the land under cultivation in India was irrigated; the remainder was dependent upon rainfall. Moreover, some of the largest increases in rice production have taken place in the same areas as increases in wheat production, suggesting that whatever factors are conducive to growth in some regions (be they the availability and management of water, or land tenure systems or the technology), benefit both wheat and rice production. Whether the growth in agricultural production, which has averaged 2.6 percent per year from 1949 to 1984, can be kept at this level for the remainder of the century depends to a considerable extent upon whether India can double the amount of land brought under irrigation, the price and availability of a variety of agricultural inputs, the effectiveness of agricultural research, the continued extension of credit, possibly a switch to high-value added crops in some states, and a host of considerations specific to each region, possibly including the land tenure systems, which in *some* states seem to have slowed agricultural growth.

In the areas of comparatively high growth, a central issue is whether the benefits have been widely shared. Some critics of the new agricultural growth strategy have suggested that growth has been at the expense of small peasant farmers losing their land to capitalist farmers, tenants losing their security, and agricultural laborers receiving lower wages. In short, the growth in productivity has resulted in greater immiseration on the part of large sections of India's rural population. Capitalist agriculture, according to this view, even as it increased productivity and enabled India to become self-sufficient, has led to a decrease in the well-being of a majority of the countryside.

At best, say the critics, the poor are marginally better off in some absolute sense, but their relative economic position has worsened.

[2] According to one study, procurement prices for wheat in some years was close to the market price, while the procurement price for rice was 20 percent below the market price. See C.H. Hanumantha Rao, *Technological Change and the Distribution of Gains in Indian Agriculture*, Delhi, Macmillan Co. of India, 1975.

Moreover, the number of poor, it is said, has grown and among the poor some are even worse off.

One scholar, Francine Frankel, assessing the distributive effects of the Green Revolution in high growth districts in the late sixties and early seventies, wrote that in Ludhiana district in the Punjab, 'it is the bottom 20 percent of cultivators, with holdings of less than 10 acres, who have fared worst as a result of the Green Revolution. These farmers may have been able to make some marginal gains in good weather years by applying small doses of chemical fertilizer to Mexican wheats, but, in general, they have not been able to sustain the indivisible inputs—tubewells and agricultural machinery—required for the efficient cultivation of the new varieties. Actually, there is some reason to believe that their position may have suffered an absolute deterioration as a result of the Green Revolution.'[3] In Thanjavur in Tamil Nadu, another high growth district, she found that 'it is in contrast to the large landowners that the landless workers have experienced the greatest relative decline in their economic position. In some cases, moreover, negative changes have added up to an absolute decline in the standard of living . . . payments for harvesting and even cash payments for day labor have remained stationary in the face of rising prices.'[4] And in Burdwan district in West Bengal, employment has increased as a result of multiple cropping, but 'any additions tend to be cancelled out by rising costs of essential commodities.'[5]

It is not always easy to distinguish between those scholars who argue the immiseration thesis, saying that there has been an *absolute* increase in poverty, and those who argue that *inequalities* are increasing. Sometimes scholars themselves do not make the distinction and some have shifted from one position to the other. Among those who have focused on the negative consequences of the Green Revolution are Pranab Bardhan, Keith Griffin, Asok Mitra, C.T. Kurien, Asok Rudra, T. Byers, B. Farmer, and Francine Frankel.

Other scholars argue that the introduction of the new agricultural technologies and policies to provide incentives has improved the well-being of small farmers and agricultural laborers, as well as the larger farmers. They add that poverty has increased primarily in areas where economic growth has not kept pace with population growth. This

[3] Francine R. Frankel, *India's Green Revolution: Economic Gains and Political Costs*, Princeton, Princeton University Press, 1971, p. 39.

[4] *Ibid.*, p. 108.

[5] *Ibid.*, p. 177.

position is taken by Theodore Schultz, David Hopper, John Mellor, Raj Krishna, Inderjit Singh, S. Bhalla and Montek Ahluwalia. While these scholars generally support the new agricultural strategy and reject the immiseration thesis, they also recognize that larger farmers have often been better able than smaller farmers and tenants to gain access to agricultural inputs, and that improvement in the well-being of the rural poor remains marginal at best. The debate involves more than an academic assessment of a particular strategy for agricultural development. The two sides have divergent views as to what policies should be pursued, and what strategies political parties should follow to support or undermine policies. The position taken by policy makers— on how far to push the policy of price incentives to producers, how much subsidy on inputs should be provided, and how much investment should be made on improving the technological bases of agriculture, especially irrigation—will have a profound effect on India's future agricultural productivity, its politics, and the well-being of its vast rural population.

Capitalist Agriculture: A Matter of Definition

Capitalism is a term ordinarily used to describe a particular kind of industrial system, but Marxists (and others) have used the word to describe agriculture as well. Marxists usually define capitalist farmers as having four characteristics: they produce for the market, employ wage labor, have mechanized their farms, and re-invest the surplus within their own farms. The capitalist farmer is distinguished from the peasant small holder who does not employ labor (he depends upon his own and family labor), is engaged in subsistence agriculture, and has too few resources to mechanize or re-invest. A fundamental consequence of capitalism in agriculture is a change in scale. Capitalist farming implies, at least from the Marxist perspective, large-scale production.

Marx and his followers argue that peasant farming is bound to be replaced by capitalist farming. Peasants might survive for a while through self-exploitation, but in time the increased productivity and profitability of large-scale farming will force peasants off the land. Marx believed this process had taken place in Germany and elsewhere in Europe, and Marxists believe that the process is now taking place in the third world. Marx himself did not lament this development. To the contrary, he believed that large-scale capitalist farming was efficient, that the growth of large estates facilitated mechanization, and that the proletarianization of agricultural labor was an important step toward a socialist revolution. A socialist state would nationalize land and peasants would become an agricultural proletariat. But in the meantime, socialists cannot afford to alienate the peasantry. To win their support socialists should promise 'land to the peasants.' The small holder has to be politically separated from the capitalist farmers (or *kulaks*) just as the petty bourgeoisie has to be separated from the industrial capitalist class.

Critical to any Marxist conception is the distinction between the exploiting classes—landlords and rich peasants—and the exploited classes—the poor peasants and agricultural laborers. Capitalist farmers exploit wage laborers by appropriating a surplus. There is also an important distinction between 'feudal' landlords and the rich 'capitalist' peasants. Some Marxists point to contradictions between capitalist farmers and feudal landlords, while others maintain that the main class divisions are the agricultural laborers and small peasants against both.

The Marxist view in its varied forms has a powerful influence on contemporary scholarly analysis of India's agrarian system. It shapes political perspectives and at various times has influenced Indian policy makers. Many scholars, politicians, and policy makers who would not describe themselves as Marxists are nonetheless affected by a Marxist perspective on agriculture. Within this perspective there are, of course, many different views so that characterizing the common view is not easy. But there is a shared perspective expressed in the pages of the professional economic journals in India, by economists within the government, and by many Marxist minded scholars abroad. These views—portions of which are shared by those who reject the Marxist paradigms—can be summarized as follows:

1. India's agrarian system is characterized by substantial inequalities in land ownership and use. A small fraction of India's rural population owns and operates more than half of India's arable land, while the remainder are small holders, tenants, and agricultural laborers. On this point there is no disagreement among observers of rural India.
2. The introduction of the new technology known as the 'Green Revolution' has accelerated the process of turning this small class into capitalist farmers. They produce for the market, evict

tenants and turn them into agricultural laborers, adopt labor displacing machinery which forces down the wages of agricultural laborers, push small farmers out of production because they cannot afford the costly inputs of modern agriculture, and displace village artisans as the new rural rich purchase urban, mass-produced consumer goods.

3. The result of the expansion of capitalist agriculture is thus greater *relative* inequalities in the countryside and among substantial sections of the rural poor, an *absolute* decline in their well-being through a process of immiseration.

4. In the absence of fundamental institutional changes—that is, radical land reform—increases in agricultural productivity within this capitalist framework will still further worsen the lot of the poor and increase the concentration of land in the hands of a growing capitalist class.

Among those who share this perspective, there is considerable disagreement as to what should be done about it. Some argue for arresting the process of capitalist development until the country carries out a radical restructuring of the land system. Others would continue the Green Revolution but modify it so that it does not worsen rural inequalities—by limiting the use of machinery, and by establishing minimum wages for agricultural laborers while pressing for land reform. Still others use this analysis of agrarian change to formulate a political strategy for the left. It enables them to make predictions as to which agrarian classes are likely to be responsive to radical appeals.

Before one turns to an assessment of how capitalist agriculture has affected income distribution and well-being in India, it is important to ask how meaningful is the Marxist definition of capitalist agriculture and whether a distinction between 'capitalist' farmers and 'peasant' farmers is useful.[6] For Marxists, the question of what kind of classes or sub-classes exist among the peasantry is important for ascertaining the contradictions or conflicts within the countryside and what the implications are for a political strategy on the part of the left. Indeed, for

[6] For a review of the Marxist debate on agrarian classes and modes of production in rural India, see the three-part series by Alice Thorner, 'Semi-Feudalism or Capitalism,' *Economic and Political Weekly*, Dec. 4, 11, 18, 1982. Thorner deals with three issues in this debate: (1) Is Indian agriculture capitalist, pre-capitalist, semi feudal or dual; and if not capitalist, do these modes impede agricultural growth? (2) What are the principal rural classes and to what extent do they conflict? (or in Marxist terms, what are the 'contradictions' in rural India? (3) What are the implications for political action by left parties that follow from the answers given to these questions?

some Marxists the *absence* of polarization indicates that agrarian capitalism has not yet developed. 'There has not yet been among the farmers of Punjab,' writes Asok Rudra, 'any strong polarization and I have expressed doubt whether it serves any important purpose to talk about capitalist development before polarization has reached a sufficiently high degree.'[7]

Answering the question of what is a capitalist farmer has proven to be difficult in India. Rudra excludes from his definition of capitalist any farmer who gives his land out for lease and does not himself cultivate. Like other Marxists (and on this point, classical economists as well) he insists that laborers must be able to sell their labor. If laborers are bound to landlords, if they work to pay off their loans or are tied in some other fashion, then labor is not free and capitalist agriculture does not exist. Other Marxists, such as Utsa Patnaik, place greater emphasis on whether there is an 'accumulation and re-investment of surplus value in order to generate more surplus on an ever-expanding scale' so that there is an increasing 'capital intensification.'[8]

The question of whether wage labor is employed and how much capital intensification and investment in farm machinery there is, is particularly troublesome when one considers India's middle peasantry. India is a country of small farmers. Three quarters of India's cultivators own less than two hectares (five acres). In fact, only three percent of all rural households own more than eight hectares. It is the small and medium holdings (five to fifteen acres) that have gained in both numbers and area, while what Indians describe as 'large holdings' (fifteen acres or more) have declined. (What is considered large capitalist farming in India, is elsewhere often considered small family farms.) The middle peasants no longer produce only for subsistence but also produce for the market, but they do not necessarily hire labor. Unlike the rich peasants who rely heavily upon agricultural laborers, the middle peasants often do their own manual work, though they may hire agricultural laborers during the harvest. In some areas the middle peasants may even hire out their own labor or that of family members.[9]

The questions of whether the number of middle peasants is increasing and whether they employ wage laborers are significant in the

---

[7] Quoted by Thorner, *ibid.*, p. 1965.   [8] *Ibid.*, p. 1964.
[9] The importance of the middle peasants is described by Pradhan Prasad, Pranab Bardhan, Kalpana Bardhan and John Harriss. For a review of their positions, see *ibid.*, p. 1996.

debate over what is capitalist agriculture and whether it is growing in India. The notion of scale or size of land-holding as a mark of capitalist agriculture was central for Marx, since he believed that peasant farming would be replaced by capitalist farming. He distinguished between 'petty commodity production' characterized by the unity of labor and capital, and capitalist production 'predicated on the very separation of labor and capital.'[10] For Marx, capitalist agriculture is essential for capital accumulation. Thus small traders, shopkeepers, artisans, small manufacturers, and peasants would (and should) disappear; they stand in the way of accumulation and therefore are standing against History.[11] The self-employed small farmer thus is condemned.

However, in Germany, France, Japan, and in the United States small family farmers have diminished in number, but not disappeared, any more than have small businessmen. Since the Marxist conception of capitalism emphasizes scale it does not see the small sector, including peasant agriculture, as an inherent part of the capitalist economy (which implies accumulation). And since small farmers do not employ wage laborers, they do not exploit and hence by definition are not capitalist. The Marxist definition of capitalism, by emphasizing the class division between small and large farmers, suggests that the smaller farmers who are being squeezed out, should politically ally themselves with the exploited landless laborers. Marxists thus distinguish between peasants on the one hand and exploiting landlords and capitalist farmers, money lenders, and traders on the other. They see the introduction of commercialization of agriculture as facilitating the conversion of semi-feudal landlords into capitalist farmers or *kulaks*. This political conception of what constitutes capitalist agriculture was articulated in the Sixth Congress of the Communist International in 1928. This conference set the framework for subsequent radical interpretations of Indian agrarian developments by emphasizing the conflict

[10] For a discussion of the Marxist view of the family farm as a non-capitalist form of agriculture, see Susan A. Mann and James M. Dickinson, 'Obstacles to the Development of a Capitalist Agriculture,' *Journal of Peasant Studies*, July 1978, pp. 466–481. The argument is that if there is no separation of labor and capital there is no capitalism and, by definition, no class exploitation.

[11] Asok Mitra, 'The Terms of Trade, Class Conflict and Classical Political Economy,' *Journal of Peasant Studies*, January 1977, p. 189. The impoverished peasant proprietor, writes Mitra, who 'tenaciously clings to his individual plot, thereby reducing the scope of higher output and larger capital formation, is to be excommunicated,' according to this perspective.

between the upper layers of the peasants and the poor peasants and the landless. The Marxist views on agrarian issues were subsequently developed in the works of several well-known Indian Marxists, but, writes P.C. Joshi, all of these 'drew upon the penetrating and perceptive analysis of the agrarian problems offered in the political thesis called "The Revolutionary Movement in the Colonies and Semi Colonies by the Communist International" of 1928.'[12]

The question of whether hiring agricultural laborers is an indication that a farmer is a capitalist is particularly complicated in India. Some small farmers, especially those without sons, or whose family members have left to work elsewhere, hire workers even when their holdings are small, while some larger farmers make greater use of *family* labor. The latter may accumulate more capital than the former and, in fact, may be more mechanized. Which one is capitalist?

To most non-Marxists, these are arcane distinctions that throw little light on the central questions of what makes agriculture more productive, whether production for the market is squeezing out smaller farmers, and whether the rural landless are becoming better off. But for Marxists, these distinctions are central because, in theory at least, they predict class polarization and provide the left with the basis for formulating a political strategy.

The use of the term 'capitalist' to refer to agriculture is further confused by the failure to distinguish between 'capitalism' as a *system* of production and the capitalist as the individual entrepreneur who operates within that system. In a developing country, capitalism as a system often operates side by side with pre-capitalist modes of production, and within pre-capitalist systems there are also individuals who behave as capitalists. Moreover, even among non-Marxists there is a tendency to define the capitalist not only by how he behaves but by the scale of his operation—to think of the large industrialists and farmers as capitalists, but not those who run small manufacturing shops or small farms.

The definition one employs is thus shaped by the questions one asks. For our purposes, we shall define capitalist agriculture as production for market and for profit, without regard to whether wage labor is employed or how much mechanization there is. The definition thus excludes the rent collecting landlord, the 'gentleman' farmer producing for pleasure, and the 'feudal' farmer more concerned with

[12] P.C. Joshi, *Land Reforms in India—Trends and Perspectives*, Bombay, Allied Publishers Ltd., 1975, p. 19.

his status and power than with profit-maximization, but it may include as capitalist farmers the small farmers, though some employ labor, some mechanize, and some do neither.

It should be recognized that in the real world of peasant farming in India, theoretical distinctions do not readily fit: some peasants may be engaged in subsistence farming as well as in production for the market, while some farmers may be both rent-collecting landlords and cultivators. This is not to suggest that it is not useful to distinguish between small and large farmers, just as it is useful to distinguish between small and big businesses. They have different needs, and government policies may affect them differently. But it does not follow that one is capitalist and the other is not, with its implication of the withering away of the so-called non-capitalist small farmer.

Agricultural Growth and Changes in Rural Well-Being

There are a number of hypothetical reasons why capitalist agriculture might decrease the well-being of the rural poor. For one thing, farmers oriented toward producing for the market at a profit may turn to labor-displacing machinery, resulting in a decline in the use of agricultural labor and a decline in agricultural wages. In the United States and in West Europe the demand for industrial labor absorbed those who were displaced from agriculture. Most third world countries, however, have experienced population growth rates that have made it difficult for the urban sector to absorb the annual increase in the number of people who enter the labor force. A second possible negative consequence is that capitalist agriculture tends to be capital intensive. Smaller farmers, lacking savings or adequate access to credit, may be unable to purchase the new costly inputs, with the result that they either remain subsistence farmers or will leave cultivation by selling out to larger, more efficient farmers. A third possibility is that agricultural prices increase as a result of the rising costs of inputs in agriculture, to the detriment of the urban and rural poor. Still another possible negative consequence is that as the income of the richer farmers increases they purchase urban consumer goods rather than consumer goods produced in the village and they no longer need village artisans to repair traditional agricultural implements. These latter two arguments are not persuasive: an increase in agricultural output and a reduction in cost per ton of output is likely to result in a reduction in prices. And a rise in the income of the middle size and richer farmers is likely to result in an increase in demand for rural services, resulting in an expansion of employment in the non-agricultural rural sector.

In addition to these presumed inegalitarian features of capitalist agriculture one should also consider the traditional agrarian system out of which capitalist agriculture emerges. Traditional agriculture is often characterized by inequalities in land ownership and use. A small fraction of the rural population may own and operate most of the land as non-cultivating landowners, while the majority of the rural population consists of small holders, tenants, and agricultural laborers. The introduction of new agricultural technologies and market-oriented agriculture may turn this small class of landowners into capitalist farmers, producing for the market, turning evicted tenants into agricultural laborers, adopting labor-displacing machinery to force down the wages of agricultural laborers, and buying out smaller farmers who cannot afford the costly inputs of modern agriculture. Larger landowners may no longer perform their traditional functions of maintaining irrigation channels now that they have their own tubewells and pumps, with the result that poor farmers suffer. Moreover, the larger farmers are able to use their political influence to monopolize credit, marketing, and irrigation facilities.

In evaluating these arguments for India, we shall focus on three major dimensions of the impact of agricultural growth on the rural poor:

1. How has capitalist agriculture affected the landless and near landless—that is, those who have holdings of less than an acre?
2. What has been the impact on the number of middle sized holdings? Is this group growing and, if so, is it because larger holdings are fragmenting, or small landowners are buying land, or is this group being squeezed out? In other words, is polarization taking place in land ownership?
3. Is the employment of agricultural labor declining as a consequence of the growing mechanization of agriculture, and are wages dropping?

Landlessness and Landownership

Has landlessness increased or not? There are two conflicting interpretations of the data. K.N. Raj, a distinguished Indian economist, has
argued that capitalist agriculture in India has increased polarization by
increasing the number of dispossessed landless and by turning small
farmers into the near landless. He draws these conclusions by examining data collected by the National Sample Survey, India's most
reliable national data source, for the years 1954–55, 1961–62, and
1971–72. But another distinguished Indian economist, V.S. Vyas,
drawing from precisely the same data, concluded that the number of
small owners has increased and that the middle peasantry has grown.
He concludes that many of the landless have become small farmers
while some of the larger farmers have sold or forfeited land.

In a study for the Population Council reviewing the arguments of
both Raj and Vyas, Mead Cain[13] concludes that neither argument can
be verified. One reason is that the data do not distinguish between
land that is used for housing, and land used for cultivation. Both sides
agree on one point: 45 percent of India's rural population is either
landless or owns less than one acre, a figure that has more or less
remained constant during this period. But the percentage that owned
some land *increased* from 14.2 percent to 19.2 percent, while those
who remained completely landless *declined* from 30.8 percent to 25.6
percent. What is not known, however, is whether the land that is now
owned is a houseplot of less than an acre, or arable land used for
productive purposes. In any event, an increase in the percentage of
those who own even land for houseplots is of some significance for, as
Cain writes, 'the market price for a unit of land that is suitable as a
houseplot is normally several times the price of the best arable land.'[14]

There is no evidence that for India as a whole the percentage of
landlessness has increased, or that those who have land have become
near landless. To the contrary, for most of the country the number of
ownership holdings below one hectare (2.5 acres) has increased.

A decline in the *percentage* of landless is not inconsistent with the
finding of scholars that in some parts of the country (particularly
eastern U.P. and Bihar), the *absolute* number of landless has increased.
Apart from the obvious fact of regional variations, rapid population

[13] Mead Cain, *Landlessness in India and Bangladesh: A Critical Review of the Data
Sources*, New York, Population Council, May 1981.
[14] *Ibid.*, p. 8.

growth can lead both to a *decline* in the percentage of landless and to an absolute *increase* in their *numbers*. This simple distinction between percentages and absolute numbers is particularly important in a country where population has increased nearly 25 percent per decade in 1961–71 and 1971–81. For the same reason, it should be noted, the percentage of literate persons has increased in India since 1961, but the absolute number of illiterates has also increased.

There is some evidence of a decline in the inequality of land ownership throughout India. Holdings of less than one hectare constituted 5.4 percent of the land in 1953, 6.9 percent in 1961 and 9.2 percent in 1971. Still, there is a substantial concentration of land holdings. In 1971–72, 78 percent of all rural households owned either no land or less than two hectares (five acres) and these accounted for only 25 percent of the area owned. At the other end, 3 percent of all rural households owned more than eight hectares (20 acres), accounting for nearly 30 percent of the area owned. Cultivated holdings in excess of ten acres account for 10 percent of the holdings, but nearly 54 percent of the owned area.

In the Punjab, according to a study by Inderjit Singh of the World Bank,[15] the number and area of both the smallest and largest size farms have declined, while the number of medium size holdings has increased.[16] Singh concludes that there is no evidence that big farmers are purchasing the land of small farmers or that small farmers are becoming landless laborers, though there has been an increase in the number of agricultural laborers. Singh's arguments are supported by Sheila Bhalla's data from Haryana. She reports that 35 percent of cultivating households owned fifteen or more acres in 1961, but this declined to only 19 percent of the households in 1971. Small holdings under five acres increased from 16 percent to 45.6 percent from 1961 to 1971.[17]

One likely explanation for an increase in the number of agricultural laborers is that many tenants have been evicted. In the 1960s, state

[15] Inderjit Singh, *Small Farmers and the Landless in South Asia*, Washington, D.C., World Bank, 1981. This massive study brings together data from an exceptionally wide variety of sources.

[16] In personal letters Ronald Herring and Pranab Bardhan dispute Singh's findings on land ownership. They argue that the reason land ownership distribution data shows a decrease in inequality is that there is an increase in the under-reporting of land in the larger size class induced by the land legislation.

[17] Sheila Bhalla, 'Agricultural Growth: Role of Institutional and Infrastructural Factors', *Economic and Political Weekly*, November 5, 1977, p. 1901.

governments, under pressure to carry out land reform, imposed ceilings on landholdings. The legislation was intended to end absentee land-lordism and to bring about a greater distribution in land ownership. The legislation permitted non-cultivating landowners to 'resume' cultivation of lands that had previously been cultivated by tenants. Under this loophole many landowners evicted tenants on the pretext that they were themselves becoming cultivators, but in reality they merely converted their tenants into agricultural laborers. The result was an increase in the number of agricultural laborers and a corresponding decline in the number of tenants.

In a series of field reports conducted while he worked for the World Bank, the noted agricultural economist Wolf Ladejinsky described how land reform legislation was being evaded.[18] The legislation, he pointed out, was intended to provide tenants with security of tenure, reduce rents, confer ownership by limiting the size of holdings, and distribute the surplus. Some three million tenants and sharecroppers did become owners of seven million acres of land, but there were also wholesale evasions of the ceiling provisions and widespread evictions of tenants. Ladejinsky concluded that security of tenure for tenants rather than redistribution of land would have been a more realistic legislative goal.

India continues to have a serious problem of maldistribution in land ownership, with attendant effects on income distribution. Maldistribution may in itself be a constraint upon increasing productivity. In parts of Bihar, for example, the upper caste Brahmins and Thakurs have converted their tenants into sharecroppers or agricultural laborers. Large landowners do not themselves personally cultivate and remain more concerned with the rent they receive and the prestige and power that comes from land ownership than in increasing productivity and

[18] See Wolf Ladejinsky, *Agrarian Reforms as Unfinished Business*, New York, Oxford University Press, 1977. This important collection of papers contains Ladejinsky's field reports on Bihar and Punjab, as well as his more general writings assessing the impact of the new agrarian policies. Written between 1968 and 1974, these essays still remain among the most valuable assessment of the Green Revolution. In his articles on Punjab, Ladejinsky reports that demand for casual labor had increased, wages for landless laborers were up, small farmers had begun to produce for the market, and the yields attained from the new technology, given the availability of water, were the same for small as well as for larger farmers. But Ladejinsky remained concerned over the worsening position of tenants, the greater benefits obtained by larger landowners, the failure of the credit system to adequately help small farmers and tenants, and the structural impediments to the technological changes in some areas, especially in Bihar.

profit.[19] With producers subordinate to owners, tenants without secure rights, land rent acquiring more importance than profitability, and land dominance by castes that do not cultivate, it is no wonder that the Green Revolution has not taken hold in the semi-feudal conditions that characterize portions of Bihar, Orissa, and West Bengal. But where land ownership has shifted from the *rentier* class to owner-cultivator farmers, there is a greater prospect that capitalist agriculture, with its orientation toward the market and production for profit, will take hold. And where capitalist agriculture has emerged, there is no evidence that it is resulting in the ouster of the small farmer by the large farmer. To the contrary, the number of middle sized farmers is growing.[20]

Raj Krishna, one-time chief economist for the Indian Planning Commission, reports that, according to the Agricultural Census of 1970–71, nearly 70 percent of rural households had operational holdings of five acres or less, and 51 percent had 2.5 acres or less. In all, 49 million holdings belonged to the category of small farmers out of a total number of 70.5 million holdings. Though 70 percent of operational holdings were small, they constituted only 21 percent of the country's arable land. Contrary to what one might expect, the small farmers had *more* access to irrigation, fertilizers and credit than their share of land. Though their share of total cultivated area was only 21 percent, their share of net irrigated area was 31.4 percent. Their share of total fertilizer use was 32 percent. And their share of agricultural credit was 33 percent. Krishna writes:

[19] For a description of agricultural stagnation in Bihar, see Kusum Nair in *Defence of the Irrational Peasant: Indian Agriculture after the Green Revolution*, Chicago, University of Chicago Press, 1979. See also Ladejinsky, *ibid.*, pp. 442–462.

While land reform in Bihar may be a precondition for rapid growth, there is, of course, no assurance that land reform in itself need make a difference. Kerala, for example, is widely regarded as having passed the most stringent land reform legislation of any state, but its rate of agricultural growth is well below that of the high growth Green Revolution states. Clearly, other factors can be at least as critical—the availability and management of irrigation, technology, credit, etc.

[20] There can be a variety of reasons for an increase in the number of middle size farms, including at least one spurious one. A farmer with twenty acres may put ten acres in his wife's name in order to evade ceiling legislation; a multiplication of middle size holdings has taken place, but there is no change in the concentration of land by families. The same farmer may also divide his land among his three sons. The result may again be an increase in the number of holdings (a legal concept), but not in the number of household farms (an operational concept). However, the sons may in fact partition the holdings. In this case, demographic factors lead to an increasing sub-division of operational holdings in India.

This means that small farmers, as a class, command more productive assets and inputs per unit of land than large farmers. But, of course, since they constitute 70 percent of agricultural households, assets and inputs availability per household is less in the small farm sector than in the large farm sector. As a result, income per household, and even more, income per capita, is less in the small farm sector: . . . Poverty persists in the small farms because they support a much larger population per unit of land.[21]

Since small farmers apply more input per unit of land than large farmers, with 21 percent of the land they produce 26 percent of the value of agricultural output.[22]

Agricultural Wages and Employment

How has the Green Revolution affected the *real* agricultural wages in India? Have they declined or gone up? The issue is very contentious. Part of the difficulty simply is that an adequate, uniquely acceptable deflator is hard to evolve. Depending on what weightages are assigned to different commodities in the deflator, different answers can be given. Tyagi, in a much noted article, has effectively brought out the problems inherent in the existing consumer price index for agricultural laborers (CPIAL).[23] A detailed discussion of this issue and the scholastic debate that surrounds it need not detain us here. What is important to note is that an increasing number of scholars have come to the view that while *real* wages may not have gone up *in the Green Revolution belt*, they have certainly not declined and, more important, most scholars now believe that the availability of employment has gone up in areas that have experienced the Green Revolution.[24]

[21] Raj Krishna, 'Small Farmers Development', *Economic and Political Weekly*, May 26, 1979, p. 913.

[22] John W. Mellor, *The New Economics of Growth: A Strategy for India and the Developing World*, Ithaca, Cornell University Press, 1976, p. 82.

[23] See D.S. Tyagi, 'How valid are the estimates of trends in rural poverty?' *Economic and Political Weekly*, June 26, 1982, pp. 54–62.

[24] See among others, I.J. Singh, *op. cit.*, Chapter 1, George Blyn, 'The Green Revolution Revisited', *Economic Development and Cultural Change*, Vol. 31, No. 4, July 1983, pp. 705–726. Blyn, however, has a mixed conclusion on employment. According to his micro-study, it has gone up in the Punjab but not in Haryana. He suggests, however, that this may not apply to the entire Haryana state. Blyn also has useful references to the scholarship on the subject of wages and employment in Punjab and Haryana.

Montek Ahluwalia, in two important studies, has dealt with the related but larger issue of rural poverty and agricultural growth.[25] In his first study which covered the period 1956–57 to 1973–74, he found no evidence of either an increase or decrease in the incidence of rural poverty for India as a whole. His recent study extends the period to 1977–78, only to confirm the lack of a time trend in rural poverty over the twenty-year period since 1956–57. However, and this is important, he does find a trend decline since 1967–68, that is, since the onset of the Green Revolution. And on further disaggregation, he finds that agricultural growth rate and extent of poverty are inversely related. While this does not mean, according to his analysis, that growth *alone* would suffice for reduction of poverty, it does unambiguously mean that the poor have not been made poorer because of agricultural growth. Similarly, John Mellor and Gunwant Desai, summing up many studies of rural poverty in an important recent volume, conclude:

. . . . Poverty sharply declined between 1967/68 . . . . It then rose for a period of three years, after the first flush of Green Revolution had run its course. It fell again between 1974/75 and 1977/78. Therefore, the problem for the poor was not the rise of Green Revolution but rather its subsidence. When this evidence is combined with the need for productivity-based, accelerated growth in agricultural production, it lays to rest the question about the relevance of the Green Revolution in combating poverty.[26]

There has been a marked increase in the number of agricultural laborers in India, but this indicates neither a growth in the demand for labor nor an increase in landlessness. In part, the increase reflects population growth and in part it reflects a shift of many rural people from the category of tenants to the category of agricultural workers—the consequence of loopholes and evasion of land reform legislation. While some decline in tenancy is an indication that tenants have acquired ownership rights, much of the decline reflects the resumption

[25] Montek Ahluwalia, 'Rural Poverty and Agricultural Performance in India,' *Journal of Development Studies*, April 1977, pp. 298–323; and 'Rural Poverty, Agricultural Production and Prices: A Reexamination,' in John Mellor and Gunwant Desai, eds, *Agricultural Change and Rural Poverty*, Baltimore, Johns Hopkins University Press, and Delhi, Oxford University Press, 1986.

[26] Mellor and Desai, *ibid.*, p. 200. Also see studies by Mellor, Srinivasan, Bardhan, Hanumantha Rao *et al.* in this volume.

of land by owners from sharecroppers and tenants. The onset of the Green Revolution may have been a factor impelling some landowners to evict tenants, but it is worth noting that the decline in tenancy in the Punjab took place largely in the 1950s, prior to the onset of the Green Revolution. Moreover, tenancy continues to remain high both in Punjab and Haryana.

In assessing what changes have occurred in the well-being of agricultural laborers, two factors must be kept in mind. One is that many agricultural laborers are also small farmers—about twelve million households, or 15 percent of all rural households in India. A second consideration is that many agricultural laborers have other income sources—not only from land, but from dairying, poultry, and from non-agricultural employment. For India as a whole, the landless and near landless derive only 50 percent of their income from agricultural labor. Agricultural wages are thus not the only measure of rural income among the poor.

Rural unemployment and under-employment remains high in India. The high population growth rate of the past fifteen years assures an annual growth in the number of people entering the rural labor force. Rural employment may increase faster than the growth in the labor force, if there is a growth in demand for farm employment as a consequence of multiple cropping and more labor intensive agriculture, an increase in employment in ancillary farming activities such as dairying, poultry, fisheries and forestry, or an increase in non-farm employment. But for the country as a whole there does not thus far appear to be any significant diversification of the rural occupational structure along these lines.

However, in areas where there have been high rates of agricultural growth over a considerable period of time there is some evidence of an increase in rural employment.[27] Increasing employment has resulted from multiple cropping and from what economists describe as 'forward' and 'backward' linkages. Forward linkages refer to the increased economic activity and resulting employment for marketing, processing and transporting farm outputs. Backward linkages create labor demand as a result of a growing demand by farmers for inputs like fertilizers, fuel, machinery, pesticides, and the systems to produce, transport, market and repair them. Employment is also generated by the growth in credit and extension services and power and transport infrastructures.

[27] I.J. Singh, *op. cit.*, Chapter 8.

There are also multiplier effects: the increased demand for bicycles, furniture, bricks, utensils, improved farm implements, irrigation pumps, and electric motors are often met by small engineering workshops located in rural towns.

Against these positive effects on employment of agricultural growth one must also assess the possible negative consequences of increased mechanization. While some mechanization may increase agricultural employment by making multiple cropping possible, some mechanization, especially of harvesting and processing, may reduce agricultural employment. After reviewing the many studies that have been conducted on this subject, Singh concludes that the net effects on rural employment are positive, but that they can be dampened considerably by the use of capital intensive technologies.[28]

Capitalist Farming in Punjab

What have been the distributive effects of agricultural growth in Punjab? This state, with nearly seventeen million people, was among the first to feel the impact of the Green Revolution and it has had the highest agricultural growth rate. An assessment of what has happened here may throw some light on the distributive effects of the Green Revolution elsewhere in the third world.

Early reports on the distributive effects of the Green Revolution in Punjab were generally negative. The large farmers adopted the new technology while the small farmers did not. Some small farmers sold out to the larger farmers. The new technologies, especially the use of tractors, initially appeared to be labor saving. Some landowners 'resumed' cultivation, forcing tenants to become agricultural laborers. Some of the early reports indicated an absolute increase in rural poverty. Two widely read studies, one by Wolf Ladejinsky, the other by Francine Frankel, provided evidence that the lot of the rural poor was deteriorating.

Recent studies suggest that the initial reports were alarmist. Smaller farmers, as we have noted earlier, have adopted the new technology. The number of agricultural laborers tripled from 1961 to 1981 and real agricultural wages rose, though only by a modest 15 percent from 1961 to 1981. The percentage of landless households declined between

[28] *Ibid.*, Chapter 8, p. 33.

1954–55, 1961–62 and 1971–72 from 37 percent, to 12 percent to 9 percent. The percentage of farmers with less than five acres rose from 32 percent to 58 percent to 60 percent of the rural population during this period while the larger farms with over twenty-five acres declined from 37 percent to 30 percent to 23 percent. What negative displacement of labor resulted from the use of tractors seems to have been offset by rapid agricultural growth.

The impact of the Green Revolution on income distribution among cultivating households in Punjab is the subject of a study by G.S. Bhalla and G.K. Chadha. This study is based upon a survey of 1,663 farming households in 180 villages. Bhalla and Chadha report that small and marginal farmers 'compare very well with farms of larger sizes as regards output per acre.'[29] They note that small farmers also derive some income from non-agricultural activities, from poultry and dairy farming and wage employment in and outside of agriculture. They find no evidence of distress land sale among small farmers. There has been some increase in the proportion of agricultural laborers, but it appears to be due to an influx of workers from other sectors of the economy or immigration of labor from outside the state, not to a decline in the number of owner cultivators. They conclude that 'all categories of cultivators have been able to record substantial increases in their output and income through the adoption of new technology.'[30] While there are inequalities in the distribution of gains, they report that small farmers record almost as much of an increase in productivity as the bigger farmers.

A much cited study by Montek Ahluwalia, however, though generally optimistic about the effects of agricultural growth on reducing the incidence of poverty throughout India, concludes that 'the most disquieting feature of our results is the evidence from Punjab and Haryana which does not support the hypothesis that improved agricultural performance will help reduce the incidence of poverty. This region has experienced a dramatic growth in agricultural output per rural person but there is no evidence of a downtrend in the incidence of poverty . . . . The poorest 25 percent of the rural population experienced stagnant levels of real consumption.'[31] But Ahluwalia

[29] G.S. Bhalla and G.K. Chadha, 'Green Revolution and the Small Peasant—A Study of Income Distribution in Punjab Agriculture,' *Economic and Political Weekly*, May 15, 1982 (part 1) and May 22, 1982 (part 2), p. 831.

[30] *Ibid.*, p. 876.

[31] Montek S. Ahluwalia, 'Rural Poverty and Agricultural Performance in India,' *The Journal of Development Studies*, Vol. 14, No. 3, April 1978, p. 315.

suggests that the explanation may be that an increasing portion of the bottom 25 percent consists of migrants from other states, an argument supported by evidence of increased in-migration and increased labor demand. 'This group consists increasingly of individuals whose consumption is higher than it would have been if they had not migrated. In other words, "trickle-down" benefits have taken the form of increased employment benefiting migrants from other states, rather than increased wages benefiting the pre-existing poor.'[32]

Finally, a variety of reports on life in Punjab villages describe an improvement in food consumption, clothing, medical care, and housing for the poor. Most striking of all is the growth of urban employment which increased by 50 percent between 1971 and 1981. Agricultural growth has apparently been a stimulus for the entire economy, especially for the numerous small workshops that produce consumer goods.[33]

[32] *Ibid.*, p. 316.

[33] John Westley and M.C. Gupta, *Agricultural Growth in India: Policies, Performance and Impact*, USAID, India, May 1982, pp. 52–74. Other assessments include M.S. Randhawa, *Green Revolution: A Case Study of Punjab*, New Delhi, Vikas, 1974; Richard H. Day and Inderjit Singh, *Economic Development as an Adaptive Process: The Green Revolution in the Indian Punjab*, Cambridge University Press, 1977; Biplab Dasgupta, *Village Society and Labor Use*, Delhi, Oxford University Press, 1977; Sheila Bhalla, 'Real Wage Rates of Agricultural Labourers in Punjab,' 1961–1977, *Economic and Political Weekly*, Review of Agriculture, June 1979; Murray J. Leaf 'The Green Revolution in a Punjab Village, 1965–1978,' *Pacific Affairs*, Winter, 1980–81, pp. 617–625: Gilbert Etienne, 'India's New Agriculture: A Survey of the Evidence,' *South Asian Review*, Vol. 6, No. 3, April 1973. For two studies focusing on agricultural wages and employment, see Robert W. Herdt and Edward A. Baker, 'Agricultural Wages, Production and the High Yielding Varieties,' *Economic and Political Weekly*, Review of Agriculture, March 1971', p. A 23-A 30, and D.S. Tyagi, 'How Valid are the Estimates of Trends in Rural Poverty,' *Economic and Political Weekly*, June 26, 1982, which challenges the view that the incidence of poverty has been increasing.

In this paper I have cited only a small portion of what is now a substantial cottage industry of literature on the Green Revolution and its impact. Several other books and articles, not already cited, were particularly useful to me: Biplab Dasgupta, *Agrarian Change and the New Technology in India*, Geneva, UN Research Institute for Social Development, 1977; T.N. Srinivasan and P.K. Bardhan, *Poverty and Income Distribution in India*, Calcutta, Statistical Publishing Society, 1974; Donald W. Attwood, 'Why Some of the Poor Get Richer: Economic Change and Mobility in Rural Western India,' *Current Anthropology*, Vol. 20, No. 3, September 1979; Dharma Kumar, 'Changes in Income Distribution and Poverty in India: A Review of the Literature,' *World Development*, Vol. 2, 1974; and *Poverty and Landlessness in Rural Asia*, Geneva, International Labour Office, 1977.

A distressing (but true) comment made by Ronald Herring in a personal communication—'For every source you cite in the text, there are contradictory sources not

The Argument Recapitulated

Efforts to assess the impact of the growth of market-oriented capitalist agriculture in India have proved difficult for five reasons. One is that scholars often disagree as to the validity of the evidence. National surveys are sometimes at variance with intensive village investigations, with the latter generally more positive about the effects on the rural poor than the former. Moreover, some scholars question the data on changes in land ownership, while others question data on increasing impoverishment among the rural poor. Secondly, even when there is agreement on facts, there are disagreements as to causes. How, for example, does one decide whether an increase in the number of agricultural laborers is the result of land reform legislation that has led to the eviction of tenants, or market agriculture that has led to the selling of land by small landowners, or a population increase among the rural poor? Agrarian changes can often alternatively be explained as a consequence of agrarian policies, demographic factors, or by the growth of capitalist agriculture. The scholar's interpretation is often determined by his theoretical orientation. Third, agricultural growth rates have been high in India by both historical and comparative standards, but the growth rates on a *per capita* basis, nonetheless, remain low because of high population growth. Even in high growth areas, per capita growth rates have been modest when viewed from a twenty year perspective. Under these conditions, whatever benefits might accrue to the poorest classes are bound to be limited. Agricultural wages are up, but only modestly. More agricultural workers are employed, but not nearly enough to provide employment for all those entering the labor force each year. Elsewhere in the world it has been the urban industrial sector and urban services that have been labor absorptive. Green Revolution areas in India have made greater use of labor, but given the already intense use of labor, it is hard to conceive of any agricultural strategy or agricultural growth rate that could absorb the projected increases in manpower. As we have noted, the sharp decline in mortality rates during the past several decades, while an indication of improved well-being, also increases the absolute number of people in the lower income categories. If population growth

cited'—is a reminder not only of how difficult it is to assess the equity consequences of north India's modest per capita agricultural growth, but how undramatic these effects have been thus far, one way or the other.

rates are greater among the lower than among the middle or higher income groups, other things being equal, one would expect a proportionate increase in the number of poor, even though a high agricultural growth rate may absorb *some* additional labor.

A fourth difficulty in assessing costs and benefits is that the effects are not limited to those who live within the areas experiencing high agricultural growth. An end to below-market procurement prices, for example, may temporarily increase food prices to the detriment of the urban poor, but increased purchases by peasants of urban consumer goods, farm machinery, fertilizers, and pesticides benefits urban employment. Moreover, an increased demand for agricultural workers may provide employment opportunities for the rural poor from other regions by inducing migration. Finally, there continues to be confusion over the difference between equality as a *relational* notion, and well-being (or immiseration) as an *absolute* notion. Inequalities can be growing, but the poor may be better off in an absolute sense while in a situation of low economic growth, policies could increase equality but make the poor worse off.

Nonetheless, I am persuaded that a close examination of the evidence from areas in India where the growth of market agriculture has resulted in increased productivity leads to the conclusion that the population of these areas, including many among the rural poor, are better off than in those areas that have not experienced comparable rates of agricultural growth. There is persuasive evidence that in the high growth areas the number of middle size farmers has increased, that many who were landless now own some land (if only houseplots), that agricultural wages and employment have gone up, and that nearby towns have prospered. At the same time, India continues to have a vast impoverished population whose numbers are increasing, for even in high growth areas the number of poor has grown. But it is critical to note that in the absence of the agricultural growth that India has maintained over the past twenty years, the rural poor would be even more numerous and poorer.

One striking statistic is that India's mortality rate has declined from twenty-three to fourteen per thousand from 1960 to 1979, a decline of 40.5 percent. In contrast, in the average low income countries of the third world mortality rates dropped by 35 percent. In Africa, where agricultural growth rates have been lower than that of India, mortality rates have declined at a lower rate.

A second point that needs emphasis is that the introduction of market agriculture does not necessarily ensure an improvement in the well-being of the rural poor. The position of small farmers, for example, can improve or worsen depending upon government policies. Small farmers need assistance in acquiring technical know-how, and in gaining access to transportation, warehouses, and a variety of agricultural inputs. Most of all, they need access to credit on terms comparable to those given to richer farmers. The market does not ensure equal access to small and large farmers alike.

Nor should one assume that allowing cultivators the right to acquire any and all forms of labor-saving machinery will necessarily lead to greater productivity on the land and more employment for all. Farmers may choose to utilize machinery because it is more profitable to do so, because it may be more reliable than employing agricultural workers, or for reasons of status. It is not unreasonable that policy makers permit farmers to import some machinery (for example, diesel pumps for tube wells, and tractors) but not other equipment, such as harvesters, which may reduce labor use without increasing productivity per acre.

Nor is it unreasonable for policy makers to impose a ceiling on the acquisition of new land, otherwise small farmers may be induced to sell before they have acquired the wherewithal to make their land more productive and more profitable. The land ceiling legislation in India may not have resulted in any massive redistribution of land, but it probably prevented an increase in the concentration of land holdings.

Finally, an increase in procurement prices paid by government can be an important incentive for the growth in investment by farmers, but it can present a cruel dilemma for policy makers. Price incentives are not only necessary for producers, but they are also necessary if agricultural wages are to rise. But high agricultural prices leave the underemployed and unemployed worse off. The alternative, of course, can be worse. Artificially maintained low food prices mean lower agricultural wages, a low rate of agricultural growth, an increase in food imports, a reduction in resources available for industrial investment, and reduced demand by farmers for urban produced consumer goods. Moreover, it is critical to recognize that as productivity increases and the unit cost of producing food declines, the free market price for the consumer goes down.

There is no hidden hand which ensures that any and all forms of capitalist agriculture must necessarily improve the well-being of the poor. On the other hand, there is no evidence that capitalist agriculture must necessarily lead to immiseration. One can even be more positive: capitalist agriculture, at least as it has developed in India, increases the possibility that the lot of the rural and urban poor can be improved. But what kind of growth takes place and how the benefits are distributed, ultimately depends upon the package of public policies adopted. An extension of irrigation to dry regions, public investments in roads and in electricity, more research and development on the improvement of agricultural technologies, a progressive agricultural income tax, and various land reform measures are all compatible with a market-oriented system of agriculture.

The Consequences of Alternative Perspectives

The belief that market-oriented agricultural policies must necessarily worsen the position of the rural poor can be an impediment to the adoption of policies that do in fact ultimately improve rural well-being. A case can be made that this, indeed, happened in India. In the 1950s and 1960s many Indian policy makers and economists argued that agricultural growth in the context of capitalist agriculture would result in growing immiseration. This belief in the inequalitarian consequences of capitalist agriculture led many policy makers to oppose price incentives that would enable farmers to invest in the HYV seeds, fertilizers, pesticides, and other agricultural inputs. The issue was sharply drawn in 1966, when neo-classical critics within the government took issue with the government's agricultural policies.[34] Their arguments were strengthened by the reality of India's growing dependence upon imported food and by pressure from the international aid community, including the World Bank, the International Monetary Fund, and the U.S. Agency for International Development. Opposed to the new agricultural policies were those who argued that higher agricultural prices would adversely affect the poor. They maintained that the use of high yielding variety seeds would benefit rich farmers and increase rural inequality, that increased imports of fertilizers, pesticides, and machinery would drain foreign exchange reserves, and

[34] For an interesting first-hand report on the opposition to the introduction of HYV seeds and price incentives in 1966, see David Hopper, 'Distributions of Agricultural Development Resulting from Government Prohibition,' in Theodore W. Schultz, ed., *Distortions of Agricultural Incentives*, Bloomington, Indiana University Press, 1978, pp. 69–78.

that by making the larger farmers more prosperous, they would become politically more powerful, making it still more difficult to carry out land reforms.

The advocates of the new agricultural policies won. But even their strongest supporters recognized that additional measures had to be taken to improve the well-being of agricultural laborers and small marginal farmers. Thus, the Janata government (1977–79) pursued policies of expanding rural works programs, providing credit for small farmers, encouraging new programs for animal husbandry, and a variety of other measures to increase employment and income for the rural poor.

Nonetheless, from time to time policies that reflect the older point of view have been adopted. At various times in the 1970s, paddy prices were kept low. A 1977 study by the Asian Development Bank reported that paddy prices in India were below that of other developing countries and below the prevailing market price, while procurement prices for wheat were close to the market price.[35] At other times the government, viewing the private trader as a threat to its control over procurement, issued rice-milling licenses primarily to cooperative and to public sector firms and threatened to nationalize the entire grain trade. The result, according to one analyst, was that there was little private investment in either storage or milling facilities, even though the marketing costs of private traders had been well below government agency costs.[36] Though government officials asserted that their primary purpose was to reduce costs by eliminating the middle man, critics believed that their primary objective was the political one of increasing control over the grain market.

Government also imposed restrictions on the interstate movement of grains (known in India as 'zonal' restrictions) to prevent grain moving privately from low price surplus to high price deficit areas. To prevent grain from moving out of high producing districts and states, the government would throw a cordon around the region; prices would fall when crops arrived in the market. The government would then buy wheat at the 'prevailing' market price which had been arbitrarily forced down. The system, according to one analyst,[37] actually

[35] Schultz, *op. cit.*, p. 16.

[36] Uma Lele, 'Considerations related to optimum pricing and marketing strategies in rural development,' in *Proceedings*, 16th International Conference of Agricultural Economists, Nairobi, Kenya, 1976.

[37] Prem Shankar Jha, *India: A Political Economy of Stagnation*, Oxford, Oxford University, 1980, p. 32.

forced the smaller farmers who needed money to sell more readily than the richer farmers who could sit out the blockade.

When world foodgrain prices rose and production costs went up in 1972–73, the Government of India banned private trade in wheat and imposed zonal restrictions to secure a monopoly on procurement. Government was then able to procure wheat at less than the real market price, but some of the wheat moved into a free market underground. Subsequently, government shifted its policy and bought half of the farmers' output and permitted the remainder to be sold in the free market.

One prediction of the critics of the new agricultural policy has proven to be correct. The better off farmers have acquired more political clout and have made it increasingly difficult for government to pursue policies that hurt their interests. Wheat farmers are now able to obtain better prices from the government. As the farmers of the better irrigated paddy fields, both in Punjab and in the Krishna and Kaveri deltas in South India, have become more powerful, they have also successfully pressed government for more remunerative prices for rice. It has become increasingly difficult for government to adopt policies that run counter to the interests of the millions of Indian peasants now cultivating for the market. Moreover, some of the earlier critics of the Green Revolution have modified their position, recognizing that India's rural poverty is not the consequence of, nor made worse by, capitalist agricultural growth. Land reforms are advocated, but few would now argue that capitalist agriculture should be halted until land reforms are adopted. Indeed, more attention is given to how irrigation can be extended, access to credit broadened, what can be done to strengthen the position of small farmers, and what assets (for example, milk producing cattle) can be made available to the landless and near landless.

But even many of the most ardent supporters of capitalist agriculture are prepared to put some brakes on the demands of the farmers. One issue is *how much* incentives need to be provided? To what extent should inputs be subsidized and support prices raised? A second issue is the question of agricultural income taxes, currently so low as to leave the increases in income earned by the agrarian sector virtually untaxed. And the third issue is the question of what kinds of restrictions should be imposed on the import and use of farm machinery that might significantly reduce the use of farm labor in a country where the prospects of absorbing surplus labor into the urban sector remain so slim.

There is also the question of what policies can best *extend* high growth capitalist agriculture to areas that, often for many different reasons, have not yet felt its impact. In some areas the constraint is the lack of assured irrigation and dependence upon rainfed agriculture. But in some areas where irrigation is available, land tenure systems deprive non-owning cultivators of incentives. How best to extend capitalist agriculture is, for some of the relevant ministries and for the international aid agencies, a central issue.

Capitalist Agriculture, Class Formation, and Political Behavior

The impact of the spread of capitalist agriculture on the class structure in a society characterized by social hierarchy has been a major issue in India and among scholars of India. Many Marxists (and those influenced by Marxism) take a reductionist position, inferring the emergence of certain 'class' attitudes and behavior from new class formation. Indeed, as we have noted earlier, for some Marxists the *absence* of class conflict even suggests that capitalist agriculture has *not* emerged.

Some Marxists advocate agrarian policies that would squeeze out the small farmers in order to create a polarized class structure. Eager to win support from the peasants, both rich and poor, who seek better terms of trade with the city, India's communist parties have actually advocated *higher* procurement prices for grain, but their support is over the objection of many Marxists who believe that low prices, by squeezing out the smaller farmers, would intensify class struggle within the countryside. One Marxist supporter of higher prices admitted that 'a better price situation would help the peasants to cling on to and cultivate their parcels of land . . . and that this (would) retard the development of capitalism,' but only, he adds, the 'landlord path of capitalist transformation.'[38]

One of the most interesting theoretical questions is whether the creation of capitalist agriculture in an overwhelmingly agrarian society with such a large and rapidly expanding population will set in motion forces (or in Marxist terms, 'contradictions') ultimately leading to its own destruction. The positive answer given by Marxists rests on the assumption that agrarian capitalism leads to class polarization, which in turn leads to class conflict. Neither of these arguments holds for

[38] Dev Nathan, 'On Agricultural Prices,' *Economic and Political Weekly*, December 25, 1982, p. 2104.

India ('not *yet*,' Marxists may retort). In a country of nearly seven hundred million, India has experienced virtually every kind of political conflict imaginable. Those who want to find examples of conflicts between agricultural laborers and landowners, between tenants and landowners and money lenders, and between small cultivators and large landowners, can readily do so. But one can also find numerous examples of rural coalitions that cut across class lines, or sharp political cleavages based upon caste, religious or linguistic differences that are also independent of class. In fact, some of the most articulate and influential political movements of the past few years have been more closely related to regional than to class issues: in Assam, for example, a major political movement developed to protest the infiltration of large numbers of illegal migrants from Bangladesh; in Punjab, a minority of Sikhs disrupted the state by demanding an enlarged autonomous and virtually independent state; in Goa, a 'sons of the soil' movement erupted, leading to the forceful ejection of substantial numbers of Kannada-speaking workers; in Andhra, a regional party defeated the Congress in state elections. In some areas, especially in the north, there have been Hindu-Muslim tensions, and conflicts between ex-untouchables and some of the lower Hindu castes.

The most significant class-oriented rural movement has been by farmers demanding higher procurement prices and subsidized inputs. Farmer agitations have assumed mass proportions in Karnataka, Tamil Nadu and especially in Maharashtra, where one farmer leader articulated the slogan 'Bharat versus India,' using the Hindi word for India as a symbol of the rural areas, and the English word for the urban centers.

If any one feature characterizes these various forms of politics, it is that protest and demand making is advanced among the more modern and mobile sectors of Indian society—farmers who gained from the Green Revolution, the urban middle class, and the more advanced, upwardly mobile sectors of the Muslim, ex-untouchable and tribal communities. There are no indications thus far that the lower social classes, especially those who are worse off, are in the forefront of political agitations. Earlier arguments that the Green Revolution would turn red as immiseration among the lower classes grew do not appear to be valid. The farmer movements in Andhra, Karnataka, Tamil Nadu, and Maharashtra, the regional movements in Punjab, Andhra, Assam, Goa, and elsewhere, and the workers' movement in Bombay are all within the more developed regions or among the more advanced social strata.

Some scholars have argued that the erosion of traditional reciprocal obligations between landlords and their tenants and agricultural laborers and sharecroppers, and its replacement by wage relations (from 'status' to 'contract,' in the terms of modern sociology) would liberate the lower classes for class struggle against their exploiters. The fallacy of this argument is not only its presumption that class interest will be paramount over religious, caste, regional, and sectoral identity, but that any *single* form of political identity will prevail. In fact, political identity is quite contextual. Agricultural workers may support the claims of farmers for higher procurement prices, persuaded that only if farmers earn more can laborers' wages go up; at other times, agricultural workers may be mobilized along ethnic lines, or as untouchables, or as Muslims engaged in conflict with middle and higher caste Hindus. At still other times, agricultural laborers may band together to demand higher wages. Much depends upon leadership, opportunities, circumstances. Small farmers may clash with larger farmers over gaining access to irrigation facilities or credit from the local banks, but they may join together in demanding high procurement prices from government; indeed, some smaller farmers, given their lower margins, may be as anxious about higher agricultural prices as larger farmers.

Moreover, in India's democratic electoral system there is virtually no limit to the kind of appeals made by party leaders. Competing political leaders belonging to the same class, caste, or religious community may pull their group in different political directions. It is well known that in democratic systems there are strong tendencies for political parties to make appeals that cut across classes. In short, given India's social complexities, the structure of its political life, and the presence of overlapping rural interests, there is no reason to expect rural politics to take a *class* form, although they may take a *mass* form.

Here and there class conflicts may erupt in the Indian countryside and, in some instances, especially when urban radicals take the lead, a local political movement may even call for revolutionary change, but neither past experience nor any well-founded contemporary theory should lead us to expect any mass movement for the overthrow of agrarian capitalism.

Opposition to India's emerging agrarian capitalism is more likely to surface in urban areas. Urban dwellers have an obvious interest in keeping food prices down; urban radicals look upon the rural poor as a potential revolutionary army; and Westernized intellectuals have a preference for 'modern' class politics rather than 'traditional' politics based upon religion, caste, and tribe. Moreover, many intellectuals, as Schumpeter once wrote, have a vested interest in social unrest, while large state-run bureaucratic structures often try to undermine independent entrepreneurship and innovation. The pervasiveness of neo-Marxist perspectives is so great among Indian intellectuals that it is widely assumed that a pro-equalitarian outlook must necessarily be anti-capitalist. Equality and capitalism are assumed to be incompatible.

A former governor of the Reserve Bank of India, for example, concluded an analysis of agricultural policy by saying:

> Growth and equity will not be adequately harmonised (under capitalist farming, and) the only answer then—whether feasible or not—would be some form of collectivisation of agriculture not so much because it is superior to a capitalist form of agriculture in terms of efficiency or production but because it offers, if I may put it that way, better chances of disguising unemployment in a socially acceptable form. In developing countries with a slow rate of growth and considerable unemployment, socialization of the means of production and particularly of land may thus have its primary justification not so much in the interest of growth as in the interest of equity.[39]

It is striking that many Indian intellectuals and bureaucrats refer to India's better off farmers as *kulaks*—a term with its unmistakable implication of a class that is to be liquidated. Agrarian capitalism in the Soviet Union, it should be recalled, was destroyed not by the uprising of poor peasants, but by the *state* when peasants refused to sell it grains at unremunerative prices. Unable to feed the urban areas and the army and to export, and unwilling to pay higher prices to the peasants, the Communists launched their war against the peasantry in the name of repressing capitalist *kulaks*. No such move is possible in a country that remains democratic. For this reason the vitality of India's capitalist agriculture is closely linked to the persistence of its democratic system.

[39] Dr. I.G. Patel, 'On a Policy Frame Work for Indian Agriculture,' Coromandel Lecture, New Delhi, December 18, 1980, p. 38.

5

The Political Economy of Industrial Growth

Industrial Deceleration

Why has industrial growth decelerated in India since the mid-1960s? Is it the result of a resource constraint, leading us to look at policies affecting savings and taxation? The result of a demand constraint, leading us to look at income distribution policies? Or the misallocation of resources, leading us to look at the politics of allocation and regulation? Has India suffered from too much bureaucratic control rather than profiting from the allocative efficiencies of the market? Or has there been too little public investment?

For the past several years, there has been a debate over these questions among Indian economists. The debate began during Prime Minister Indira Gandhi's last years in office, as she quietly initiated a process of economic liberalization. But with Rajiv Gandhi as Prime Minister, the issue of industrial policy moved to the center of the political state.[1] Through his speeches, his appointment of liberal economic advisors, and the announcement of a new budget by a

---

Appeared originally in *World Politics*, Vol. XXXVIII, No. 4, July 1986. This is a review essay of two important recent books: Pranab Bardhan, *The Political Economy of Development in India*, Oxford, Basil Blackwell, 1984; and Isher Judge Ahluwalia, *Industrial Growth in India: Stagnation Since the Mid-Sixties*, Delhi, Oxford University Press, 1985.

---

[1] These lines were written in February 1986. Rajiv Gandhi's increasing political difficulties since then reconfirm many of the points in this essay. For a fuller assessment of Rajiv Gandhi's performance as Prime Minister, see Chapter 11.

liberal finance minister, the Prime Minister in effect declared that his government is committed to making the economy more competitive both internally and internationally, that many bureaucratic controls would be replaced by market processes, and that more productive and efficient economic behavior would be stimulated through tax policies. Are these the right policies for accelerating industrial growth? And if so, are they politically feasible? If the previous policies were not working, why were they retained for so long, what were their political as well as economic consequences, and what are the likely constraints and consequences for the alternative policies proposed by Rajiv Gandhi's government? These are the issues raised in the books under review. They lead us to consider some of the fundamental questions concerning the political economy of development in India.

The major economic facts are not in dispute. From 1956 to 1966, India's annual growth rate in manufacturing was 7 percent. From 1966 to 1982, it declined to 5 percent. The overall economic growth rate has been 3.5 percent per year. It is impressive when compared with India's near-stagnant economy during the fifty years prior to Independence. It is impressive, too, when compared with the growth rates of most European countries in the nineteenth century. If the economic growth rate has not led to as significant an increase in the well-being of most Indians as of Europeans, it is because the higher population growth rate has meant a smaller increase in per capita income. With a 2.2 percent population growth rate, per capita income has increased at a mere 1.3 percent per year—too little to have a significant impact on the level of poverty. It should be noted that, had the economic growth rate been slightly higher (say about 5 percent per year), per capita income would have increased at twice the rate.

When one looks at a number of other developing countries, India's record is a poor one. The country's industrial growth lags far behind that of South Korea, Taiwan, Mexico, Brazil, Indonesia, Malaysia, and Egypt, whose industrial growth rates ranged from 7 percent to 14 percent per year in the 1970s. In India, the share of the gross domestic product (GDP) derived from industry increased from 20 percent to only 26 percent between 1960 and 1982. By contrast, it increased from 20 percent to 39 percent in South Korea, from 14 percent to 39 percent in Indonesia, from 29 percent to 38 percent in Mexico, from 21 percent to 31 percent in Turkey, and from 24 percent to 34 percent in Egypt. In 1950, South Korea had a per capita income of $146. Taiwan at $224, and Brazil at $373, were better off than South Korea or India, but not by a great deal. Had India's GDP grown as rapidly from 1960 to 1980 as South Korea's, it would stand at $531 billion today rather than $150 billion—surpassing that of the U.K., equal to that of France, and more than twice that of China. India's per capita income would have been $740 instead of $260; even with the benefits of growth inequitably distributed, it is not unreasonable to believe that most of the poor would have been substantially better off. India's standing in the world economy and as a world power would be quite different—especially, to pursue this imaginary projection, if India's share of world trade had grown in the same proportion as that of Korea. Instead, India's exports in 1983 were $9.7 billion, as compared with South Korea's $24.4 billion, China's $22.2 billion, Hong Kong's $21.9 billion, and Singapore's $21.8 billion; they were slightly below Yugoslavia's $9.9 billion.

India has many of the preconditions that are widely regarded as facilitating rapid industrial growth. Savings and investments have increased. Oil price rises notwithstanding, India has not had a major balance-of-payments problem, in part because of remittances sent by its overseas migrants. Nor does India have the debt problems that beset many of the countries of Latin America. Natural resources, especially coal, iron ore and water, are available in abundance. And the country has a large reserve of skilled manpower, including engineers and managers.

Moreover, India has at least two requisites for effective policy making and implementation: a well-developed civil service and a stable government. Jawaharlal Nehru was Prime Minister for seventeen years, Indira Gandhi for fifteen. There have been religious, linguistic, and caste conflicts, but they were episodic and generally confined to limited regions of the country. For all of the time Mrs. Gandhi was Prime Minister—from 1966 to 1977 (except 1969–71), and again from 1980 until her assassination in October 1984—she had a solid majority in parliament and was therefore free to pursue an industrial policy of her own choosing.

Bardhan and Ahluwalia's Explanations

What went wrong, then with industrial policy? Pranab Bardhan, in his slim volume originally prepared as a series of lectures delivered at All Soul's College, Oxford, argues that the problem has been a decline in public investment—the consequence, he believes, of constraints imposed on the state by India's dominant proprietary classes. Bardhan thus offers a neo-Marxist interpretation, but not until he dismisses a number of alternative Marxist (and non-Marxist) explanations.

Advocates of the dependency theory will find no support for their position in Bardhan's analysis. India's deceleration in industrial growth can hardly be the result of a decline in foreign demand and the worldwide recession since, as Bardhan notes, India has had a relatively closed economy. Trade as a proportion of national income is quite small, and India's share of exports in world trade has actually declined over the past three decades. Moreover, many of the countries with the most rapid industrial growth are in fact those with an increasing share of world trade.

Nor are the multinationals the villains; Bardhan points out that multinationals are insignificant in India. Of the top twenty-five industrial firms, only four are foreign: the Indian Tobacco Company, Hindustan Lever, Dunlop India, and Ashok Leyland. None of these are in the top ten (Union Carbide is not among the top twenty-five). Plantations and mines, once foreign-owned, have been sold to Indian businessmen or nationalized. Government licensing policies and regulations on foreign share holdings have discouraged foreign investors, and new foreign private direct investment has been minimal.

Bardhan also persuasively dismisses the argument that income inequalities are a constraint on the growth of demand, especially for consumer goods. Elsewhere in the third world, he writes, income inequality has often induced faster economic growth. Besides,

> if the rich get richer at a sufficiently rapid rate and spend their booming income on 'luxury' consumption and reinvest their profits, industrial growth may not be broad-based or wholesome, but it can be fast (p. 20).

He does suggest, however, that the country's slow per capita agricultural growth rate has had a dampening effect on the demand for consumer goods; but that is only a partial explanation for the deceleration of industrial growth.

Nor is the savings rate an explanation. India's gross domestic savings as a percentage of the gross domestic product was over 22 percent in the early eighties, about equal to that of middle- and even some high-income countries, and significantly higher than the 15 percent it had been in the mid-sixties. But Bardhan notes that the high savings rate has not led to a high growth rate, partly because capital-output ratios are rising. Productivity on investment has declined in almost all industries, notably in state-controlled industries such as electricity generation, steel, and transport equipment.

According to Bardhan, the rise in capital-output ratios is particularly prominent in the public-sector industries; their performance has had a devastating impact on the economy as a whole.

> There is no question that over the last three decades the state has accumulated power of direct ownership and control in the economy to an extent unparalleled in Indian history, both in the spheres of circulation (banking, credit, transport, distribution and foreign trade) and of production—directly manufacturing much of basic and capital goods, owning more than 60 percent of all productive capital in the industrial sector, running eight of the top ten industrial units in the country, directly employing two-thirds of all workers in the organized sector, holding through nationalized financial institutions more than 25 percent of paid-up capital of joint-stock companies in the private sector, and regulating patterns of private investment down to industrial product level and choice of technology (p. 38).

Bardhan goes on to point out that the public sector has failed to generate a surplus for investment. Thirty public-sector units of the central government have recorded losses for ten consecutive years, and the State Electricity Boards and State Road Transport Corporations have lost billions of rupees each year. Public financial institutions have used their resources to take over 'sick' firms, bailing out unsuccessful private companies at public expense, even when these sick firms have little prospect of becoming viable. The share of non-development expenditures in the government's budget has also been growing, while the real earnings of central government employees have increased at an annual rate that is two-and-a-half times that of the per capita income of the country. In short, the government has been 'consuming' resources that might otherwise go to public investment.

So, concludes Bardhan, the growth deceleration is the result of a deceleration in public investment.

> Fixed capital formation in the public sector . . . grew at the annual rate of 11.3 percent in the period of 1950–51 to 1965–66, but in the

second period of 1966–67 to 1981–82 it dropped to a rate which is less than half, 5.5 percent (p. 23).

The cutbacks were in power generation and in transportation, with major consequences for industrial growth, since shortages in infrastructural sectors have a cumulative impact. Thus, Bardhan's argument is that the state has a stranglehold on the industrial sector, and that the public sector has not been efficiently run; nonetheless, the cutbacks in this sector are the primary reason for the deceleration.

The author's prescription consists of more resources for the public sector. 'Massive doses of public investment in basic industries and infrastructural facilities and public credit,' he writes, 'are crucial at the early stages of industrial and agricultural transformation.' Why is public investment inadequate? His answer is that

> pressures from heterogeneous elements in the dominant coalition for budgetary subsidies fritter away much of the investible public surplus. This is a kind of 'fiscal crisis' . . . blocking the necessary accumulation function of the state (p. 68).

Bardhan's critics agree with him on two points: first, the public sector has been mismanaged and, as a consequence of subsidies and protection, much of the private sector has also been inefficient. Second, public-sector investment in such critical areas as railway rolling stock and power generation has declined, to the detriment of the economy as a whole. Beyond that, there is disagreement. On Bardhan's left are those who, like the eminent Indian economist Sukhamoy Chakravarty, not only argue that there should be a larger volume of public investment, but that there has been inadequate aggregate demand which, in addition to higher public investment, needs to be remedied through better income distribution policies.[2] Two eminent liberal scholars. T.N. Srinivasan and Jagdish Bhagwati, agree that the decline in infrastructure investments has been a problem, but they point to inefficiencies in the use of resources as the central issue.[3] Both are particularly

[2] Chakravarty, 'Aspects of India's Development Strategy for the 1980s,' *Economic and Political Weekly*, Vol. 19, May 19–26, 1984, pp. 845–52. Professor Chakravarty chaired an economic advisory panel to Indira Gandhi. The demand constraint position is advocated by K.N. Raj, P. Patnaik, D. Nayyar, and, among American economists, Lance Taylor.

[3] Jagdish N. Bhagwati and T.N. Srinivasan, 'Indian Development Strategy: Some Comments,' *Economic and Political Weekly*, Vol. 19. November 24, 1984, pp. 2006–08.

system of patronage. Although these classes have some competing interests (the private sector, for example, resents many of the bureaucratic controls, and rural and urban groups clash over prices of agricultural produce), all three welcome state subsidies. In short, public investment in India has declined because the proprietary classes have expropriated resources in the form of subsidies. From this political analysis, Bardhan draws the conclusion that 'in the context of economic growth it is . . . the capacity of the system to insulate economic management from political processes of distributive demands, rent-seeking and patronage dispersement that makes the crucial difference' (p. 72). While not arguing for the South Korean model, he explains the success of the Korean economy: 'more important than the discipline of the market mechanism has been the ability of the system in the last two decades to largely insulate the framework of economic policy-making and implementation from the clientelist demands of the political process' (p. 72). Bardhan thus sees democratic politics, not industrial policy, as the problem. He considers mismanagement of the economy to be the result of inter-elite accommodation, while Ahluwalia argues that the problem lies in the inefficient use of resources as a result of insulation from market forces.

But is it, to use Bardhan's terminology, the 'dominant proprietary classes' that have impeded the adoption of an alternative industrial strategy?

India's industrial policies are hardly unique. There are a number of countries that have pursued an import substitution policy, maintained an inefficient public sector, developed a system of government allocation of licenses in accordance with plan priorities and targets that proved to be inefficient, created a system of controls and high marginal tax rates that produced a growing underground economy,[5] and subsidized inefficient producers—that have, in short, sought to eliminate both competition within the economy and competition by their producers in the global market place. In recent years, socialist Yugoslavia,

---

[5] The existence of a large, unreported black economy means, of course, that much of the country's increased industrial production is not included in the growth rate. The deceleration thesis would be partially undermined if there had been an acceleration of growth in the black economy during the past fifteen years, but there is no evidence one way or another. It would be only *partially* undermined, that is, since the evidence on the poor performance of the public sector and the worsening of the capital output ratio is not disputed. If India's national income is significantly higher than the official estimate, however, the savings rate as a proportion of national income (estimated at 22 percent), may be overestimated.

Hungary and Czechoslovakia, and the People's Republic of China have attempted to revamp their economic systems to make more effective use of market mechanisms as a means of providing incentives for producers and creating more efficient means of allocating resources. Several non-Communist countries—South Korea, Taiwan, and Brazil—have gone through painful transitions from import substitution to export-oriented policies, from policies intended to protect producers from competition to policies aimed at enabling firms to compete in both domestic and world markets.

Bardhan's use of a class analysis of politics and public policy leads him to focus on interests rather than on ideology, and to ignore the question of how and why India chose its industrial strategy. The present policies have their roots in the socialist ideologies of Jawaharlal Nehru. The foundations of the public sector, of state regulation of the private sector, and of import substitution policies were laid in the mid-fifties. Indeed, Nehru and his economic advisors wanted to pursue a socialist strategy in agriculture as well; they advocated 'cooperative' joint farming, with the village as the unit of production. But their proposals, embodied in the famous 1959 Nagpur Congress resolution on agrarian organization, were defeated by supporters of peasant farming. In the mid-sixties, a new agricultural strategy was adopted. It involved increased public investment in irrigation and fertilizers, the development and use of new high-yielding varieties of wheat, and an agricultural price policy intended to provide incentives to farmers for investing in agricultural inputs. The new policy represented a major defeat for the socialists who had called for asset redistribution, either by giving 'land to the tiller,' or through collectivization, Chinese-style. The aim of the socialists to restructure India's rural society was not realized primarily because India preserved an open, participant political system that enabled the peasant proprietor classes to resist both asset redistribution and collectivization.

The socialists were more successful in getting their industrial policies approved.[6] Their goal of expanding state control over the means of

---

[6] The major legislative milestones in industrialization policy in India were: (1) the Industries (Development and Regulation) Act of 1951, with provisions for industrial licensing for producing any new product (the Act has been amended frequently to increase the regulatory authority of the government); (2) the Industrial Policy Resolution approved by Parliament in 1956, categorizing industrial sectors reserved for the state, those in which the private sector would also be permitted, and the remainder that would be left to the private sector; (3) the Monopolies and Restrictive Trade Practices (MRTP) Act of 1969, enabling the government to place restrictions on new licenses for larger

industrial production, either through public ownership or public control, was attained partly because they had the support of the middle classes, and partly because the state bureaucracy proved to be one of their major allies. Mrs. Gandhi reversed her father's agricultural policies, but she moved further to the left on industrial policy. Under her regime, the Monopoly and Restrictive Trade Practices Act was passed, sharply limiting the capacity of larger firms to expand. She nationalized banks, insurance, and the coal industry. Pressed by Mohan Kumaramangalam (a former member of the Communist Party of India, a friend during her school days in London, and one of her closest advisors in the early seventies), Mrs. Gandhi introduced the twenty-fifth Amendment to the Constitution, limiting the fundamental rights provisions, particularly as they affected property rights. The target, declared Kumaramangalam, was the 'big monopolies,' which needed to be nationalized.

Also missing from Bardhan's analysis is any recognition of the alliance that subsequently developed between the socialists and certain sections of the bureaucracy. Some of the highest bureaucrats in the government—officials like P.N. Haksar, who headed the prime minister's secretariat, and D.P. Dhar in the Planning Commission—were sympathetic to the left position. Even some 'conservative' bureaucrats welcomed the expansion of government control, and hence of their own power, over the private sector.[7] India's socialists have never acknowledged their close ties to the bureaucracy—officially, they are as critical as is Bardhan of the 'rent-seeking' proclivities of bureaucrats—but the fact is that important sections of the bureaucracy promoted nationalization, the expansion of the public sector, and licensing.

industrial houses; and (4) the Foreign Exchange Regulation Act (FERA), passed in 1973 to further regulate foreign investment. For a useful history of industrial policy, see S.S. Marathe, *Industrial Policy in India—Retrospect and Prospect*, New Delhi, Centre for Policy Research, 1984.

[7] Remarkably little has been written about the impact of the bureaucracy on the formation of industrial or agricultural policies. A partial exception is Francine R. Frankel, *India's Political Economy, 1947–1977*, Princeton, Princeton University Press, 1978. Among the important members of the civil service who influenced industrial policy under Prime Ministers Nehru and Indira Gandhi, were S. Bhoothalingam in finance and steel; C.D. Deshmukh in planning; H.V.R. Iyenger in commerce, industry, and the Reserve Bank; S. Jagannathan in economic affairs; the late L.K. Jha also in economic affairs; S.S. Khere in steel and mines; K.B. Lal in trade; P.C. Mahalanobis in planning; B.K. Nehru in economic affairs; I.G. Patel in finance; and Vishnu Sahay and Tarlok Singh in planning.

Bardhan pays too little attention to the role of the politicians in shaping industrial policy. Although party politicians, especially those from rural constituencies, had good political reasons to oppose co-operative joint farming, they clearly had much to gain from a system in which resources for development were allocated by the state, and where the business community had to turn to the bureaucracy for licenses. Patronage is the heart of Congress politics, and controls are the heart of the patronage system. Moreover, in 1969 Mrs. Gandhi moved leftward as part of her campaign to politically discredit her more conservative opponents in the Congress party and to mobilize popular support. The story is too well known to need recounting here. It is worth noting, though, that when Mrs. Gandhi and her supporters. launched their attacks against 'monopoly capitalism' in the late sixties, they also introduced legislation that prohibited contributions by companies to political parties. These restrictions enabled Congress party politicians to extract illegal payments from the business com-munity in return for 'facilitating' licenses and subsidies, and countless other benefits from the government. Thus, a symbiotic relationship developed among party politicians, bureaucrats and businessmen that was made possible by socialist policies. Ironically, this coalition is now a target of socialist critics.

In short, the industrial strategy adopted by the government not only affected the performance of the economy, but created economic and political groups with interests in the preservation of these policies. One can go even further and say that many of the least attractive features of Indian political life, including the growing corruption among bureaucrats and politicians, and the criminalization of politics, are the consequences of industrial policies. An important *political* argument for deregulation, liberalization, and ending many of the subsidies and tariffs is that these controls have nurtured corruption and crime among businessmen, bureaucrats, and politicians. Indeed, one of the strongest reasons for a new industrial policy is not only that it is necessary to unshackle the economy, but that it would help to liberalize and decriminalize politics and administration

The speed with which Prime Minister Rajiv Gandhi moved toward economic liberalization came as a surprise. His background as a pilot, his close association with school friends who have been managers in multinational corporations, his personal fascination with computers, and the fact that he was not brought up in the socialist intellectual milieu that shaped the youth of both his mother and grandfather, are all important elements in his personal outlook.[8]

In the past, a major constraint on changing industrial policy has been the mindset of the political elite. Many Indians argued, and still argue, that if socialist policies have failed, it is not because the policies themselves were inadequate, but because their proper implementation has been undermined by corruption. They do not perceive the emergence of a parallel economy, patronage by politicians, and venality of bureaucrats as the result of government policies that induce people to behave in this manner, but rather as an indication of the failure of businessmen, politicians, and bureaucrats to behave properly. The notion that institutions and policies can shape behavior is not widely held. Many intellectuals in India are critical of the growing corruption of the state and its bureaucratic inefficiencies, while at the same time continuing to support Nehru's concept of industrial policy within a socialist framework; they fail to recognize how one shapes the other. They think that socialism can be made to work if, in Bardhan's words, the state can be 'politically insulated' from conflicting interests.

To those on the left, the public sector has been ideologically sacrosanct. They believe that public sector firms could be made to operate more efficiently if they had better managers, rather than that they are inefficient because they have monopolistic control over markets and are protected against price competition. Also sacrosanct to many is the notion that only socialism can provide for a more equitable distribution of wealth, while capitalism (by definition) means a worsening of income distribution. Moreover, competition itself is seen as wasteful and inegalitarian in outcome, destructive of the ideal social order in which each social group acts in accordance with prescribed and ordained norms of conduct. Nehru, for example, chastized industrialists

---

[8] Rajiv Gandhi may also be influenced by the evident impact of liberalization in increasing industrial growth during the last two years in which Indira Gandhi was Prime Minister. When, for example, the government partially decontrolled the cement industry in 1982—previously, it was required to sell its output to the government at an administered price—production increased by 21 percent within a year. For an account of the liberalization policies during the last years of Mrs. Gandhi's government, and of the initial changes proposed by Rajiv Gandhi, see Paul Sillitoe, 'Rajiv's Reformation,' *Far Eastern Economic Review*, January 17, 1985, pp. 50–51, and P.G. Mathai, 'Towards Liberalization,' *India Today*, November 15, 1984, pp. 88–89.

for their belief in the 'profit motive of an acquisitive society.'[9] In the West, competition presumes a social order in which 'all men are created equal,' thereby facilitating policies that remove barriers to inequality so that individuals can seek to maximize their potential in competition with others. But in a social order that presupposes inherent inequalities, it is assumed that equality among individuals and groups can best be achieved, not through the removal of barriers to free competition, but rather through state intervention to regulate the social order so that groups are made equal. Indeed, it is widely believed in India that it is the function of the state to protect one group against another, and to protect firms against the competition of the marketplace. Import substitution became more than a policy of protecting infant industries; it became a way of protecting inefficient producers.

Not everyone in India shares this image of the state as protector and benefactor. In the last decade or so, a new technocratic/managerial elite has emerged, which includes graduates of the prestigious Institutes of Management and Institutes of Technology; they are prepared to compete within India and in the world economy. India now has a large number of young entrepreneurs and managers with considerable self-confidence. Within the bureaucracy itself, a number of individuals are sharply critical of the prevailing industry policy, both because of its impact on the economy and because of its corrupting influence on the administration. The opinions of these individuals might not have had much influence on industrial policy but for the fact that the new Prime Minister appeared to share much of their outlook.

The burgeoning literature on the political economy of development often has as its centerpiece the notion of 'constraints' on development—by which economists mean resource constraints, and political scientists mean the constraints of interests. Neither pays much attention to the constraints of self-imposed mindsets, the worldviews that prevent those in power from learning from their mistakes, from giving up policies based on principles that do not work, and from rethinking the differences between goals and instruments, means and ends. It is not yet clear whether the new group now governing India has completely given up the socialist mindset; but if the Indian government does

[9] Jawaharlal Nehru, *The Discovery of India*, New Delhi, Oxford University Press, 1983 ed., p. 501. Nehru went on to write that the 'Indian outlook . . . has never approved of the spirit of acquisitiveness' (p. 523), thereby expressing not an 'Indian' view, but a Brahminical one.

succeed in creating a new industrial policy that liberalizes the economy, lowers trade barriers, encourages exports, privatizes or removes from ministerial control some of the public sector firms, ends many of the licensing procedures, and generally moves in the direction of making the economy more competitive, it will be the result of this group's initiative, rather than of any powerful political interests pushing in that direction. Nor will it be the result of rethinking on the part of India's economists, few of whom anticipated the new politicies intellectually.

Obstacles to Liberalization

There are formidable political obstacles to liberalization. There is opposition from the left within the Congress party, from the left parties, and sections of the academic community. Opposition also comes from those who are the beneficiaries of the present system— businessmen in protected industries, workers in inefficient plants, and bureaucrats earning fees from businessmen. These groups are likely to use every conceivable argument to halt liberalization: they will advocate reimposing import restrictions as India's balance of payments worsens; they will call for the rescue of failing firms on the grounds that workers would otherwise lose their jobs; and they will plead to retain subsidies in order to keep prices down. Those who put forth these arguments could win popular support if the new policies are accompanied by a significant increase in inflation, or if the policies fail to improve industrial output and employment significantly.

India is likely to experience a difficult period of transition. If imports are liberalized too rapidly, protected industries will not be able to make the necessary adjustments to become competitive. Liberalization will falter if the economy is opened to luxury goods rather than to the import of capital goods and technology that will enable industry to modernize. If public sector firms remain inefficient, the high cost of steel and the unreliability of electric power and transportation will continue to push costs up for domestic industries, reduce their capacity to compete with foreign imports, and prevent them from expanding exports. The deficit in the balance of payments will grow, and it is unlikely to be reduced by an increase in remittances or foreign aid. Borrowing on commercial terms will mean higher interest rates and increased debts. If the trade deficit is to be kept manageable, India will need to cut imports, particularly in edible oils and sugar; exports will have to expand; and the country will need to attract additional capital investment from abroad. Substantial investments will have to be made to modernize such critical sectors as steel, coal, power, transportation, and irrigation, but it is not clear where the resources for such investments will be found. A reduction in subsidies could net substantial new resources; but some of these subsidies, particularly those for food and gasoline, benefit large numbers of people. Their withdrawal is politically unpopular, as the government learned in February 1986. In short, it will take a great deal of *political* as well as economic fine-tuning to make the transition. The Prime Minister and his technically oriented advisors will have to demonstrate that they have the political skills to handle the transition.

If Rajiv Gandhi proves to be successful in rationalizing the Indian economy by making it more open and competitive, the consequences are likely to be reflected in the political arena. Influence will shift from those sectors of the business community concerned with protection to those that need a more open trading economy; and the power of the bureaucracy over business, and of politicians over the bureaucracy, will surely be reduced. But the short-term consequences may also include more militant unionism and a growing antagonism toward the Prime Minister from leftist intellectuals, leftist political parties, and leftist sections of the Congress party. It remains to be seen whether the Prime Minister's new industrial policies will lead to an economic miracle for India. Meanwhile, they seem likely to arouse strong opposition.

India's experience since Independence suggests the importance of the leadership's ideology in generating industrial policies that, in turn, create interests committed to the preservation of such policies. India's socialists succeeded in creating an industrial structure in which the state is predominant, both in its direct control over basic industries and in its indirect control over the private sector. State control—though still far from the socialist ideal of central planning in the Soviet and East European sense of central allocations of resources and enforcement through centralizing command—has given the bureaucracy enormous power. The result is that a system put in place by anti-bureaucratic and anti-capitalist socialists is now sustained by the bureaucracy, by sections of the governing Congress party, and by portions of the business community. Therefore, in spite of the disenchantment with socialism by sections of the middle class, and the efforts at reform by liberals within the government, it will be difficult to dismantle many of the controls that have by now become institutionalized. A fundamental change toward market-oriented policies requires a new ideological orientation of the governing elite, an economic and political strategy for handling the transition, a strong commitment by the leadership to pursue these policies in spite of short-term losses, and the capacity of the leadership to build a new coalition of political forces to provide support for these policies. Rajiv Gandhi has met the first condition, but there are no indications yet that he is able to meet the others.

6

The Political Consequences of Preferential Policies: India in Comparative Perspective

Do preferential policies—or affirmative action programs, as they are called in the United States—have similar political consequences in very different social and cultural settings? The object of this paper is to suggest that they do.[1]

The governments of India, Malaysia, Sri Lanka, and the United States have adopted policies intended to give preferences in employment and in education to selected disadvantaged ethnic groups. The effects of these policies on the education, occupation, and income of the intended beneficiaries vary within and among these countries. But the political effects are remarkably similar, suggesting that there is a political and policy logic to such policies shared by very diverse societies and polities.

One way to study the effects of policies is to use what John Stuart

This paper originally appeared in *Comparative Politics*, October 1983.

[1] An earlier version of this paper was presented at the Ford Foundation workshop on preferential policies held in Trincomalee, Sri Lanka, from March 8 to 12, 1982. For comments on that paper I am grateful to Robert Goldmann and Donald Horowitz and to many of the other participants in the workshop, including Eleanor Holmes Norton, Charles Hamilton, Bashiruddin Ahmed, Suma Chitnis, Raghavendra Hebsur, Chandra Richard de Silva, Kingsley M. de Silva, S.W.R. de A. Samarasinghe, Neelam Tiruchelvam, T.S.A. Srinivasavardhan, and George Verghese. Many of the arguments presented here were initially developed in a book I wrote with Mary Fainsod Katzenstein, *India's Preferential Policies: Migrants, the Middle Classes and Ethnic Equality*, Chicago, University of Chicago Press, 1981.

Mill called the 'method of difference' in comparative analysis. According to this method, if we wish to examine the effects of, say, tariff policies, we should compare at least two countries 'whose habits, usages, opinions, laws and institutions are the same in all respects, except that one of them has a more protective tariff.'[2] Clearly this standard is so demanding that it makes comparative analysis impossible.

An alternative method is to look at the effects of the same policy on at least two countries 'whose habits, usages, opinions, laws and institutions' are *different*. No conclusions can be drawn if the effects are different, but if the effects are similar then a causal relationship can be established.

To test our hypothesis that preferential policies produce similar political consequences in widely different social and cultural settings, we shall draw our evidence from India and the United States, two countries that are very different but which have adopted similar policies to deal with the issue of inequalities among ethnic groups.

First, it is necessary to clarify the conceptual language.

Preferential policies refers to laws, regulations, administrative rules, court orders, and other public interventions to provide certain public and private goods, such as admission into schools and colleges, jobs, promotions, business loans, and rights to buy and sell land on the basis of membership in a particular ethnic group.[3]

By *ethnicity*, I mean the way individuals and groups characterize themselves on the basis of their language, race, religion, place of origin, shared culture, values, and history. Ethnicity is generally, but not always, a matter of birth. Many people collectively may redefine their identity; government policies are often important in shaping the identity of an ethnic group and determining who is a member.

Ethnic equality can refer to *equality of opportunity, equality of results*, or *equality of treatment*. By *equality of opportunity*, I mean that individuals, irrespective of the ethnic group they belong to, are considered for education and employment as well as other public and

---

[2] John Stuart Mill, *Logic*, quoted by Denis Thompson, *John Stuart Mill and Representative Government*, Princeton, Princeton University Press, 1976, p. 22.

[3] In the United States these policies are called 'affirmative action' or 'compensatory' policies by supporters, and 'reverse discrimination' by detractors. In India, these policies are called protective discrimination' or simply, 'reservations.' The terminology often reveals the writer's point of view. No term is completely neutral but I have used the word 'preferences' as the least value-loaded term, not specifically tied to either country.

private goods on the basis of their ability and skills or their needs. When there is *equality of opportunity*, individuals are neither discriminated against nor given benefits because of their language, religion, race, place of origin, caste, or any other ethnic category.

Equality of results, as it relates to ethnicity, means that the distribution of income, wealth, and occupations among individuals is in proportion to the population of each ethnic group in the country.

Equality of treatment suggests that individuals, regardless of the ethnic group they belong to, are treated alike, that people with more money are entitled to more material goods, but are not entitled to degrade others because of their lower income or ethnic group.

The Arguments for Preferential Policies

Virtually everywhere in the world there is now a demand for greater equality among ethnic groups. Whether it is India or the United States, Sri Lanka or Belgium, Malaysia or Canada, educationally and economically disadvantaged ethnic groups are demanding governmental intervention on their behalf. Most governments have responded either out of a concern for social justice or to mitigate political conflict. Preferential policies—or affirmative action programs, reservations, or compensatory discrimination, as these policies are variously called—are one such government response.

There is a universality to ethnic inequality. All multi-ethnic societies exhibit a tendency for ethnic groups to engage in different occupations, have different levels and often types of education, receive different incomes, and occupy different places in the social hierarchy. In some instances this ethnic division of labor reflects domination by one ethnic group over another through the imposition of its economic powers, control over the state, and assertion of central legitimizing principles and symbols intended to justify the domination. In other instances the ethnic division of labor may be the consequence of different values, preferences, and ambitions of ethnic groups. One group, for example, may have little regard for education where another values education highly. One group may prefer entrepreneurial activities, another the professions, and still another, physical labor. One group could consist of high achievers who seek to move up to whatever occupations are most valued or best paid, while members of another group could be less ambitious, preferring to live as they have in the past, and less willing to venture forth from their community or into new occupations.

Which explanation is 'true,' is often matter of debate. The debate within a country between those who see differences as a result of societal constraints and those who see them as a result of individual or group cultures, values, and preferences—between the socio-political determinants and cultural/individual behavioralists—is often at the root of different policy perspectives. The policy lever one pulls depends in part on how one explains ethnic differences. In fact, both sets of factors can be at work within the same society. Groups may be the victims of societal discrimination and lack initiative and drive; there may be barriers to education as well as indifference to education; groups kept out of certain occupations may also have occupational preferences.

Whatever the cause or explanation, what is striking is the growing contemporary concern for the removal of these differences. Until recently, however, most societies did not view these differences as a problem. That particular religions, castes, or linguistic groups in India predominated in the military, the bureaucracy, trade, and commerce, as landowners, tenant-cultivators, landless laborers, or artisans, seemed to many to be a 'natural' order reflecting, if not innate differences in ability, at least innate differences in culture. And in the United States, it struck no one as a problem that in New York City the Irish dominated the police and the Jews the school system and that municipal garbage collectors, postal workers, textile workers, and, for that matter, corporate, university, and foundation presidents tended to come disproportionately from particular ethnic groups.

Why there is a growing world-wide concern with reducing inequalities among ethnic groups, need not concern us here in any detail. Fundamentally, it is related to the broader concern with income and social inequalities among classes. But there are at least two reasons why many consider ethnic inequality more unacceptable than class inequality. One is that differences among ethnic groups are often seen as an indication of differences in opportunity, proof that society has unfairly allocated access to education and employment, and that dominant groups are using their position to restrict others from moving upward. In contrast, class differences are not necessarily viewed as an indication of inequality of opportunity. To the contrary, they may be the result of equality of opportunity. A society that provides equal opportunity is one in which the results are uneven and where the unequal results are considered legitimate. Winners believe they deserve more, losers that they deserve less, in a competitive race in which all have an equal opportunity to move up. If one has succeeded and another has failed, presumably differences in ability, skill, hard work, and ambition are reflected. If the outcome is stratified by ethnic groups, however, the presumption is made that the results may have been fixed—that is, that some groups were discriminated against while others were favored. Thus, in both India and the United States, the low status and the low income of ex-untouchables and Blacks are widely viewed as the result of discrimination by dominant ethnic groups, whereas poverty among Brahmins and Protestant Whites is ordinarily not seen as a result of prejudice.

The second reason why ethnic inequality is often of greater social and political concern than class differences is that when ethnic differences lead to ethnic conflict the result is often more disruptive to the social order than in the case of class conflicts. On a global basis more people have been killed in this century because of the ethnic group to which they belonged than because of their class. Forceful expulsion of populations, genocide, civil wars, and a variety of internal upheavals linked to ethnic conflicts have marked social and political life in the advanced industrial countries no less than in the newly independent states of Asia and Africa. Ties of blood (whether real or a social invention), have driven mankind to commit acts that exceed the brutalities committed on behalf of class.

It is this concern for both distributive justice and the minimizing of ethnic conflict, that has led some governments to turn their attention to the question of how to reduce inequalities among ethnic groups.

Various policies aimed at increasing the income and occupational equality of ethnic groups are available to governments. Preferential treatment is only one of several such alternatives. Among the others are: regional and urban development programs where disadvantaged ethnic groups are geographically concentrated; government aid for selected sectors of the economy where disadvantaged ethnic groups are concentrated in agriculture, fishing, forestry, or particular industries; social service programs for improving the health, education, and housing of low-income groups: wealth and income distribution policies, such as land reform, tenancy reform, and minimum wages, which differentially benefit one ethnic group in relation to another; and a variety of policies that increase the political power of selected ethnic groups, such as the devolution of authority, the redrawing of administrative boundaries, and electoral reform.

Such policies, though intended to benefit particular ethnic groups, do not use ethnic criteria as their basis. Preferential policies do. Under preferential policies individuals are given special benefits, not because they live in poor regions, work in lagging sectors of the economy, or are educationally and economically disadvantaged, but because they belong to a particular ethnic category—a caste, race, tribe, religion, linguistic, or cultural group which, on the average, is less educated, earns less, and has lower status employment than other ethnic groups. The advantage of such explicit policies is that only the targeted group benefits. It is also argued that the benefits accrue faster. Most important, the policies are politically attractive to the leadership and to the more advanced elements of the ethnic group, for they are the major gainers.

Preferential policies have been adopted in the United States, India, Malaysia, and Sri Lanka. They have been advocated in several European countries (particularly Holland and the United Kingdom) and in Israel. In each instance, there is a controversy not only over the efficacy of such policies, but also over the deeper philosophical question of the justice of employing ethnic criteria as the basis for the distribution of benefits, that is, whether the characteristics of the group rather than of the individuals who belong to the group should be the basis for the receipt of entitlements and preferences. At the heart of the controversy is the question of individual versus group rights. India and the United States have approached the issue of preferential policies from quite different philosophical traditions. Yet, as we shall try to argue, similar (though by no means the same) policies have produced remarkably similar political consequences.

Our account of the American debate will be highly condensed, since we shall assume that the reader is broadly familiar with the issues, while our account of the debate—and the assumptions that underlie that debate—in India will be presented in greater detail. We shall then turn our attention to the political consequences of preferential policies in India and suggest similarities in the American experience.

In the United States, advocates of ethnic equality initially directed their attention to eliminating discrimination in education, employment, housing, and civil rights. A series of Supreme Court decisions—particularly *Brown* v. *Board of Education* 1954—and legislative decisions, especially the 1964 Civil Rights Act, attempted to break the barriers to equality of opportunity and equality of treatment. A prime target of reform was school segregation. American civil rights supporters argued that the integration of Whites and Blacks in schools, combined with the elimination of discrimination in employment and housing, would enable disadvantaged Blacks to compete with Whites, and that in time most of the disparities would disappear. Others argued that since the effects of past discrimination were reflected in current individual capabilities, equal opportunity would result in unequal outcomes. They argued that the assumption that the removal of discrimination in education would equalize opportunity and bring about more equal results, was false. Holders of this view rejected the classic liberal view that the educational system could even out class barriers, and that subsequent differences in income or productivity could then be explained by examining the personal deficiencies of workers. Moreover, if cultural differences affected the ability of groups to compete, under conditions of perfect competition some ethnic groups would win a disproportionate share of the higher occupations and incomes.

Perhaps the strongest argument against a color-blind policy came from those who questioned whether there could be real equality of opportunity in a society where prejudice and discrimination were so widespread. Neither school integration nor legal measures to counter discrimination would, therefore, be sufficient to create equality of opportunity between the races.

Affirmative action programs were proposed as a way to equalize the races, but there was division between those who saw such programs as a goal and those who saw them as a system of quotas or preferences. For some, *affirmative action* meant programs of training and recruitment in support of a national commitment to equal *opportunity* in education and employment. Others stressed reserving a certain percentage of positions for exclusive use by Blacks, Hispanics and other targeted groups. The line between goals and actual quotas is difficult to draw in practice; to many non-Americans it is probably an arcane distinction with no significant difference of outcomes. Nonetheless, the issue calls attention to the widespread American belief in equality of opportunity, but not necessarily equality of results, and more fundamentally to the American preference for individual rights as opposed to group rights.

These issues were drawn in the Bakke case, involving a white male who argued that he was denied admission to the University of California Medical School at Davis because sixteen out of one hundred places in the entering class had been reserved for minorities. Supporters of affirmative action argued that the unequal distribution of benefits among races with respect to the number of doctors reflected discrimination against minorities and that group performance was a way to determine whether equal opportunities existed. Most supporters of the Davis Medical School also subscribed to the notion that it was individual performance that counted: they argued that affirmative action in education would lead to equal opportunity in employment which would ultimately bring equal results. This classic liberal position was articulated by Archibald Cox, professor of law at Harvard and the lawyer for Davis. In fact, he said, if the Davis program were to 'give rise to some notion of group entitlement regardless either of the ability of . . . individuals or of their potential contribution to society . . . I would first, as a faculty member, criticize and oppose it; as a constitutional lawyer, the further it went the more doubts I would have.'[4]

Some observers interpreted the Bakke case as a classic clash between the principle of meritocracy and the goal of racial equality, but defenders of meritocracy argued that merit was the only way to guarantee equal opportunity. Some saw the case as a test of the principle of compensatory justice, while others argued that nothing was more unfair than to measure individuals by their race. There were also arguments about the need for role models, analogies between proportionality in politics and proportionality in education, and a controversy over whether there had to be prior discrimination on the part of the Davis Medical School to justify a compensatory admissions policy. At the heart of the debate, however, lay the question: are constitutional rights for individuals or for groups? To supporters of the doctrine of individual rights, the meaning of the Fourteenth Amendment was clear and decisive: 'No state shall . . . deny to any *person* within its jurisdiction the equal protection of the laws.'

Many advocates of affirmative action policies see them not as group preferences but as an attempt by government to stop discrimination. From this perspective, Executive Orders 11246 and 11375, which required federal contractors to establish affirmative action plans, were the means by which the federal government sought compliance with Title VII of the 1964 Civil Rights Act outlawing employer discrimination. While some civil rights advocates distinguished between anti-discriminatory policies (which they support) and numerical goals or

---

[4] Timothy J. O'Neill, 'The Language of Equality in a Constitutional Order', *American Political Science Review*, 75, September 1981, p. 627.

quotas (which they oppose), others argued that 'without numerical goals Title VII is virtually unenforceable' since it is nearly impossible to prove that racial bias affects individual hiring decisions.[5]

Supporters of quotas argue that there is a 'pool' of potentially qualified applicants among minorities, and that if an employer consistently hires a smaller percentage than those in the available pool there is a pattern of discrimination. One must therefore define what the appropriate qualifications are for a particular job or for admission into an educational institution, develop appropriate measures for determining the number and percentage of qualified minorities, and then monitor employers and educational institutions to assure that hiring or admission of minorities is proportionate to the number in the qualified pool of applicants.

This view of quotas is conceptually different from one which emphasizes hiring and admissions in proportion to the size of the ethnic group within the society. Its advocates argue that it is a policy intended ultimately to create color-blind hiring and hence is consistent with an individual rather than a group rights position. But its critics argue that while goals can be consistent with an individual rights position, in practice efforts to define 'qualifications,' 'pools,' and 'numerical goals,' particularly when these are defined and set by government bureaucrats, can easily become quotas and group rights.

The case for moving from one position to the other is forcefully articulated by Franklin Thomas, President of the Ford Foundation, who argues that anti-discrimination policies in the United States have moved through three ascending stages. Stage one is 'racial neutrality,' that is, anti-discriminatory laws intended to create color-blind behavior. Stage two is an active anti-discriminatory policy requiring equal opportunity policies by employers, programs to enlarge the pool of qualified persons, and a degree of 'special treatment' for Blacks.

[5] Christopher Jencks, 'Special Treatment for Blacks?' *The New York Review*, March 17, 1973, p. 14. For other views on these issues see Nijole V. Benokaitis and Joe R. Feagin, *Affirmative Action and Equal Opportunity: Action, Inaction, Reaction*, Colorado, Westview Press, 1978; 'Evaluating the Impact of Affirmative Action: A Look at the Federal Compliance Program: A Symposium,' *ILR Review*, July 29, 1976, pp. 485–584; Nathan Glazer, *Affirmative Discrimination: Ethnic Equality and Public Policy*, New York, Basic Books, 1975; Richard A. Lester, *Reasoning about Discrimination*, Princeton, Princeton University Press, 1980; John E. Fleming, Gerald R. Gill, and David E. Swinton. *The Case for Affirmative Action for Blacks in Higher Education*, Washington, Howard University Press, 1978; Thomas Sowell, *Markets and Minorities*, New York, Basic Books, 1982.

Stage three, he writes, 'advances affirmative action by a giant's leap' to what Thomas calls a 'federally-mandated race-conscious policy.'[6] Thomas agrees that mandated numerical remedies change the relationship between the individual and the group, but he supports these remedies on the grounds that 'affirmative action in all its forms serves the most profound goal of a democratic society—equality and justice for everyone regardless of color, ethnicity, or sex. All of the sophisticated tools of regulation, enforcement and litigation are only instruments towards that end.'[7]

In any discussion of preferences it is also useful to distinguish between *procedural* and *substantive* preferences. Procedural preferences are intended to increase the access of a group to political power, education, and employment, but unlike substantive preferences do not necessarily guarantee equal results. Government policies that force employers to look at a larger pool than the known work force, define job-related standards that do not impose higher educational or physical strength qualifications than those required by the job, and set equal opportunity requirements to replace the traditional 'old boy' network are examples of procedural 'preferences.' Such procedures are generally less contentious than substantive preferences intended to assure equal results. The reason is that these procedures can also be described as ways of eliminating discriminatory practices and thus are consistent with the individual rights/equal access position

According to public opinion polls, most Americans object to the notion of group rights and quotas but support other measures to advance greater ethnic equality. Congress and, with some important exceptions, the courts have held to the individual rights position, while in effect sanctioning goals and timetables designed to achieve equality for disadvantaged groups. But some civil rights organizations and many government agencies charged with implementing affirmative action programs have tended to operate on the basis of group rights and goals. As with many political debates, code words have become a shorthand way of expressing deeper philosophical positions. *Quotas* has come to mean a group rights position, while for many liberals *goals* is a device for preserving the commitment to individual rights while advocating steps to reduce inequalities among ethnic groups.

[6] Franklin A. Thomas, *Reflections on a Multi-Racial Society*, London, Granada Publishing, 1983, pp. 12–13.
[7] *Ibid.*, p. 18.

Preferential Policies in India

The Indian position is more explicit in support of group than of individual rights, though both positions have a place in the country's constitution. Indeed, imbedded in the Indian Constitution are two conflicting notions of equality, each derived from an opposing philosophical tradition.[8]

Article 15 of the Indian Constitution states: 'The state shall not discriminate against any citizens on grounds only of religion, race, caste, sex or place of birth.' Similarly, Article 16(2) states that no citizen 'shall on grounds only of religion, race, caste, sex, descent, place of birth, residence or any of them be ineligible for or discriminated against in state employment.' This is the standard liberal position on individual rights.

But article 15(4), an amendment adopted in 1951, modifies Article 15 with a clause that states: 'Nothing in this article . . . shall prevent the state from making any special provision for the advancement of any socially and educationally backward classes of citizens or for the scheduled castes and the scheduled tribes.' Similarly, Article 16(4) modifies Article 16: 'Nothing in this article shall prevent the state from making any provision for the reservation of appointments or posts in favour of any backward class of citizens.' This is the standard group rights principle.

[8] See Weiner and Katzenstein, *op. cit.*, for a more detailed historical account of how the policies were adopted in India and how they affected employment and education in selected regions of the country. See also Barbara R. Joshi, *Democracy in Search of Equality*, Delhi, Hindustan Publishing Corporation, 1982; Suma Chitnis, *A Long Way to Go*, New Delhi, Allied Publishers, 1981; Parta C. Aggarwal and Mohammed Siddiq Ashraf, *Equality Through Privilege: A Study of Special Privileges for Scheduled Castes in Haryana*, New Delhi, Shri Ram Center for Industrial Relations and Human Resources, 1976; G.P. Verma, *Caste Reservations in India: Law and the Constitution*, Allahabad, Chugh Publications, 1980; Karuna Ahmad, 'Towards Equality: Consequences of Protective Discrimination,' *Economic and Political Weekly*, January 14, 1978, pp. 69–72; Marc Galanter, 'Equality and Protective Discrimination in India,' *Rutgers Law Review*, Vol. 16, 1961, pp. 42–74; Marc Galanter, 'Group Membership and Group Preferences in India,' *Journal of Asian and African Studies*, Vol. 2, 1967, pp. 91–124; Alan Gledhill, 'Constitutional Protection of Indian Minorities,' *Journal of the Indian Law Institute*, Vol. 1, 1959, pp. 403–415; Raj Kumar Gupta, 'Justice: Equal but Inseparate,' *Journal of the Indian Law Institute*, Vol. 11, 1969, pp. 57–86; Mohammed Imam, 'Reservations of Seats for Backward Classes in Public Services and Educational Institutions,' *Journal of the Indian Law Institute*, Vol. 8, 1966, pp. 411–466.

Thus, after boldly reconfirming the nineteenth-century liberal conception of the rights of citizens, the Indian Constitution then asserts the principle of collective rights of classes of citizens based upon religion, race, caste, sex, descent, place of birth, or residence when the claims are made on behalf of classes 'socially and educationally backward.' Other provisions of the Constitution go beyond enabling the government to give preference to specified classes of citizens by *requiring* the government to do so. Article 335, for example, provides for reservations of appointments of scheduled castes and scheduled tribes to the administrative services, and other provisions provide for reservations in parliament and the state assemblies.

Thus, the Indian government in its Constitution and in subsequent legislative and administrative decisions, confirmed in court rulings, established the policy that the government can and should allocate seats in legislative bodies, admit students into educational institutions, grant scholarships, provide employment in government services, and make available various other entitlements to individuals on the basis of membership in a group. Once this principle was established, the political controversies then centered on two ancillary questions: what groups should be entitled to preferences? What particular preferences should be provided?

An earlier legislative history largely settled the identity of the scheduled castes and scheduled tribes. These groups are widely known and locally accepted and are often specified in the census as well as various other administrative and legislative acts. The only significant controversy concerned whether ex-untouchables who had opted out of Hinduism by converting to Christianity or Buddhism qualified as members of scheduled castes since the latter were initially defined as castes within the Hindu religious framework. The controversy was ultimately settled by broadening rather than narrowing the definition of scheduled castes. Similarly, a legislative effort to exclude Christian tribals from the reservations provided for scheduled tribes, was rejected by the Indian parliament.

The issue of giving other 'backward classes' benefits and of the wav these classes should be chosen was more controversial. The 'backward class' category is an especially elastic one since the criteria for inclusion are left to the political arena.[9]

[9] Marc Galanter, 'Who Are the Other Backward Classes? An Introduction to a Constitutional Puzzle,' *Economic and Political Weekly*, Vol. 13, October 28, 1978, p. 1814.

The debate over the choice of criteria for including particular communities has been indecisive. Some government commissions argued that objective measures of 'backwardness,' such as average education or income levels, be employed. Other commissions emphasized position in the social hierarchy: a caste should be included as 'backward' on the basis of its low status or the inferior treatment of its members by other communities. Whether the test for inclusion is an economic or a caste one, the consensus was that the criteria should be applied to groups, not individuals.

Some states were highly selective, but others chose to define as 'backward' virtually any non-Brahmin caste. Efforts by the central government to develop a uniform set of criteria, if not a uniform list, were rejected by parliament and the courts, with the result that each state government has its own criteria and its own list. One consequence is that, while members of scheduled castes and scheduled tribes are given reservations in the central services and in centrally-run educational institutions as well as at the state level, reservations for the backward classes are confined to state and locally-run institutions and administrative services.

Although virtually all states provide benefits to some backward classes, several states have aggressively incorporated a substantial number of castes with large populations in their list. It is not unusual for 20 to 25 percent of the population of a state to appear on lists of backward classes, in addition to the 15 percent of the Indian population classified as scheduled caste, and another 7 percent as scheduled tribe.

In addition, most states have extended preferences to *residents* of the state, particularly in educational admissions and in employment for the state government. Although the laws and administrative rulings are usually explicit in specifying a time period as a definition of residence, it is not uncommon for residence to be used as a surrogate for ethnicity. The widely used term is 'sons of the soil,' referring to populations indigenous to a particular area, as distinct from migrants. Thus, in Assam 'sons of the soil' rules specify residence, but both private and public employers understand that the intention of these policies is to give employment preferences to Assamese over Bengalis. Similar policies in Bombay are intended to benefit those who speak the Marathi language over Tamils and other migrant communities, irrespective of the duration of their residence.

The main argument for extending reservations to 'sons of the soil' is that they, too, are 'socially and educationally backward' in relation to some migrant communities. In many regions of India an ethnic division of labor has developed, involving migrants and natives, with migrants holding positions in the state and central administrative services, the professions, the colleges and universities, and business and trade. The demand for preferential policies to protect the native middle classes over the migrant middle classes is an old one: preference was given to residents of the state in Hyderabad in the 1920s and in Bihar in the 1930s. In the 1960s and early 1970s, similar policies were adopted in Assam (against Bengalis), in Maharashtra (against Tamils), and within the Telengana region of Andhra (against people from the delta).

An interesting feature of Andhra's policies that may foreshadow developments elsewhere is that 'local' was defined not in terms of residence in the state but as residence in regions and districts of state. Demands for the 'regionalization' of preferences have already been made in other states.

There was thus a progression in the application of the principle of reservations: from scheduled caste and scheduled tribe minorities that were lowest on the social scale, to the more numerous and somewhat better-off backward castes, to autochthonous populations, a majority diverse in its social and economic characteristics yet backward in relation to its migrant competitors.

These extensions have not been without controversy, however. In some states both scheduled castes and forward castes have opposed the extension of preferences to backward castes—most notably in Bihar, where a recommendation by the state government was accompanied by massive demonstrations in colleges. 'Sons of the soil' preferences have been opposed, not only by migrant communities, but often by the governments of the states the migrants came from, along with warnings of reprisals if state governments became too restrictive.

Some critics of reservations for backward castes and for 'sons of the soil' urged the state governments to put aside all benefits for castes and linguistic groups, proposing instead that benefits go only to individuals from families that lacked education or adequate income. But this proposal for replacing group characteristics with individual characteristics was uniformly rejected by policy-makers.

Objections notwithstanding, the extension of preferences to communities previously not receiving preferences has over the past three decades moved inexorably forward. The only limitation imposed by the courts is that, with respect to scheduled castes, scheduled tribes, and backward castes, the total number of reservations for admission to colleges and for positions in the administrative services must be below

50 percent. No such numerical restriction, however, was placed on preferences for 'sons of the soil.'

There has also been a progression in the kind of reservations provided. Initially, reservations were provided for admission to schools and colleges, including engineering and medical schools. They were provided for appointments to the state administrative services and, in the case of scheduled castes and tribes, to the central administrative services. Reservations were then extended to the entire public sector, though not to private employment. Private employers, however, are under pressure from state and central governments to provide reservations for scheduled castes and tribes and for 'sons of the soil.'

The system of reservations was originally intended for admission to educational institutions and for government employment. In some instances, preferences were also extended to promotions. More recently, there have been demands that preferences in admissions to medical schools be 'held over'; that is, seats not filled one year must be added to reservations for the next.

The Indian policy, then, is to create a new kind of labor market in which each ethnic group is given a share commensurate with its population. Shares are first apportioned in educational institutions, then in various categories of employment in the public sector, and ultimately in private employment.

From this perspective, the model society is not a socialist one in which all individuals have, if not equal levels of education, at least equal incomes and wealth. Nor is it the liberal capitalist model of a society based upon equal opportunity in which individuals compete for higher education and higher incomes. Rather, it is a society in which the *upper* levels of education, income, and occupation are proportionately made up of persons from all the country's ethnic groups. This objective is to be achieved, not by an open competitive market, but by a government-regulated educational and labor market that ensures an appropriate place for each group. Social justice, according to this view, thus requires a public policy that guarantees individual mobility by means of group allocation.

The Political Consequences of Preferential Policies

To view policy options, policy choices, and program implementation simply in rational cost-benefit terms based upon an assessment of policy outcomes, its gainers and losers, is to ignore the political dimension of the policy process. On the other hand, to reduce the system of reservations to a struggle by various groups for economic position, or by one group for mastery over another, is to miss the deeper conceptual issues which underlie political struggles. Neither approach provides a satisfactory answer to the question of why two countries, the United States and India, both committed to ethnic equality, both employing similar policy instruments, nonetheless continue to deal with the question of ethnic equality in different ways. Behind such words as *ethnicity, equality, integration,* and even *preferences,* lie fundamentally different beliefs.

But at another level, there is a convergence among countries that chose to follow the path of preferential policies, a convergence dictated by the *political logic* of preferential policies. This logic is especially clear in the Indian case precisely because India has so explicitly made a policy committment to ethnic-group preferences. By 'political logic' I mean a policy decision that creates a political space, shaping the terms of subsequent policy debates and substantially influencing political responses and new policy choices. In the Indian case, the political logic of preferential policies worked as follows:

1. *Group preferences.* There has been a progression from one group to another in the allocation of preferences. As we have seen, a policy initially intended to benefit scheduled castes and tribes was extended to backward castes and to autochthonous populations.[10] There have been pressures to expand the list of backward castes and to define autochthonous in an increasingly localized manner, as well as demands that reservations be extended to Muslims, to the families and children of immigrants overseas, and to various other groups.

2. *Kinds of preferences.* The Indian Constitution asserts that

---

[10] The extension of preferences to autochthonous majorities has brought to the fore the question of when preferences are merely a rationale for discriminatory policies. In India, as elsewhere, the argument that the 'native' population has a more authentic claim to land, education and employment than people of migrant origin has raised the issue of whether there are two classes of citizens with different rights. This issue has been raised in Sri Lanka where the Sinhalese are given preferences over the Tamils, in Malaysia where the Malays ('bhumiputra' or native population) are given preferences over Chinese and Indians, and in Kenya where the prime minister recently proposed that businessmen of Asian origin who broke the law would be expelled, while 'African' businessmen would be fined or jailed.

government can make provisions for the 'reservations of appointments or posts' but leaves to the legislature the decision of what precise reservations should be provided. The result has been a debate over whether reservations should be provided in engineering and medical schools as well as in colleges, in public sector companies as well as in government services, and for privately as well as publicly owned firms. Controversy has arisen over what categories of employment to impose quotas on, and whether promotions as well as initial appointments should be by quota.

Determining which groups should be given preferences and of what kind, are not matters than can readily be resolved by some principle, especially since other widely held principles conflict with preferences. The principle, for example, that preferences should be given to local people conflicts with the principle of national citizenship. 'This is a matter,' said Mrs. Gandhi, 'in which one has to have a certain balance. While we stand for the principle that any Indian should be able to work in any part of India, at the same time it is true that if a large number of people came from outside to seek employment . . . that is bound to create tension in that area. Therefore, while I do not like the idea of having such a rule, one has to have some balance and see that the local people are not deprived of employment.'[11]

Similarly, the notion of making appointments on the basis of ethnic membership is seen as conflicting with the goal of institutional efficiency and the notion of individual merit. Heads of public sector firms, for example, have pressed for the exclusion of certain categories of employment (by skill level of rank) from reservations, but what is an acceptable balance to a manager is often not an acceptable balance to the leaders of ethnic communities.

Thus, what preferences and for whom, are political matters resolved not by legal doctrines or general principles but in the political arena, with struggles in the streets, at the polls, within the government bureaucracy, and in the state legislatures. Concessions granted to one group then become the basis of demands by another.

[11] Weiner and Katzenstein, *op. cit.*, p. 25.

3. *Mobilization.* Because the question of what groups are to be given preferences is constitutionally and politically open, the demand for preferences has become a device for political mobilization. Politicians can mobilize members of their caste, religious, or linguistic community around the demand for inclusion on the list of those to be given preferences. Leaders of ethnic groups and their supporters have demanded preferences either on the grounds that they are economically backward or that they have suffered from discrimination as a result of their low status in the caste hierarchy, or both.

As an issue around which to organize ethnic groups, the demand for reservations has been highly effective. This is particularly true in the case of the backward classes—a variety of castes diverse in their occupations, income, education, and size who (especially in northern India) have banded together politically around the claim for preferential treatment. Similarly, it has been a unifying demand for autochthonous groups (of many castes and religious affiliations) united in their opposition to 'outsiders.'

4. *Backlash.* As preferences were extended to backward castes and as more benefits were given to scheduled castes and scheduled tribes, the 'forward' castes have mobilized in opposition. In the state of Gujarat, for example, upper caste students launched a movement to end preferences for the scheduled castes when benefits were extended. In Bihar, upper castes, with the support of the scheduled castes, opposed giving reservations to the backward castes. Increasingly, political groups are now organizing either to resist further expansion of preferences or to oppose those in place.

One reason for the backlash is an awareness that some individuals receiving preferences are not themselves from educationally backward or economically deprived families. The more successful reservations are in producing a middle class within the backward community, the more such cases increase and the more resentful are members of communities denied reservations.[12]

[12] The acceptability of a preferential policy is also often based upon its rationale. It makes a difference if a policy is intended to overcome previous discrimination, is a remedy for backwardness, or is a benefit given to 'natives' because it is asserted that an

5. *Supernumerary positions.* As the number of reservations increases, categories expand, and a backlash emerges, governments seek to reduce ethnic conflict by creating supernumerary positions, both in education and in employment. In Andhra, for example, the state government agreed to reserve admissions to Osmania University in proportion to the number of people residing in each district of the state (a policy intended to increase the proportion of students from the backward western districts and to reduce the number from the more advanced eastern districts). The government then mollified the losers by creating another university, one that would be open to everyone in the state without regard to place of birth or residence. Similarly, when the state government agreed to establish regional representation in appointments to the administrative services, it also created supernumerary positions in order not to fire those who came from 'overrepresented' districts. In Gujarat, when the forward castes agitated against reservations for scheduled castes and tribes in the medical schools, the state government agreed to expand admissions in proportion to the number of reservations, so the forward castes would not feel deprived by the admission of scheduled castes and tribes.

6. *Institutional opposition.* The need by institutions—private and public firms, government departments, hospitals, universities, and research organizations—for individuals of particular skills and motivation is sometimes at variance with the requirement that appointments and promotions be based on membership in an ethnic group. Institutions may fight for the exclusion of certain categories from the system of reservations, or resist the allocation of a particular position to a less qualified member of a scheduled caste, tribe, or backward caste. Alternatively, heads of institutions may take the supernumerary route and make more appointments than are needed so that double appointments can be made—one for the reserved candidate and the second for a

---

indigenous population has greater rights. The same policies may be acceptable to those who are excluded if they are adopted on one principle, but rejected on another. In Malaysia, for example, Chinese acceptance of preferences for Malays was substantially higher when preferences were justified on the grounds that Malays were backward, than when the government announced that Malays were entitled to special benefits because they were 'bhumiputra' or 'sons of the soil'.

more skilled person who can do the work and exercise genuine authority. The result is often bitterness on the part of those holding the reserved slot for having been given rank without actual responsibility, and resentfulness on the part of others that they have been given responsibility without commensurate rank and salary.

7. *Intra-group conflict.* Preferences may lead to conflicts within ethnic groups as to whether reservations are allocated fairly. Since the ethnic category to which preferences have been given is often a composite of numerous ethnic groups, tension develops when one ethnic group receives more benefits than another. If the winners in the competition for reserved positions come predominantly from one identifiable ethnic group (say, Christian tribals as against as non-Christian, or the Oraon tribe as against the Mundas, or the Mahar caste of ex-untouchables as against the Chamars), then demands may be made for subdividing preferences or for dropping one or more groups from the list. As we have noted, some Hindu tribals want to exclude Christian tribals, and some scheduled castes want to exclude those converted to Christianity, Buddhism, or Islam. Some critics have called for the application of socio-economic criteria to individuals so as to exclude from benefits the children of prosperous members of the community. Understandably, the advanced sections of the targeted community resist such proposals by emphasizing the demands that unite their ethnic group. For this reason, it is common for the advanced sections to be among the most militant in their espousal of ethnic group rights.

8. *Social marking.* The policies strengthen ethnic group membership by establishing a new form of social marking: individuals are labeled in the occupational structure in terms of the community from which they come. This marking may ensure greater access to education, employment, and promotion, but it makes social mobility contingent upon membership in an ethnic group. Individuals are what they are because of the group they belong to—a statement that once described an individual's subordinate status but which now explains, and even facilitates, mobility. There is a kind of justice: the same principle that prevented mobility has become an instrument for mobility.

For example, an Oraon tribesman, a college graduate now employed in a government department, told me that he is looked down upon because the community to which he belongs is regarded by caste Hindus as primitive. He concluded that he could raise his social status only when the social status of his entire tribe was raised. A hierarchical system based upon caste ranking does not easily permit individuals to escape their status. Individuals are treated with condescension or deference, as impure or pure, because of the community to which they belong. This powerful linkage of individual status to community status makes this system of preferences based upon group membership as acceptable as it is. For lower castes, reservations facilitate educational and occupational mobility, but they do not remove the stigma of social rank. An ex-untouchable remains an ex-untouchable although he and 3.5 percent of his colleagues in the senior administrative services are ex-untouchables.[13] The preferential system thus helps preserve caste membership. Individuals are members of scheduled castes, scheduled tribes, or backward castes, no matter what level of education they possess, what income they earn, what occupation they practice, or what authority they exercise.

Supporters of the system argue that in a hierarchical society based upon inequality. the introduction of the merit principle would worsen inequalities, that equality among ethnic groups can take place only when individuals are accorded education and employment on the basis of the ascriptive group they belong to. Preferential policies may deepen ethnic attachments, but they can also be viewed as an adaptation to the demand for equality in a society which has a tradition of hierarchy, where status and benefits have historically been allocated on the basis of group membership and group relationships.

9. *Termination.* The politics of termination may yet prove to be one of the most explosive issues. Advocates of preferential policies see them as temporary measures to enable groups to catch up—similar to a tariff policy for infant industries. However, in practice it has proven politically difficult to find ways to terminate such policies. Proposals in India to substitute

[13] The phenomenon of stigma is generally associated with higher-level jobs where one looks for the maximum, not minimum, qualifications.

individual for group characteristics and for de-scheduling groups that have successfully moved up the educational and occupational hierarchy have been rejected by the government and by all major political parties. Political leaders seek to woo segments of the electorate by promising preferential benefits; there are no political advantages to be gained by proposing to terminate benefits.

Theoretically, one could conceive of 'anticipatory' termination measures, that is, policies that set conditions now for future termination. Distinctions could also be drawn between procedural and substantive preferences with provision for the future termination of the latter, but not the former. But given the political forces at work, it is most unlikely that the government and legislative bodies will be farsighted enough to consider anticipatory termination policies.

Conclusion: Comparative Implications

The Indian experience suggests that preferential policies facilitate the mobilization of groups to demand preferences or their extension, creating political struggles over how the state should allocate benefits to ethnic groups, generating a backlash on the part of those ethnic groups excluded from benefits, intensifying the militancy of the beneficiaries, and reinforcing the importance of ascription as the principle of choice in allocating social benefits and facilitating mobility. A major consequence of preferential policies, therefore, is that they create a political process influencing the ways in which groups organize, the demands they make, the issues over which policies are debated, and the coalitions that are formed. From a political perspective, it is the impact of preferences on ethnic group cohesion, group status, and political mobilization that is significant. Preferential policies are intended, not to destroy the system of ethnic hierarchy, but to improve the position of groups within the hierarchy. The purpose of such policies is not only to facilitate the upward movement of some individuals, but to move an entire group within the hierarchy. Positional change, not individual mobility, is the aim.

Integration thus has a quite different meaning in a hierarchical social order than it does in a society concerned with equality of opportunity and treatment. The mixing of children in schools and of families in neighbourhoods, so central to the American concept of integration, is not a goal in India, where it is assumed that linguistic and caste groups may attend their own schools and live in their own quarters. The proponents of integration in India envisage a social order in which each group has a proportional share of benefits and statuses, but in which they do not necessarily mix together socially.

By now it should be self-evident that the political process set in motion by the adoption of preferential policies in India is not confined to India. Even though American courts have abjured quotas, in practice policy skirts close to the principle of group rights, and many of the same questions raised in India have been raised in the U.S. as well:

- To what groups should preferences be given—Blacks, native Americans, Hispanics, Asians, women?
- What ethnic groups should be classified under each category? Are Portuguese and Brazilians to be classified as Hispanics? Should well-educated Chilean and Argentinian refugees be included along with less educated Chicanos and Puerto Ricans? Should African students who have recently settled in the United States be included among 'Blacks'?
- What constitutes group membership? What degree of consanguinity makes one an Indian or a Black or an Asian? What is an Hispanic? A surname? Can one become Hispanic through marriage?
- What preferences should be granted? Promotions as well as hiring? Membership on the law school journal as well as admission to law school?
- Should individuals be given preferences even when they do not come from disadvantaged families and have themselves never personally been disadvantaged?
- How far should an institution modify its admission, employment, or promotion criteria to meet group quotas?
- With respect to what kinds of positions might reservations undermine efficiency by the appointment of less qualified individuals?
- At what point do appointments based upon affirmative action goals or quotas become discriminatory against others?

These issues affect not only the courts, legislatures, and administrative agencies, but each institution engaged in the process of recruitment, hiring, and promotion. Thus, both 'mini-political processes' and a national political process are created around these issues.

The many similarities between the Indian and the American experience suggest that there is a political logic to preferential policies. However great the differences between the social systems of the two countries, and however different the effects of preferential policies on group equality, there is a convergence with respect to the kind of political process produced by preferential policies. It is this convergence that leads us to pose three questions to those who argue for the use of preferential policies, ethnic group rights, and equality of results:

1. Is the kind of society produced by a system of ethnic group preferences more just than the society that might be produced by other kinds of policies intended to reduce ethnic differences?
2. If a policy of ethnic group preferences is put in place, is it politically possible to place limits on who receives preferences and what kind?
3. If preferential policies are adopted, how, if at all, can they ever be terminated?

Supporters of preferential policies may well reply that what ultimately matters is whether the policies work. Are these policies better able than other policies to reduce the gap separating the well-being of one ethnic group from another? Opponents of preferential policies must, in turn, demonstrate that alternative policies are available—within their framework of individual rights and a commitment to the goal of equal opportunity—that will bring about a more equitable distribution of society's benefits among ethnic groups. They must show that other policies to bring about a more equitable distribution of income within society, without *explicit* regard for race, religion, or ethnic group—policies centering around sectoral and regional investments, income policies, tax policies, social welfare programs, land reforms, etcetera—are at least as efficacious.

The position one takes in this debate may ultimately depend upon whether one believes it is possible to create a social order in which the significance of ethnic group membership in gaining equal access to education and employment can be substantially reduced, or even eliminated. Those who think it can be reduced or eliminated will prefer ethnic-blind social policies and will oppose preferences as a policy that will merely reinforce ethnic differences. Those who believe that an ethnic-blind society is not possible, and that people will in practice be educated, hired, and promoted on the basis of their group membership, will advocate preferences as the most feasible way of reducing ethnic inequalities. They will see the political consequences discussed in this paper as an acceptable cost.

On one point, at least, both sides agree. No democratic political system can long tolerate a social order in which the major educational, income, and occupational divisions are along ethnic lines. The question is not whether, but how, these divisions can be bridged.

III. Electoral Politics

7

Party Politics and Electoral Behavior: From Independence to the 1980s

Only a handful of countries in the third world have sustained democratic institutions and practices. By democratic we mean countries that meet the following conditions:

1. Government leaders are chosen in competitive elections in which there are opposition political parties.
2. Political parties, including opponents of the government, have the right to openly seek public support. That is, they have access to the press, freedom of assembly, freedom of speech, and freedom from arbitrary arrest.
3. Governments defeated in an election step down; losers are not punished by the winners, nor are defeated leaders punished unless in the act of governance they have broken the law, and their punishment is based on due process.
4. Elected governments are not figureheads; they exercise power and make policies and they are accountable to the electors, not to the military, the monarchy, the bureaucracy or an oligarchy.

Applying these criteria, nineteen developing countries (thirteen with populations exceeding one million) qualified in 1983. They included

---

A slightly different version of this study appears in Myron Weiner and Ergun Ozbudun, eds., *Competitive Elections in Developing Countries*, Durham, N.C.; Duke University Press for the American Enterprise Institute, 1987, pp. 37–76. This study, written before the eighth parliamentary elections, includes data only up to the 1980 elections. Relevant references to developments after Mrs Gandhi's death have been added to what is primarily an overview of electoral and political trends till the early 1980s.

India, Nigeria, Turkey, Colombia, Venezuela, Sri Lanka, Malaysia, Costa Rica, Jamaica, Portugal, Greece, Papua New Guinea, the Dominican Republic, and six smaller countries. Had the list been prepared several years earlier, other countries would have been included. Several countries on the list in 1983 would not qualify in 1987, while several additional countries, mainly in Latin America and the Philippines, should be added.

A review of those developing countries that have sustained democratic institutions for an extended period permits a number of generalizations concerning the determinants of democracy in the third world, all but one of which are applicable to India:[1]

1. The British model of tutelary democracy has been more successful than other models in sustaining democratic institutions and processes in newly independent countries. That model has had two features: (*a*) it provided for the creation of institutionalized central authority—a bureaucracy, a judiciary, a police force, and an army—institutions that gradually became indigenous; and (*b*) it provided for the creation of representative institutions and periodic elections. The United States, it should be noted, played a similar role as an occupying power in creating a system of central authority and representative institutions in postwar Germany and Japan.

2. The transition from non-colonial authoritarian military government to democracy has most often occurred when there was an earlier experience with political parties, elections, and democratic rule; the transition almost always requires the approval, or at least the acquiescence, of the military.

3. The institutional framework for democracy helps create conditions for its own persistence by (*a*) making possible the emergence of social classes attached to these institutions that have an interest in their maintenance and (*b*) nurturing popular attitudes that are supportive of democratic procedures. It is in this connection that time becomes important. It takes time to create the journalists, academics, lawyers, and party activists who are committed to a free press, an independent judiciary, an autonomous university system, political parties, and voluntary associations. And it takes time to create larger publics supportive of those institutions.

[1] Based on 'Empirical Democratic Theory,' *ibid.*, pp. 31–32.

4. The characteristic and strengths of the individual political parties and the nature of the party system are decisive in whether a democratic system persists. There are striking similarities in the kinds of parties and party systems that now exist in democratic developing countries. One such similarity is that the cleavages among parties do *not* fully mirror a country's class, ethnic, religious, and regional cleavages. Another is that at least one national party or a stable coalition of parties wins a majority of. seats in parliament and one or more opposition parties are able to win substantial electoral support. The party system is not so fragmented as to preclude the creation of a stable government or so centralized as to preclude electoral competition.

5. Among members of the political elite there is an agreement that adversarial politics takes place within certain procedures. This agreement may spring from many years of experience with a democratic system; it may be the consequence of a period of violence or authoritarian rule that leads members of the elite to set boundaries to their own disagreements; or it may be the result of formal consociational arrangements to bridge sharp subcultural cleavages.

Except for the second proposition concerning the transition from military to democratic rule, which is obviously inappropriate for India, these generalizations are applicable to India. An examination of the role played by the British in creating the institutional framework for electoral politics, the circumstances under which political parties developed in India, the determinants of political participation, and the social bases of party support helps us understand some of the fundamentally stable elements in the Indian party system as well as some of the forces for change.

The Origins of the Electoral Process

The British introduced the elective principle into local bodies in India in 1884 and into provincial councils in 1892. In England and in India, support for both the introduction of the electoral process and for the expansion of the powers of local government came from the Gladstone liberals who saw the introduction of an elected local government as a first step leading eventually to national self-government. The central question to these liberals was what proportion of municipal and other local boards and provincial councils were to be elected rather than nominated. Indian liberals were eager to move toward national self-government as quickly as possible. The issue of the size of the electorate was of secondary importance.

Many English officials, however, believed that the principle of elections was inappropriate for India. They argued that the various social cleavages in India made the country incapable of maintaining representative government. Lord Salisbury, Britain's Prime Minister, said that elective or representative government was 'not an Eastern idea' and that its introduction into India would put an 'intolerable strain' on a society divided into hostile sections. Lord Kimberley, Secretary of State for India, said that 'the notion of parliamentary representation in so vast a country, almost as large as Europe, containing so large a number of different races, is one of the wildest imaginations that ever entered the minds of men.' And A.J. Balfour said:

> We all admit that representative government . . . is the best form of government when it is suitable but it is only suitable . . . when you are dealing with a population in the main homogenous, in the main equal in every substantial and essential sense, in a community where the minority are prepared to accept the decisions of the majority, where they are all alike in the traditions in which they are brought up, in their general outlook upon the world and in their broad view of national aspiration.[2]

The conservative view was that an electoral system along British lines—one person, one vote; territorial representation; and majority rule—would be disastrous for India's Muslims. Conservative concern for India's largest religious minority was based less on an abstract notion of justice than it was on the awareness of the need to sustain Muslim support for British rule in India. Since the liberals had won on the issue of whether the elective principle should be introduced into India, the conservatives turned their attention to the issue of how best to ensure representation for the Muslim minority.

This issue and the decisions that resulted from the ensuing debate had a decisive impact on the subsequent development of India's political parties, on the forms of social and political conflict, and,

[2] Sir Reginald Coupland, *The Indian Problem, 1833–1935*, Oxford, Clarendon Press, 1968, p. 26.

ultimately, on the number of states to be carved out of British India. Few policy decisions in twentieth century India were as important.

The debate was joined by John Morley, the Secretary of State for India, a liberal, and Lord Minto, the viceroy, a conservative, who together had responsibility for recommending constitutional reform to the British parliament. Lord Minto put the issue starkly in a letter to Morley: 'I am firmly convinced as I believe you to be that any electoral representation in India would be doomed to mischievous failure which aimed at granting a personal enfranchisement, regardless of the beliefs and traditions of the communities composing the population of this continent . . . . The Mohammedan community may rest assured that their political rights and interests as a community will be safe-guarded by an administrative re-organization with which I am concerned.'

Morley opposed making religious affiliation the basis for electoral representation and preferred protecting the Muslims through some form of territorial representation. Minto, however, argued that only communal electorates, in which Muslims could vote for their own candidates, could assure them of effective representation. To the British the religious cleavage between Hindus and Muslims was analogous to the historic schism in Europe between Protestants and Catholics, manifested in Britain by the persistent, festering quarrel between the two religious communities in Ulster. Many English people believed that the Muslims were in a position comparable to that of the Protestant minority in Ireland.

Though most Hindus opposed Minto's proposals for separate electorates, many Indian liberals agreed to accept his proposal as a practical solution for India. Indian liberals turned their attention not to the principle of communal representation itself but to the question of whether Muslims should be represented in direct proportion to their population or 'overrepresented,' as demanded by Muslim political leaders.

The Muslim view—one ultimately supported by British authorities—was that the Act of 1892, which extended elections to provincial legislatures, threatened their position. The Muslims argued that their representation should be 'commensurate not merely with their numerical strength, but also with their political importance and the value of the contribution which they make to the defense of the Empire.'[4] The

[3] Stanley Wolpert, *Morley and India, 1906–1910*, Berkeley, University of California Press, 1967, p. 189.

[4] Statement by the Muslim deputation to Lord Minto in October 1906, quoted by Coupland, *The Indian Problem*, p. 34.

British, recognizing the link between Muslim loyalty and their demand for 'weightage,' that is, more seats than they were entitled to by virtue of their numbers, agreed both to the principle of communal electorates and to the principle of overrepresentation.

In 1909 the Morley-Minto reforms were introduced. They provided an extension of the elective principle to the legislative councils in the states. Suffrage was extended, though it remained limited, and the system of communal electorates was introduced into all elected bodies.

The Act of 1909 thus freed Muslim leaders from dependence on Hindu votes. Thereafter, neither Hindu nor Muslim politicians needed the support of the other community. Had Muslim candidates been dependent on Hindu votes, then candidates who sought to bridge differences between the two communities would have had the prospect of electoral victory. Communal electorates assured Muslim leaders that they could win elections solely by appealing to the interests and loyalties of Muslims. The system of communal electorates thus guaranteed that two party-arenas, one for the Muslims and the other for the Hindus, would develop. Since each religious community could choose its own representatives, India now had a system of political dualism in which social cleavages were institutionalized. The Morley-Minto reforms thus created the electoral framework for two party-systems— not for a two-party system. Within each community there could be competitive parties, but parties seeking support within one community could not win support within the other.

Thus the Morley-Minto reforms confirmed the electoral principle, established communal electorates, extended the principle of representation, and allowed for representative government in the provinces. The reforms also provided the basis for a further debate on three political and constitutional issues: whether suffrage should be extended, whether the principle of elected representation should be applicable to all members of legislative bodies, and, most controversial, how much power the elected provincial governments should be given.

The Montague-Chelmsford reforms dealt with each of these issues at the close of World War I. These reforms, approved by the British parliament in 1919, extended the suffrage to include more property-tax payers, persons with educational qualifications, and landholders. The landless and urban workers were still not included; in most municipal areas the electorate was about 14 percent and in the rural areas it remained a tiny 3.6 percent.[5] The reforms did, however,

---

[5] Hugh Tinker, *The Foundations of Local Self-Government in India, Pakistan, and Burma*, London, The Athlone Press, 1954, p. 148.

increase Indian representation in provincial councils. But the most important feature of the reforms was that local and provincial governments were given greater power in what the British described as a system of dyarchy. Selected powers were transferred to state governments with departments run by elected ministers responsible to provincial legislatures with elected majorities.

The reforms of 1919 established the federal structure. No longer were provinces the administrative agents of the central government, but they had substantial powers of their own. Thus, two major transformations in the political process had occurred: the decentralization of power from the center to the provinces, and the growth and extension of the principle of elections and representation. Together these two principles and the institutional changes that accompanied them had a powerful influence on the kinds of political parties and the party system that emerged in modern India.

The Emergence of Political Parties

Political parties and organizations in India are an outgrowth of an historical process, not a foreign transplant. Even before the British introduced the elective principle into India, there were already two influential groups of political organizations. One group represented the interests of the landholders and included organizations such as the British Indian Association and the Zamindar Association of Calcutta. The other group represented the interests of the new urban middle classes. The organizations in this group were concerned with achieving greater equality with the British in India with respect to appointment in public services, civil status, and representation in public bodies. The Indian National Congress, founded in 1885 from several such urban groups, was the most important of these middle class associations.

The Indian National Congress was itself divided into various interests and ideologies. There were the moderates, with their liberal ideology and commitment to social reform, and there were radicals, less committed to constitutionalism but often socially conservative on matters of Hindu social customs. In the main, the moderates tended to be an upper middle class group, whereas the radicals came from the lower middle classes. Many British officials in India hoped that the establishment of elective bodies and the expansion of Indian representation would strengthen the moderates and weaken the radicals.

Much of the early history of the Congress revolved around internal political struggles among groups that differed on how best to wrest power from the British—whether constitutional tactics should be employed, whether Indians should or should not take part in elective bodies, and what position they should take on matters of Hindu social reform and on economic issues. Until the 1920s these debates were confined to the middle and upper castes in India's expanding middle classes.

Whereas Hindu leaders had every reason to advocate a broader suffrage and an expansion of representative government, Muslim leaders resisted both. Muslims were not attracted to the Indian National Congress. From the beginning of organized political life in modern India, Muslims formed their own organizations. In 1906 the first major national Muslim organization, the Muslim League, was formed. Unlike the Congress, which had its roots in the middle classes, the League had its roots in the landholding aristocracy. The League leadership thus had two reasons for opposing the electoral process, reflecting both their communal (religious) and class origins. Muslim leaders regarded elections both as an instrument by which the Hindu majority would dominate the Muslim minority and as an attack by the Hindu middle classes against the Muslim aristocracy.

Stirred by the introduction of elections to legislative bodies, the Congress began to take on the characteristics of a political party, with provincial and district offices, dues-paying members, internal elections, and fund raising. In the early 1920s Mahatma Gandhi began to turn the Congress into a mass movement by his appeals to the peasantry and to industrial labor. In 1920 he launched his first *satyagraha*, or non-cooperation, civil-disobedience movement.

Other political movements also sought mass support. In 1924 the Communist party opened branches in several major cities. In Madras a non-Brahmin party, the Justice party, was formed. There was hardly a state that did not have a regional party competing for control over the newly elected provincial governments.

The Congress was divided on the question of whether it should contest provincial elections. The Moderates, as the Gladstonian liberals were called, formed a party of their own, the National Liberal Federation, which won elections in the two large provinces of Bombay and the United Provinces. Supporters of Gandhi, who called themselves Swarajists, arguing that the Montague-Chelmsford reforms did not go far enough, boycotted the 1920 provincial elections. But in 1923, partly because of the victory of the liberals and with the intention of destroying dyarchy by opposing the financial measures of the administration, the Swarajists contested the provincial elections.

Some Swarajists argued that they should contest elections but not form ministries if they won, whereas others argued that they should take power whenever they could. For many nationalists the electoral process was a device for attracting popular support, not a mechanism for taking power, for they wanted to do nothing that might legitimize British authority. These nationalist Congressmen viewed the adversarial electoral process as a means of mobilizing the electorate, strengthening the party organization, and asserting their own personal leadership.

But because the franchise remained limited—in most states it was only 3 percent of the total population—mass politics was not yet part of the electoral scene. What was important, however, was that the electoral process changed the structure of organized groups. Parties had to form local organizations; a machinery for choosing candidates had to be established; and party leaders had to be selected, platforms prepared, funds raised, and electoral campaigns conducted. In short, the 1920s was the decade in which parties learned how to engage in electoral politics. That the electorate was small and the power of those who were elected was still limited, was, in retrospect, less important for the future of the parties than the fact that the parties participated in the electoral process.

Several recent studies have called attention to the development of peasant, tribal, and other non-urban, non-middle class movements that emerged outside the framework of political parties and electoral politics in the late nineteenth and early twentieth centuries. A.R. Desai, a Marxist sociologist, wrote that 'the Indian rural scene during the entire British period and thereafter has been bristling with protests, revolts and even large-scale militant struggles involving hundreds of villages and lasting for years.' Kathleen Gough, a Marxist anthropologist, counted seventy-seven revolts reflecting an extraordinary variety of local discontent.[6]

Peasant and tribal movements were directed against government tax authorities and against landlords. There were also a number of social reform movements and religious revitalization movements that remained outside the framework of political parties and electoral politics. Religious movements were divided between those that wanted to rescue and revitalize religious traditions and those that sought the

[6] A.R. Desai, ed., *Peasant Struggles in India*, Bombay, Oxford University Press, 1979, p. xii; Gough in *ibid.*, pp. 85–126.

reformation and modernization of traditions. And among the lowest castes were some who advocated a radical social transformation, whereas others sought to change the status of their group within the social hierarchy by obtaining greater education and employment.

The revolutionary potential of these movements was never realized. Most were short-lived protests, and others were absorbed by political parties. Typically, educated middle class members of a social movement led their group into a political party and electoral politics. B.K. Roy Burman, a scholar of tribal India, wrote of one movement among the tribals of Bihar that 'an agrarian movement that started with a bang ended with a whimper of middle class opportunist politics with a frill of philanthropism. More or less the same is the story of the Jharkhand movement in Chotanagpur proper, the plain tribals movement in Brahmaputra valley, and the tribal youth movement of Tripura.'[7]

The Government of India Act, passed in 1935, further expanded the realm of Indian political participation, not only at the provincial level but also in the central legislature. Once again there were sharp divisions among nationalists as to how far they should participate in a government created by an imperial authority whose removal was their central political objective. But Jawaharlal Nehru concluded that 'under the circumstances we have no choice but to contest the elections to the new provincial legislature . . . . We should seek elections on the basis of a detailed political and economic program, with our demand for a Constituent Assembly in the forefront. I am convinced that the only solution of our political and communal problems will come through such an assembly, provided it is elected on an adult franchise.'[8]

The 1936–1937 elections proved to be a watershed in the development of Indian political parties. The Congress won a majority of seats in six of the eleven legislative assemblies. In all, it won 706 out of 1,585 legislative assembly elections. Many small regional parties were virtually wiped out. The elections were a major triumph for the Congress party: a measure of the importance of nationalism, an indication of how effective the Congress party organization was in reaching the electorate, and a tribute to Gandhi's and Nehru's appeal.

The Congress formed ministries in seven of the eleven provinces.

[7] B.K. Roy Burman, 'Challenges and Responses in Tribal India,' in M.S.A Rao, ed., *Social Movement in India*, Vol. 2, Delhi, Manohar Book Service, 1979, p. 110.

[8] C.H. Philips, ed. *The Evolution of India and Pakistan: 1858 to 1947, Selected Documents*, London, Oxford University Press, 1962, p. 248.

The socialist wing of the Congress opposed taking office anywhere, a position that proved costly because it deprived the socialists of the patronage and popularity associated with officeholding. Many of the Congress leaders who assumed positions in the provincial governments in 1937 became senior figures in the state and national government after Independence.

But the issue was not only whether (and when) the British would leave India and turn authority over to elected Indians, but whether India would be one country, as advocated by the Congress, or two, as proposed by the Muslim League. In the next decade these two struggles took place side by side. In 1939 when the British went to war against the Germans, units of the Indian army were sent to strengthen British forces. The Congress opposed the British policy of bringing India into the war without the consent of India, and in 1939 the Congress ministries resigned. In August 1942, the Congress launched the 'Quit India' movement, calling for the complete withdrawal of the British from India. Gandhi, Nehru, and other Congress leaders were arrested, and for most of the war years the nationalists were either in jail or taking part in an underground movement against the British. Electoral politics was suspended.

The Muslim League had not fared well in the 1937 elections. In no province did the League win a majority of the reserved Muslim seats. But, as Independence approached, the League's demand for safeguards for Muslim minorities, then its call for a Muslim state, won popular Muslim support. At a historic meeting in Lahore in 1940 the League passed its famous resolution calling for the partition of India and the creation of an independent state of Pakistan in the northwest and in the eastern regions of India. The Congress remained committed not only to one country but to a strong unitary, central government. In the 1946 elections the country was polarized. The League won 428 of the 492 provincial seats reserved for Muslims and in the elections for the central assembly the League won all 30 reserved Muslim seats. Similarly, the Congress won a majority of the non-reserved seats in both the state and central assembly elections. The political cleavage between Hindus and Muslims was now complete. The Muslim League, a weak elite organization until as late as 1937, won so much support from the Muslim electorate in 1946 that it became a force that could no longer be ignored either by the Congress or by the British.

When the British withdrew from India in 1947, they left behind an army, a judiciary, an administration predominantly staffed by Indians, and a federal structure with power distributed between the states and central government. The British also left behind a political party that had led (and won) the struggle for Independence and led (and lost) the struggle for a single country. The leadership of the Congress was in the hands of those who had won the battle within the party over whether they should take part in electoral struggles. They were men who had built an electoral organization and had had experience as ministers running provincial governments. Like other nationalist movements, the Congress had fought for Independence. But, unlike many other nationalist movements, it had done so through an electoral process as well as through civil disobedience. The country was governed by a leadership committed to parliamentary institutions, representative government, electoral process, and political parties. Neither the history nor the commitment guaranteed the future of democratic institutions for India. But they did provide a more promising framework for the development of competitive electoral politics than any that existed in neighboring Pakistan or in many other newly independent countries in the third world.

A cabinet mission sent by the British to India at the end of the war attempted to bring the League and the Congress together over various constitutional arrangements for the transfer of power. But proposals by the British to decentralize power went too far for the Congress leadership, which was committed to a united India with a strong center, and did not go far enough for the League. Politics soon moved to the streets, with violent clashes in Calcutta and in the Noakhali district in East Bengal. Some political organizations created private armies of young people, civil war erupted, and the country appeared to be on the verge of a cataclysmic upheaval. In early August 1947 the British transferred power to two governments, one in India led by the Congress party, and the other in Pakistan led by the Muslim League. The British, by now with support from both parties, had created two new nations. Religion, a false consciousness to Marxists and a sideshow for what many believed (and hoped) would be the more fundamental division of class, proved to be the great divider.

Parties in Post-Independence India

The constitution of 1950 reconfirmed the federal, parliamentary, and democratic structure. Suffrage was made universal for all men and women twenty-one years of age and older, with neither property nor literacy requirements. The system of communal electorates was abolished. The constitution provided that parliament and state assemblies were to be elected at least every five years. An independent election commission was created with responsibility for delimiting more than 500 parliamentary and more than 3,000 state assembly constituencies. The commission was also responsible for registering all eligible voters, for recognizing state and national parties, for establishing procedures for the nomination of candidates, and for managing all elections.

India's first election for the national parliament was held in 1952. Subsequent elections were held in 1957, 1962, 1967, 1971, 1977, 1980, and 1984. State assembly elections were held simultaneously with the parliamentary elections from 1952 to 1967 and separately thereafter.

The election commission has recognized several parties as national, but only one, the Indian National Congress, has actually contested seats in all the states and in almost every constituency. The Congress has won every parliamentary election and most of the state assembly elections, except those in 1977. Two communist parties have been recognized as national parties, and, for most elections, one or two socialist parties and one Hindu nationalist party, the Bharatiya Jana Sangh, have been recognized. A conservative party, the Swatantra Party, flourished for a while but eventually merged with other parties. On several occasions the Congress party split, and each part claimed to be the true successor; but only one, Mrs. Indira Gandhi's Congress, has retained a national following. National recognition by the election commission does not mean that a party competes in all constituencies, or even in all states; it only means that the party has received a large enough percentage of the national vote to be recognized by the election commission. In fact, each of these national parties has had support in only a few states or a single region. Communist strength has been largely confined to West Bengal, to the small neighboring states of Tripura and Manipur, and to the southern state of Kerala, with pockets of strength in Assam, Bihar, and Andhra. The socialist parties have had support in Bihar, Uttar Pradesh, and Bombay. And the Jana Sangh's strength has been limited largely to the Hindi-speaking states.

Several other parties are significant only in a single state. Two parties in populous Tamil Nadu—the Dravida Munnetra Kazhagam (DMK) and its splinter, the All India Anna Dravida Munnetra Kazhagam (AIADMK)—received so many votes that their percentage of the national vote legally entitles them to recognition as national parties. In Punjab, the Akali Dal, and, in Kashmir, the Jammu and Kashmir National Conference are parties that alone, or with others, have controlled the state government. In several smaller states, especially in the northeast, local parties have been quite powerful.

It is useful to distinguish, then, between the national party system and the state party systems. Although the Congress, before its defeat in 1977, overwhelmingly dominated the electoral scene, won two-thirds of the seats in most parliamentary elections, and controlled most of the state assemblies, opposition to the party varied greatly from state to state. Moreover, the level of competition was very high in some states; indeed, there were few states in which the Congress won elections with a majority of the vote. More often the fragmentation of the opposition parties enabled the Congress, with a bare plurality of votes, to win a solid majority of seats. For example, in 1980 in the fifteen major states (those with ten or more seats in parliament) the Congress won a majority of the vote in six states, a plurality in seven states, and lost one state (elections were not held in one state). The closest competitors to the Congress were the Janata party in seven states, the Lok Dal in three, the Communist Party of India (Marxist, or CPI[M]) in two, and the AIADMK and the Akali Dal in one state each. In the ten state assembly elections held in 1980 the pattern was quite different. The Congress won a majority of votes in only one state, a plurality in seven states, and lost two states. The Janata was its closest competitor in only one state; the Bharatiya Janata party, which split from the Janata, was the closest competitor in two states. The Lok Dal was the closest competitor in three states, and the CPI(M) was the closest in one state. The Congress (U), which broke away from Mrs. Gandhi's Congress, the AIADMK, and the Akali Dal were the closest in one state each.

Political Participation

States have been categorized as strong or weak, hard or soft, but to understand why people participate in politics, perhaps a more useful dichotomy for states is: active or passive. The more active a state is, that is, the more its actions intrude upon the lives of its citizens, the more likely it is that citizens will in turn attempt to influence government. In India, government and politics affect the daily lives of very large numbers of people. Consider some of these more characteristic examples:

1. Most Indians depend upon the government for their livelihood. To open a shop or business, to import, to export, to start a school or college, to form a cooperative society, and sometimes even to get into a college or obtain admission into a government hospital, one needs government permission. A large part of the middle class is employed by state or local government. Whether these workers get a job, where they work, whether they are transferred to another locality or not, whether they can obtain a loan from the government, whether they can obtain government housing, and, if so, what kind, and whether they get promoted, all depend on decisions of other government officers. Businessmen can do hardly anything without government approval. Large firms cannot expand without government permission. Textile factories are limited to a specified number of looms. The amount of cement, steel, coal, and electricity a factory gets is a matter of government approval. Public sector monopolies—railroads, airlines, coal, iron and steel, electricity, cement, telephones—control all essential services. One must have influence to deal with the public sector, sometimes even to obtain an airline ticket.

2. Peasants depend on the government for their seeds, fertilizers, electricity, diesel fuel, and irrigation. The government decides what farmers shall pay, and, by setting procurement prices, what they shall be paid for their produce. Peasants obtain credit from government-run banks and cooperatives. And some of the marketing and warehousing is handled by government agencies.

3. The government decides whether a village gets a school, a road, a fair-price shop for buying food at government-fixed prices, irrigation facilities, tubewells for drinking water, and a dispensary. The state-run public transport company decides whether the bus will stop in a village, and the state-run electricity board decides whether the village will have electric power. The irrigation department decides whether an irrigation canal should be built from the main canal, how much water the village should receive, when the village will receive it, and at what price.

4. There are rules about leaving the country. Government regulates how much foreign exchange can be taken out. Professors and other government employees must obtain permission from the government before accepting an invitation to attend a conference abroad. Research institutions must obtain permission before

accepting contracts or awards from foreign institutions. Much research funding comes directly from government agencies, and the funding agency must grant permission before any findings can be published.

5. The press is free, but newspapers depend on government for allocations of paper and for government advertising. Radio and television are run by government departments, and films must be reviewed by a board of censors before release.

6. Former untouchables and other low-income groups receive government-financed housing sites, employment through rural works, and special access (through reservations and financial assistance) for their children in schools and colleges.

Government is thus a provider and a regulator. It is, to use the Hindi term, a *Mai Baap*—a mother and a father. Good government is not one that governs least but one that provides the most. Good government, it is widely believed in India, ensures proper conduct in a world in which, without such restraints, individuals would act only to benefit themselves and their families without regard for others. Without proper authority, relationships would fall apart and conflicts would erupt into violence.

Persons in authority also bestow status. In a social order in which individual status is largely determined by the social group to which the individual belongs, with each group marked by a position in the social hierarchy, the struggle for individual power is also a struggle for group status. As the Indian economy and social order have become more politicized by state intervention, groups have seen more clearly that political action is necessary for their economic well-being and social status. For example, when one group obtains more education than another and agriculture technologies improve the income of one group more than that of another, long-standing group relations are disrupted. The political arena provides groups with an opportunity to correct what they perceive as an imbalance in the social order. For example, a backward caste—as they are widely designated, as distinct from the scheduled castes (former untouchables) below, or forward castes above—that has prospered from agricultural development may seek political power to improve its social status, to increase its access to education, or to influence government pricing policy. A higher caste, fearful of losing its social status, may fight back by using its political influence to undermine land reform or to gain access for its children into higher education or into positions in the bureaucracy. The more the state has to allocate, the more the incentive for groups to attempt to influence who gets what.

The most widespread form of political participation is through direct contact with local officials, members of the state legislative assembly, members of parliament, and local party leaders. Access may be direct or through a village patron who has connections within the government. To get what one wants, one may appeal to friendship or to ties of blood, caste, or community; one may have to pay a bribe or promise a vote. For most voters and politicians, politics is not a matter of ideological principles and policies but one of patronage and administration.

The local Congress party organizations provide groups with direct access to government administration. Patronage is what the Congress party offers and what local communities and groups seek. Members of the state legislative assemblies (MLAs) are among the most sought-after elected officials since they are in direct contact with government administration. In a few states where substantial resources are given to elected district councils, the elected members of the councils are influential because of their access to patronage. Turnout for district council elections and for state legislative assembly elections is often higher than for parliamentary elections, and the coat-tail effect carries members of parliament into office, quite the opposite of the American electoral pattern.

Elected politicians, most often from the Congress party, are in a position to arrange for a road here or a school there, to get a permit or license for a local businessman or merchant, to fix up admission into the local college for the child of a voter, and to help a sugar-cane grower obtain a loan from local authorities. Politicians are concerned not with social transformation but with the delivery of services. As long as services are delivered, the policies of the state governments and of the national government seem to be of little importance to the local party or to voters.

Rival village·factions, various castes, and assorted interests have sought to control the local Congress party. In the fifties and the sixties, party elections for local, district, state, and All-India Congress committees were as intensely contested as the state and national elections. This was because the group that won the party elections would control the nominations for seats to the state legislative assemblies and to parliament.

Paradoxically, the struggles within the Congress party often strengthened the party as each faction attempted to mobilize more of the populace to enroll some party members. Local village factions and castes that wanted greater access to the government were encouraged by dissident groups within the Congress to join the intra-party struggles. As a result, new social groups and new local elites joined the party.

From the first parliamentary election of 1952 through the election of 1967—before the Congress party split in 1969—turnout increased. The struggles within the Congress and the effect these conflicts had on the broader community were only two of several factors that increased the turnout. Politics became pervasive. Almost all significant institutions in public life—the schools and universities, the cooperatives, the voluntary associations, the administration, and later the courts—were permeated by political conflicts, often along party lines.

Participation in the electoral process grew. In the 1952 elections, 46.6 percent of the electorate participated. Participation continued to rise in 1957 and 1962, and it reached its peak in 1967 with 61.1 percent of the electorate. It has not reached that level since. In 1980, 57 percent of the electorate, or 201.7 million Indians, voted in the parliamentary elections (see Table 7.1).

TABLE 7.1
Indian Parliamentary Elections (1952–1980)

Year	Seats	Candidates	Electorate (in millions)	Polling Stations	Votes Polled (in millions)	Turnout (percent)
1952	489	1,864	173.2	132,560	80.7	46.6
1957	494	1,519	193.7	220,478	91.3	47.1
1962	494	1,985	217.7	238,355	119.9	55.1
1967	520	2,369	250.1	267,555	152.7	61.1
1971	518	2,784	274.1	342,944	151.5	55.3
1977	542	2,439	321.2	373,908	194.3	60.5
1980	525	4,611	345.0	437,166	201.7	57.0

Source: Myron Weiner, *India at the Polls, 1980: A Study of the Parliamentary Elections*, Washington, D.C. American Enterprise Institute, 1983, p. 146.

Turnout has varied substantially from one state to another, but some states have consistently had a higher turnout than the national turnout, and some have consistently had a lower turnout. The turnout in the four southern states—especially in Kerala—has been generally higher than that in the rest of the country. In the north, Punjab and Haryana have had a high turnout. The less developed regions of the country have had the lowest turnout. In the 1980 elections only 47 percent of the electorate in Orissa voted, ten percentage points below the national average. Other states with consistently low turnout are Madhya Pradesh, Rajasthan and Bihar—all states with below-average literacy levels, poor transportation, widely dispersed populations, and relatively inaccessible polling stations. But even in these states, turnout has risen since 1952.

Differences between urban turnout and rural turnout have narrowed, and in some states have disappeared. For example, in 1980 the turnout in Calcutta, Bombay, Hyderabad, and Bangalore was actually less than that in the rural areas of their states, whereas in Delhi, Madras, and Ahmedabad turnout was slightly above that in their rural hinterland. Rural-urban differences were comparatively large in the 1950s and early 1960s and have since become small. India's constituencies in the cities have been more politicized than those in the countryside; but since the earliest elections, turnout in rural areas has increased more rapidly than that in the cities. For example, in 1957 the turnout in urban areas was 55 percent and in rural areas was 46 percent. By 1972 urban turnout had risen five percentage points to 60 percent, but rural turnout increased twelve percentage points to 58 percent.[9]

India's scheduled castes and tribal population have become increasingly politicized. India's election law provides for the establishment of reserved constituencies for former untouchables (called scheduled castes) and for the tribal population (scheduled tribes). In reserved constituencies, only members of scheduled castes and tribes may run, but all adults within the constituency irrespective of caste and community may vote. Before 1977 turnout in scheduled caste constituencies was significantly below that of the states in which they were located. For example, in 1971 in Uttar Pradesh turnout in the eighteen reserved constituencies was 39.1 percent compared with the statewide turnout of 46.1 percent, and in Bihar in the eight reserved constituencies turnout was 43.4 percent compared with the state turnout of 49 percent. In the 1977 elections, however, these differences were much smaller, and in Bihar and West Bengal the turnout in the reserved constituencies was actually higher than that in the rest of the state. In

[9] These urban-turnout data are from state assembly elections.

1980 in both states turnout in reserved constituencies continued to exceed the statewide turnout.

Of the Indian population, 14.6 percent belongs to the scheduled castes. In Uttar Pradesh,, West Bengal, Punjab, Haryana and Himachal Pradesh they form a fifth of the population. Their increased politicization accounts for a significant portion of the increase in turnout.

Unlike the scheduled castes, which are widely dispersed, India's tribal population is concentrated. Tribals form 5.9 percent of the population, approximately 47 million people; but they are a majority in the small states of Nagaland (89 percent), Meghalaya (80 percent), and Arunachal Pradesh (79 percent) in India's northeast, and they are a substantial portion of Manipur (31 percent), Tripura (29 percent), Orissa (23 percent), and Madhya Pradesh (20 percent). In the tribal majority states, turnout in 1980 surpassed the national turnout. In the reserved tribal constituencies in the larger states, turnout in 1980 remained below the statewide turnout, though in some states—namely, Gujarat, Rajasthan, and West Bengal—the differences were small.

One feature of the rising turnout, however, remains puzzling. As we have seen, turnout has increased throughout the country; and there has been a growing convergence of urban and rural, reserved scheduled caste, and tribal constituencies. But, at the same time, differences among the states remain as large as ever. Whatever factors have led to an increase in turnout—more polling stations, more effective mobilization on the part of political parties, or a general increase in political awareness as a result of greater exposure to government or to the media—they seem to have affected all states more or less equally. And yet differences among the states remain.

Elections are only one form of political participation. Indians have perfected the art of protest; and, as one journalist wrote, Indians have as many native words for protest as Eskimos have for snow. There can be *satyagraha*, or civil disobedience; *gherao*, or forcibly locking an official in his office; *dharna*, or general strike; *morcha*, or march; and there can be fasts„ blackflag demonstrations, work stoppages, slowdowns, strikes, one-day walkouts, silent marches, and long marches across the state to the legislative assembly or government secretariat. These forms of collective protest take place for many reasons, not the least important of which is that they are ways in which parties mobilize supporters in anticipation of elections. These protest movements are based on the assumption that elected officials will be responsive because they fear losing votes. The existence of an electoral system, therefore, facilitates non-violent protests.

India's brief experience with authoritarian government from June 1975 to January 1977 shows some of the effects of suspending the electoral process, and, indirectly, some of the effects of having an electoral process. At the time citizens were unable to press politicians to restrain bureaucrats. When government officials bulldozed Muslim-populated squatter settlements in Delhi and imposed compulsory sterilization on many low-income villagers in north India, elected officials did not restrain the government. Government soon lost contact with public sentiment. The government was not aware of the magnitude of discontent among Muslims and scheduled castes. The resumption of elections in February 1977 revealed which groups most resented the loss of political rights. Contrary to the widespread belief that the westernized middle classes would be the only groups opposing the Emergency, the scheduled castes, Muslims, and scheduled tribes turned against Mrs. Gandhi and the Congress party.

In the 1977 elections turnout soared in some areas. Evidently the restrictions on political participation and the repressive acts of government motivated those who had previously not taken part in electoral politics. Voting turnout increased more among the lowest income groups than in general constituencies. In Bihar and Madhya Pradesh, for the first time, the average turnout in scheduled caste constituencies actually exceeded the turnout of the state as a whole. Similarly, north Indian constituencies, in which Muslims constituted 20 percent or more of the population, experienced turnout well above that of statewide voting. In Uttar Pradesh, for example, turnout in the twenty-three Muslim constituencies was 61 percent as against a statewide turnout of 56.4 percent.

Though turnout did decline in the scheduled caste, scheduled tribe, and Muslim constituencies in the 1980 parliamentary elections (though no more than in other constituencies), it still remained well above pre-1977 levels. Evidently, the increased politicization stimulated by the Emergency has persisted.

The Social Bases of Voter Alignments

In any consideration of India's social cleavages, voter alignments, and party systems, it is well to keep in mind that India is a vast subcontinent with more than 700 million people, a population equal to that of Africa and western Asia combined. It is slightly more populated than all of Europe, including the European portions of the Soviet Union, and has the diversity to match. At least ten languages, particularly Hindi and Bengali, are spoken by as many people as are the major languages of Europe. Hinduism, with its many sects and castes, is the dominant religion; but Islam has 75 million adherents, giving India more Muslims than any Middle Eastern country. Even in a world of multi-ethnic states, India stands alone in its diversity.

Most significant social cleavages can be found in India. There are conflicts between peasant proprietors and their tenants and agricultural laborers; between the middle class and the business community; and between one caste, religious community, tribe, or linguistic group and another. Hardly a day passes that newspapers do not report violent clashes somewhere in the country—a struggle between the Assamese and Bengalis one day or between scheduled castes and highcaste Hindus on another. Outsiders point readily to a conflict in one part of India as a forerunner of a national political schism. In the 1950s an outburst of linguistic regionalism in several states was interpreted as the beginning of a period of national disintegration. In the early 1970s reports of a protest movement among agricultural laborers in a district of Tamil Nadu led some observers to predict rural warfare between peasants and agricultural laborers, or the Green Revolution's turning red. The religious, regional, ethnic, and class conflicts that in other countries are often sequential are in India all present simultaneously. The task of analysis is to map out the various cleavages and to show how and why they vary from one region to another, how they are manifest in party alignments and electoral behavior, and under what conditions they change.

Partisanship

Variations in voter preferences from one election to another have been relatively small, suggesting that many parties have a core of partisan supporters.[10] The vote for the Congress in six of the seven parliamentary elections ranged from a high of 47.8 percent in 1957 to a low of 40.7 percent in 1967. Only in the post-Emergency election of 1977

[10] Two useful studies containing data on partisanship in India are Samuel J. Eldersveld and Bashiruddin Ahmed, *Citizens and Politics: Mass Political Behavior in India*, Chicago, University of Chicago Press, 1978, and John O. Field, *Consolidating Democracy: Politicization and Partisanship in India*, Delhi, Manohar Book Service, 1980.

did the vote for the Congress fall lower—to 34.5 percent (see Table 7.2). The vote for the Communist Party of India (CPI) and the Communist Party of India (Marxist), varied from 9 percent to 10 percent from the 1957 to 1971 elections, then dropped to 7.1 percent and 8.5 percent in the 1977 and 1980 elections respectively. The two communist parties have been consistently strong in West Bengal and Kerala.

TABLE 7.2
Congress Party Results in Parliamentary Elections (1952–1980)

| Election | Percentage of Vote | Seats | |
		Number	Percent
1952	45.0	357	73
1957	47.8	359	73
1962	44.7	358	73
1967	40.7	283	54
1971	43.7	352	68
1977	34.5	153	28
1980	42.7	351	67

Source: Myron Weiner, *India at the Polls, 1980: A Study of the Parliamentary Elections*, Washington, D.C., American Enterprise Institute, 1983, p. 157.

The Jana Sangh is the one national party that has shown steady growth in the parliamentary elections. Starting with a miniscule 3.1 percent of the national vote in 1952, it garnered 5.9 percent in 1957, 6.4 percent in 1962, and 9.4 percent in 1967. Its vote dropped to 7.4 percent in 1971. The Jana Sangh did not stand as a separate political party in 1977 and 1980 because it had been absorbed into the Janata party, but in both elections candidates of the party pulled a sizable vote. The Jana Sangh (under the new label, Bharatiya Janata party) again became an independent party in the state elections in 1980, when it won 30.3 percent in Madhya Pradesh (compared with 28.7 percent in 1972, when it last stood in state assembly elections) and 18.6 percent in Rajasthan. The party has been consistently strong in six states: Bihar, Haryana, Madhya Pradesh, Punjab, Rajasthan, and Uttar Pradesh.

The Socialists also ceased to be a separate political party in 1977, but their electoral position had been declining since the mid-1960s. The two major socialist groups, the Samyukta Socialist party and the Praja Socialist party, and their earlier incarnation, the Socialist party, collectively won 10.6 percent of the vote in the first parliamentary election, 10.4 per cent in 1957, 9.3 percent in 1962, 8 percent in 1967, and then plummeted to a mere 3.5 percent in 1971, with a following mainly in Bihar.

Several state parties have demonstrated an enduring base of support. In Tamil Nadu, the DMK won 35.8 percent of the vote in 1967, 33.9 percent in 1971, and with its splinter AIADMK, 48.7 percent in 1977 and 48.4 percent in 1980. The vote of each of these Dravida parties in Tamil Nadu was sizable enough to give the two parties 4.7 percent of the national vote in 1977 and 4.5 percent in 1980. In the Punjab the Akali Dal, a regional party of the Sikhs, has won a fifth to a fourth or more of the vote—24 percent in the state elections in 1952, 20.7 percent in 1962 (it did not contest in 1957), 20.5 percent in 1967, 29.5 percent in 1969, and 26.9 percent in 1980.

From 60 to 65 percent of the electorate has consistently voted for the three major national groups—the Congress, the Communists, and the Jana Sangh—and the two major regional groups—the Dravida and the Akali parties (see Table 7.3). These parties evidently have partisan supporters. The remaining vote, a third to two-fifths of the electorate, has been cast for independent candidates and for a scattering of small regional parties, some of which have also developed a solid base of electoral support.

What we know about the attachments of various groups of voters to particular political parties is based largely on an ecological analysis of electoral returns,[11] some intensive anthropological field investigations of particular constituencies, and reports by journalists. In India there are no large-scale national surveys of voters comparable to the surveys in Europe or the United States, though there are some surveys of particular regions and communities for particular elections that supplement our other data.

The most rigorous statistical data we have is derived from state

[11] For an ecological analysis of elections, I have drawn from studies by Paul R. Brass, Marcus Franda, Francine Frankel, John Osgood Field, William Richter, Craig Baxter, Marguerite Ross Barnett, and Robert Hardgrave, whose papers appear in Myron Weiner and John Osgood Field, eds., *Electoral Politics in the Indian States*, Vols. 1–4, Delhi, Manohar Book Service, 1975–1977. I have also drawn from Ramashray Roy, *The Uncertain Verdict*, Delhi, Orient Longman, 1973; Centre for the Study of Developing Societies, *Context of Electoral Change in India: General Elections 1967*, Bombay, Academic Books, 1969; Biplab Dasgupta and W.H. Morris-Jones, *Patterns and Trends in Indian Politics*, Bombay, Allied Publishers, 1975; and Centre for Developing Societies, *Party System and Election Studies*, Bombay, Allied Publishers, 1967.

TABLE 7.3
Parliamentary Election Results (1971, 1977, and 1980)

	1971		1977		1980	
Party	Seats Won	Percentage of Valid Vote	Seats Won	Percentage of Valid Vote	Seats Won	Percentage of Valid Vote
Congress (I)	352	43.7	153	34.5	351	42.7
Congress (U)	—	—	—	—	13	5.3
Janata[1]	—	—	298	43.2	31	18.9
Congress (O)	16	10.4	—	—	—	—
Jana Sangh	22	7.4	—	—	—	—
Swatantra	8	3.1	—	—	—	—
Socialists	5	3.5	—	—	—	—
Bharatiya Lok Dal	2	3.2	—	—	41	9.4
CPI	23	4.7	7	2.8	11	2.6
CPI(M)	25	5.1	21	4.3	35	6.0
DMK	23	3.8	1	1.7	16	2.1
AIADMK	—	—	18	3.0	2	2.4
Akali Dal	—	—	8	1.3	1	0.7
Independents	14	8.3	9	5.7	8	6.5
Other Parties	28	6.8	24	3.5	16	3.4
Total	518	100.0	539	100.0	525	100.0

Source: Myron Weiner, *India at the Polls, 1980: A Study of the Parliamentary Elections*, Washington. D.C., American Enterprise Institute, 1983, p. 149.

Note: Dash indicates that the party did not run.

[1] Seats won in 1971 by groups later forming the Janata party totaled 53; percentage of valid votes for the groups in 1971 was 27.6.

assembly rather than from parliamentary elections. With only 542 parliamentary seats, the parliamentary constituencies are too large (average number of eligible voters per constituency is 650,000) for most ecological analyses. But there are approximately 3,500 state assembly seats, each with about 100,000 eligible voters (with an average turnout below 60,000). By sorting these constituencies for some regions of the country into categories—rural-urban, scheduled tribe and scheduled caste, size of landholdings, and religious and caste composition—it has been possible to infer how certain social and economic groups in India vote.

Ethnic-Based Parties

The organization of political parties around linguistic, religious, tribal, and caste affiliations has a long history in India. As we have seen, the system of communal electorates established in 1909 enabled Muslim political organizations to appeal exclusively to a Muslim electorate. The existence of separate electorates probably exacerbated communal cleavages by making it impossible for non-Muslim parties to appeal to Muslim electorates.

It has been argued that elections and parties intensify linguistic, religious, tribal, and other ethnic cleavages precisely because political leaders can use ethnic loyalties to mobilize voters and hence may deliberately exacerbate cleavages to rally support. If, however, political parties succeed in crossing ethnic lines, if ethnic and class cleavages are cross-cutting rather than mutually reinforcing, then tension is reduced, bargaining among groups becomes possible, and more stable governments are likely. An examination of the major ethnic political parties in India may enable us to consider the impact of the electoral process on intensifying or modifying group conflict.

Hindu Nationalism: Bharatiya Jana Sangh

At the time of Independence the Muslim League was by far the largest, most powerful ethnically based political organization in India, but with the creation of the state of Pakistan the League virtually closed down in India. The Hindu Mahasabha, first formed in Punjab in 1907 and then reorganized as an all-India party in 1915, was initially formed as a reaction against both the Muslim League and Indian liberals. It was equally hostile to liberal, secular ideas imported from the West and to Muslim communalism. Its membership, strongly Brahmin, opposed social reform legislation and devoted much of its effort to discouraging low caste Hindus from converting to Islam or Christianity. With the demise of the Muslim League in post-Independence India and with increased secularization and westernization among the highest castes, the Mahasabha declined as a political force. The party won four seats in the first parliament but had less than 1 percent of the national vote, and it faded away thereafter. One other Hindu communal party, the Ram Rajya Parishad, sought support on a platform of

Hindu revivalism, unsuccessfully. Clearly, there has thus far been no electoral support in India for Hindu revivalism or for an explicitly anti-secular, anti-western political party. Perhaps the absence of a religious tradition of exclusivity—which marks Christianity, Islam, and Judaism but not Hinduism—or the absence of a hierarchical clerical class has prevented the emergence of the kinds of religiously based Hindu parties comparable to such movements in Western · Europe, Iran, Israel, and elsewhere in the Middle-East.

Because the Hindu religious tradition does not prescribe any universal behavior, no political organization has campaigned for the enforcement of a sabbath, the establishment of rules determining who is a Hindu, or the imposition of religiously sanctioned penalties for criminal behavior. There has been no active campaign on issues of abortion, birth control, divorce, or usury, or on religiously prescribed norms of conduct that characterize other religions. As Will Rogers once quipped that he belonged to no organized political party for he was a Democrat, so, too, many Indians could say that they belong to no organized religion for they are Hindus.

The Bharatiya Jana Sangh comes closest to being a Hindu party. It was formed in 1951 as a party committed to *Bharatiya Sanskriti* (or Indian culture), which for many of its members and supporters meant Hindu nationalism. Much of its organizational impetus came from the Rashtriya Swayamsevak Sangh (RSS), a paramilitary organization founded in 1925 and concerned with the regeneration of India as a Hindu nation. The RSS had been banned after a Hindu assassinated Gandhi in January 1948. When the ban was lifted, the RSS leadership decided to enter active politics by supporting a former president of the Hindu Mahasabha and creating a new political party, the Jana Sangh. The new party, although eschewing an anti-Islamic position openly, took positions that were loosely identified with a Hindu perspective: support for cow protection; promotion of Ayurvedic or traditional medicine; advocacy of Hindi as the country's official language and opposition to the use of Urdu, the language of India's Muslims; and advocacy of a more powerful defense with nuclear capability.

The Jana Sangh's entrance into electoral politics suggested that these positions lacked popular support. The party won only three seats in parliament with 3.1 percent of the vote. In subsequen: elections its vote and seats increased. In the 1967 elections, its electoral high point, it has thirty-five seats in parliament, making it the third-largest party, with 9.4 percent of the popular vote.

As the party has grown it has moved toward the political center. It has taken a less strident posture toward Muslims and toward Pakistan, and it has even nominated Muslims for state assembly and parliamentary elections, but it still remains avowedly more militant and more nationalist than other parties, on matters of defense and nuclear policy. Its strength has been largely in the six states of the Hindi region: Punjab, Haryana, Rajasthan, Uttar Pradesh, Madhya Pradesh, and Bihar. Except for a slight downturn in state elections in 1969 and in the parliamentary elections of 1971, it has shown impressive growth. It has been more successful in the cities than in the countryside, except in Madhya Pradesh, and it has grown more rapidly in the urban than in the rural areas. In urban areas it has received support from shopkeepers and merchants and from the lower middle classes, particularly those who are in government employment. In Bihar and Uttar Pradesh it has support from the Rajputs, the traditional martial caste that is attracted to the Jana Sangh's militant nationalism. The party also attracts many urban students, and its student organization, the Akhil Bharatiya Vidyarthi Parishad, is one of the largest student organizations in the country.

The Jana Sangh played an important role in forming the Janata party in 1977. A Jana Sangh leader, Atal Behari Vajpayee, was the Minister of External Affairs in the Janata cabinet. The Jana Sangh participated in five coalition governments in the Hindi states between 1967 and 1971, and after the Janata took power the Jana Sangh group took control of Himachal Pradesh, Rajasthan, Madhya Pradesh, and Delhi. The Jana Sangh remained within the Janata after the party split in 1979, but after the 1980 elections the Jana Sangh members withdrew to form their own party once again, now renamed the Bharatiya Janata party. The party did well in the state assembly elections in mid-1980 and again in 1982, and emerged as the second-largest party in Madhya Pradesh, Rajasthan, and Himachal Pradesh.

In the last few years, the Jana Sangh has been winning rural support in Uttar Pradesh and Bihar. Like the Congress party, the Jana Sangh draws its support from the upper castes, the Brahmins, Rajputs, and Kayasthas, and from the merchant castes, the Vaishyas, in the towns. Its strength in Uttar Pradesh is substantial in the central districts of Oudh, where it won the support of the *talukdari*, or former landlord families. It has recently sought to extend its influence to portions of the middle peasantry, the backward cultivating castes. Its support for Hindi and its opposition to the use of Urdu have attracted newly educated Hindus to the party, who see English and Urdu as the language of social classes competing for positions in government bureaucracy.

Much of the organizational strength of the Jana Sangh derives from its close affiliation to the RSS. This paramilitary organization is more explicitly militant and Hindu than the Jana Sangh. It is organized into paramilitary units whose members pay a great deal of attention to physical fitness through gymnastics. As the Jana Sangh broadened its electoral base and began to compete with other groups within the Janata party—especially the Lok Dal, the party of the middle peasantry— its opponents within the Janata party demanded that the Jana Sangh break its ties with the RSS. But the Jana Sangh leaders refused, recognizing that without the RSS ties they would be organizationally weakened.

Some Indians view the Jana Sangh as an important counterfoil to the Communists, since both parties appeal to newly educated urban youth. The Jana Sangh offers a radical right appeal with elements of Hindu revivalism, equality with the West through armed strength, and a strong national center. The Communists offer the radical left appeal of social transformation, struggle against the propertied classes, and anti-Americanism. Although they both appeal to educated youth, their main appeal is to different social strata. The Jana Sangh's appeal has been to those who held authority in the old social order—the former maharajas in Madhya Pradesh, the Rajput-warrior castes of Uttar Pradesh and Bihar, the former *talukdar* landlord classes—and to the middle-propertied strata, particularly the merchants and, in some areas, the middle peasantry and the newly urbanized lower middle classes. The Jana Sangh has little influence upon the lowest social strata, either in the cities or in the countryside, and, except for a few pockets of support in Karnataka and Kerala, it has yet to break out of its regional standing as a party of the Hindi-speaking region.

Cultural Regionalism: The Dravida Parties

The two Dravida parties of Tamil Nadu, which together have been the dominant political parties in the state since 1967, provide an interesting example of how a political movement initially based on an appeal to caste, successfully broadened itself into a regional nationalist movement. The Dravida movement has its origins in the historic social cleavage between Brahmins and non-Brahmins. Brahmins dominated the administrative services and the newly created urban professions in the nineteenth and early part of twentieth century. Opposition to the Brahmins came initially from 'forward non-Brahmins,' largely land-owning groups with dominance in rural areas. At the turn of the century, the Brahmin urban middle classes in India, as the urban middle classes elsewhere, took the lead in advocating Home Rule and then Independence. Brahmins dominated the administration, the universities, and the nationalist movement. In the 1920s, the Brahmins were challenged by the newly formed South Indian Liberal Federation (later renamed the Justice party), a non-Brahmin organization that emphasized its Dravidian (south Indian) identity and an anti-Brahmin ideology. The Justice party drew its political strength from the newly urbanized non-Brahmins. These non-Brahmin elites, wrote Marguerite Ross Barnett, 'rejected Home Rule and territorial nationalism, em-phasizing the primacy of Dravidian cultural authenticity, a common non-Brahmin identity, and an incipient Dravidian cultural nationalism.'[12] But behind the rhetoric was the straightforward class interest of the non-Brahmins that they be given greater representation in the British bureaucracy and that their social status be elevated. (The more radical wing of the non-Brahmin movement called itself the 'Self-Respect League.') The non-Brahmins proved so effective at mobilizing the numerous backward castes that in the 1920s they defeated the Congress party and took control of the provincial government. But, with the growing popular appeal of nationalism in the 1930s, the Justice party declined as a political force and did not revive until after Independence. By then the Tamil Nadu party itself fell under the control of non-Brahmin castes. In 1949 several Dravidian groups joined to form the DMK under the dynamic leadership of C.N. Annadurai, a young nationalist who had supported the movement for Independence and opposed the separation of south India from the north (as advocated by some of the Justice party leaders) but who was committed to the cause of the non-Brahmin castes and to Tamil nationalism. In the late 1950s the DMK appealed to the backward castes and to the young people in the urban areas with its attack against Hindi imperialism and northern domination. The DMK became one of the first political parties in India effectively to use mass media and popular culture. It attracted support from film stars and Tamil poets, staged parades and mass rallies, and

[12] Marguerite Ross Barnett, 'Cultural Nationalist Electoral Politics in Tamil Nadu,' in Weiner and Field, *Electoral Politics*, p. 4:29.

had its speakers use popular rather than bookish Tamil. A major transformation occurred in the middle and the late 1960s, when the party dropped its anti-Brahminism and declared its identification with all Tamil-speakers. By becoming so explicitly the party of Tamil nationalism, by directing the region against northern domination, by asserting the claims of the state against the center, the DMK was able to undermine the position in the state of the Congress party, which had identified itself with all-India nationalism.

The DMK most effectively damaged the Congress party in Tamil Nadu by its campaign against the use of Hindi as an official language. It was an issue that appealed not only to Tamil nationalist sentiment but also to the practical interest of young people, who saw the growing use of Hindi in the central government as undermining their access to jobs in the national civil service.

The great political breakthrough for the DMK took place in the 1967 state assembly elections, when the DMK won 138 and the Congress won 50 out of the 234 seats. The victory was made possible by an alliance between the DMK and the Swatantra party led by C. Rajagopalachari, an elder, former Congress leader, who was the leading Brahmin politician in the state. This alliance once and for all legitimized the DMK's claim that it was the party not of the non-Brahmins but of Tamil nationalism. The DMK reconfirmed its position with its electoral victory in 1971. Following the death of its leader, Annadurai, the DMK split; but the two parties, the AIADMK and the DMK, represented merely two rival versions of Tamil nationalism. Throughout the 1970s the two parties dominated Tamil politics, squeezing out the Congress and other parties. The DMK governed the state through 1976, and the following year it was replaced by the AIADMK. In the 1977 elections the Janata party allied itself with the DMK, whereas the Congress party of Mrs. Gandhi allied itself with the AIADMK. The AIADMK won 30.6 percent of the vote (and 18 of the 39 parliamentary seats), and Mrs. Gandhi's Congress won 22.3 percent (and 14 seats). The DMK won 18 percent of the vote. In 1980 the alliances were reversed: the Congress party joined with the DMK, and the governing AIADMK formed an electoral alliance with the Janata. Once again, the coalition around Mrs. Gandhi's Congress won: her party won 31.6 percent of the vote with 20 seats, and her ally, the DMK, won 23 percent of the vote with 16 seats. Each of the two parties allied itself with a national party in an effort to get support for the state assembly elections. Although the AIADMK failed to win popular support in the parliamentary elections, it demonstrated its electoral power in the state assembly elections several months later when it emerged as the largest party in the state, with 38.7 percent of the vote. The Congress vote declined from 31.6 percent in the parliamentary elections in January to 20.5 percent in the state assembly elections in June, whereas the AIADMK reversed its position from 25.4 percent to 38.7 percent. A substantial portion of the Tamil electorate seems to have distinguished between its preferences for the national government and those for the state government.

Religious Regionalism: The Akali Dal

Punjab has a significant regional party known as the Akali Dal, but unlike the DMK parties it has not made the transition from the party of an ethnic group to the party of regional nationalism. Once again, it should be noted that, like many other parties, the Akali Dal has its roots in pre-Independence politics. A political movement exclusively of the Sikhs, it was first organized to establish popular community control of the Gurdwaras, or Sikh shrines. In 1925 the Akali Dal succeeded in placing the Gurdwaras under the control of a committee elected by universal adult suffrage. Because the Gurdwaras have substantial endowments, the Akalis gained access to considerable patronage. The Akalis subsequently became a significant force in Punjab in the struggle with the Muslims over control of the state. In 1947, when India was partitioned, Punjab, too, was partitioned. The Sikh population living in west Punjab, in Pakistan, fled to Delhi and to the Indian Punjab, with the result that the concentration of the Sikhs in the Indian portion of Punjab sharply increased.

The Akali Dal vote in the state assembly elections ranged from a fifth to a quarter of the population. In the predominantly Sikh areas the Akalis received nearly half of the Sikh vote. A majority of the Sikhs supported the Congress party.

Many Sikh leaders were concerned with strengthening the cohesion of the Sikh community and arresting the movement of young Sikhs into secular life or to Hinduism. Sikh leaders organized their own schools, emphasized the need to write the Punjabi language in the Gurmukhi script (the script of Sikh scriptures), and sought to draw young people into the life of the Gurdwaras. Sikh leaders wanted to sharpen the boundaries between Hindus and Sikhs, and political action seemed an appropriate way to proceed.

The Akalis called for the creation of a separate Sikh state carved out of the Sikh majority areas of Punjab. Territorial division, the Akalis hoped, would not only strengthen their own political power but also create solidarity within the community. Their electoral influence was substantially undermined by Pratap Singh Kairon, a Sikh and a leader of the Congress party who successfully forged an alliance between Hindus and a substantial portion of the Sikh community. Moreover, as Paul Brass writes:

> Although the boundaries between Hindus and Sikhs have become more sharply defined during the past century, there remain Hindu and Sikh sects and individuals in both religions who do not consider the differences between the two creeds to be substantial . . . . Allegiances of many of the low caste or scheduled caste groups in the Punjab, who comprise more than 20 percent of the population of the state, are by no means clear . . . . Moreover, the language division between Hindus and Sikhs in the Punjab is more symbolic than real . . . . Finally, factional politics and personal political opportunism have often cut across both communal and ideological differences among the parties and have provided a basis for movement, communication, and alliances of individuals and groups across party lines.[13]

In short, the Akali effort to segment the two communities through party politics and electoral struggles did not succeed in the sixties. The Akalis did, however, succeed in persuading the central government to partition Punjab into predominantly Sikh and Hindu states. The central government agreed to the demand, partly because it had already acceded to the principle of linguistic states elsewhere in the country, and the Akalis had redefined their demand for a Sikh-majority state to a Punjabi-speaking state; partly because the growing popularity of the demand among Sikhs threatened to erode the position of the Congress party, and the Congress party itself was divided on the issue; and partly because the center recognized that a violent clash between the central government and the Sikhs could disrupt the Indian army, a substantial portion of which is recruited from the Punjabi Sikhs and Hindus. The movement for a Punjabi-speaking state was suspended during the war with Pakistan in 1965, then acceded to by the Congress at the close of the war. In the 1969

[13] Paul R. Brass, 'Ethnic Cleavages in the Punjab Party System, 1952–1972,' in Weiner and Field, *Electoral Politics*, p. 4:110–12.

elections the Akalis emerged as the single largest party in the Punjab assembly, with 41 percent of the seats, and formed a non-Congress coalition government. Akali support was confined almost entirely to the Sikh community, and its main strength was among the Jat Sikh peasants, the landowning class. The Akalis did poorly among the Sikh scheduled castes. Moreover, a substantial number of urbanized Sikhs voted for the Congress party.

The Akalis thus remained a significant regional party with the capacity to form governing coalitions with other groups when support for the Congress was on the wane. Because the Akalis opposed the Emergency, they were natural allies of the Janata party in 1977; and they were subsequently able to form a coalition government in the state. Class divisions among the Sikhs, and the readiness of the Congress party to reach out for Sikh as well as Hindu support, prevented the Akalis from exacerbating religious cleavages. In this respect the situation has changed in the last few years, which we shall examine below. Nor were the Akalis willing, as were the Dravida and several other regional parties, to move from an exclusive base within a single social group to the larger community, using regional rather than religious nationalism as the basis for their appeal. The Akali Dal and the Dravida parties thus stand at opposite ends of the pole.

Other initially narrow-based parties have sought a broader base of social support with varying degrees of success. In the mid-1950s several parties starting with a narrow social base won substantial public support for the reorganization of states along linguistic lines, but most of these parties faded away as the new states were created. In the city of Bombay an anti-foreign party, the Shiv Sena, won substantial support in its campaign for employment for Marathi-speaking people, but it never succeeded in winning support outside Bombay; even within the city its support has dwindled. In southern Bihar the Jharkhand party, a party of the local tribal population, has from time to time tried to broaden its base by calling on all the residents, both tribals and non-tribals, of southern Bihar to support the demand for regional development or a separate state. However, it has not attracted support from the non-tribal population. Several small tribal-based parties in the northeastern states, on the other hand, have built coalitions of tribes around regional nationalism.

What one sees in India is a well-known phenomenon in countries with competitive electoral politics: small ethnically-based political parties, too small to win power by themselves, either seek coalitions with others or attempt to broaden their appeal to include other ethnic groups. In India these attempts focus on regional nationalist identities. Clearly, not every party will attempt to do so. Those that chose not to do so remain small sectarian parties or, alternatively, eschew electoral politics and turn to militant methods for achieving political power. In 1981 the Akalis, excluded from power by their electoral defeat a year earlier and their electoral appeal arrested at a quarter of the population, spilt. One faction, taking a militant position, called for a separate nation, Khalistan. The other faction called for the redress of their grievances (the inclusion of Punjabi-speaking areas of neighboring states, more representation in government services, and central government support for creating more industries in the state) through collective action on the part of Hindus and Sikhs in the state.

By 1983 the pro-Khalistan Sikhs had attracted substantial support within the state. A decision by Mrs. Gandhi's government to send armed forces into the Sikh holy temple at Amritsar after it had been occupied by armed militants, led to many deaths and an increasing radicalization of the Sikh population. Mrs. Gandhi herself was assassinated by two of her Sikh guards, and in the days following her death the city Delhi was torn by violence. Rajiv Gandhi, Mrs. Gandhi's successor as Prime Minister, took steps to win back the moderate elements in the Sikh community, and in 1985 elections were held in Punjab, bringing the moderate section of the Akali Dal back to power. By now, however, the moderates are out of power too, and President's Rule has replaced the Akalis.

Middle Peasant Caste Politics: The Lok Dal

Only one of the regional parties, the Lok Dal, has been able to convert its power at the state level into a significant share of power at the center. The Lok Dal originated in Uttar Pradesh, India's most populous state, in the mid-1960s as a party of the middle peasantry. In 1967 a Congress leader, Charan Singh, broke from the Congress to organize his own party, the Bharatiya Kranti Dal (BKD), to speak for the middle farmer and individual ownership, representing especially the Jat caste of peasant proprietors to which he belonged. In the state assembly elections in 1969 the party emerged second with 21 percent of the vote and, as a result of factional conflicts within the state Congress, Charan Singh formed his own coalition government. Eight years later, Charan

Singh's party (renamed the Lok Dal), combined with the Jana Sangh, the socialists, and the Congress dissidents to form the Janata party. Charan Singh, convinced that his party played a decisive role in defeating Mrs. Gandhi, especially in the states of Uttar Pradesh (where the Janata won 68 percent of the vote), Bihar (65 percent), Haryana (70 percent), Rajasthan (65 percent), and Orissa (52 percent), believed that he, not Morarji Desai, should be the leader of the Janata party and Prime Minister of India. In mid-1979 Charan Singh led his party out of the Janata party and brought down the Janata government and Morarji Desai. By holding the balance between the Janata and the Congress, Charan Singh was able to become India's Prime Minister, as the head of an interim coalition government. And by refusing to form an electoral coalition with the Janata in the 1980 parliamentary elections, Charan Singh's party contributed substantially to the re-election of Mrs. Gandhi and the Congress party.

What gave the Lok Dal such extraordinary influence? Why has it built up a strong and loyal following among the peasants of northern India? The middle peasantry grew in importance in Uttar Pradesh with the abolition of the *zamindari* (landlord) system and the transfer of title to new owner-cultivators who paid land-revenue taxes directly to the government. With the introduction of the Green Revolution technology, the economic situation of the middle peasants improved. The middle peasants became a class of small capitalist farmers producing grains and other commodities for a commercial market. They sought agricultural supplies at low cost and wanted agricultural procurement prices that would ensure them a profitable return on their investment. Because almost everything they needed in agriculture—credit, diesel fuel, tubewells, storage facilities, fertilizers, pesticides, irrigation, and new varieties of seeds—involved dealing with government or quasi-government institutions such as banks and cooperatives, an elaborate system of state patronage developed. The middle peasants in Uttar Pradesh were dissatisfied with the Congress government, which did not pay enough attention to their interests and which was dominated by Brahmin and Rajput castes who controlled much of the patronage.

Most of the middle peasants belong to the middle and backward castes. The Jat caste is the largest and most influential of the middle castes, and the Ahirs (or Yadavs) and Kurmis are the principal backward cultivating castes. The middle and backward castes are as concerned with their social advancement as they are with their economic interests. The social identification of the upper caste Brahmins and Rajputs is with Congress while their traditional rivals in the middle and backward castes—Jats, Ahirs and Kurmis—identify with Charan Singh's Lok Dal. On the eve of the 1980 elections, Charan Singh's interim government proposed that 25 percent of all jobs in the central services be reserved for the backward castes. It was a blatant caste appeal to peasants who wanted government jobs for their educated sons and daughters.

With the formation of the BKD in 1967, Charan Singh brought together the middle peasants into a formidable political force. The party proved to be particularly strong in western Uttar Pradesh, which is the most agriculturally prosperous region of the state and is the center of the Jat community. Though Charan Singh's party commanded only a fifth of the vote, the decline in the vote for the Congress (from 53 percent in 1952 to 46 percent in 1957, 38 percent in 1962, and 33 percent in 1967) placed the new party in a pivotal position in the state. Moreover, given the pivotal position of Uttar Pradesh in parliament (Uttar Pradesh holds 16 percent of the seats), Charan Singh was able to play a significant role in national politics.

Though in 1980 Charan Singh's party won only 9.4 percent of the national vote, it won forty-one seats, second only to the Congress, and continued to demonstrate its strength in Uttar Pradesh and in several other north Indian states. It won 29 percent of the vote in Uttar Pradesh (second only to the Congress), a third of the vote in Haryana (making it larger than the Congress), 19.5 percent in Orissa, 16.6 percent in Bihar, and 12.1 percent in Rajasthan.

In the 1980 elections Mrs. Gandhi rebuilt the electoral coalition in Uttar Pradesh that had made the Congress the winning party in 1971 and earlier—the Brahmins and Rajput landowning castes, the Muslims, and the landless laborers, especially the scheduled castes and scheduled tribes. But the Congress failed to win the vote of the middle peasantry. Elsewhere in India, especially in the southern states of Andhra and Karnataka, the Congress had more success in winning support from the middle peasants and the middle castes. Charan Singh himself was so strongly identified as a regional (and caste) leader that dissatisfied peasant proprietors in the non-Hindi-speaking states have not been attracted to the Lok Dal. But the continued weakness of the Congress party in Uttar Pradesh and in neighboring states assures the middle peasant castes (whether in the Lok Dal or in some other political party) an important independent political role in the Hindi region and perhaps in national politics. In an analysis of the elections in Uttar Pradesh, Paul Brass concludes that there has been 'politicization and increased cohesion of the middle castes of peasants . . . for the Lok Dal of Charan Singh in 1980' and that 'the principal underlying conflict in the north [is] between the middle peasantry and all other social forces.'[14] Given the pivotal role that elections in northern India have played in national politics, Brass argues that the future of the Indian parliamentary system itself will be determined by the outcome of that conflict. This might seem like a bold generalization after the Lok Dal defeat in the 1984 elections but the subsequent Lok Dal victory in Haryana despite the party split after the death of its founder and leader, Charan Singh, suggests that the social cleavages in northern India described by Brass remain a central determinant of electoral behavior and party conflict.

The Social Bases of Congress Support

India's largest multi-ethnic, multi-class party is, of course, the Congress party. The only party that ever defeated the Congress nationally, the Janata party, was similarly diverse, though ultimately it failed to remain united as a single party. In view of this occurrence, two important questions can be addressed. One is the question of what communities, classes, and regions have made up the winning coalition for the Congress in the seven elections in which the party won 40 to slightly over 50 percent of the electorate. The second question is how a party with such diverse and even conflicting social support has been able to cope with its internal differences.

In the 1980 parliamentary elections the Congress won 351 seats with 42.7 percent of the popular vote. Support came from a broad spectrum of the populace: from the very rich to the very poor, from Brahmins to former untouchables, from well-to-do businessmen and government bureaucrats to tribal agricultural laborers and Muslim weavers. For example, the Congress won fifty of seventy-nine reserved scheduled caste constituencies and twenty-nine of thirty-seven scheduled tribe constituencies, but it also carried the prosperous sections of New

---

[14] Paul R. Brass, 'Congress, the Lok Dal, and the Middle Peasant Castes: An Analysis of the 1977 and 1980 Parliamentary Elections in Uttar Pradesh,' *Public Affairs*, Vol. 54, (Spring 1981) p. 1:41.

Delhi. Mrs. Gandhi won the support of the class and caste extremes in the social structure, ironically with a centrist program.

The Congress also did better than other parties among religious minorities. It won a majority of the vote in the predominantly Sikh state of the Punjab, carried the Christian-populated constituencies of Kerala, and won a plurality of seats in which Muslims constituted at least 20 percent of the population. A breakdown of India's population in terms of religion and caste indicates the extraordinary electoral advantages to a political party with substantial bloc support from religious minorities, scheduled castes, and scheduled tribes. Muslims form 11.2 percent of the national population, Christians 2.6 percent and Sikhs 1.9 percent. Scheduled castes account for 15 percent; scheduled tribes 7.5 percent.

Although ecological analyses confirmed by field reports indicate that these groups provide the Congress with a larger share of their vote than does the rest of the electorate, no hard data are available to indicate what the percentage of the Congress vote in 1980 or earlier was from each of these communities. *But if the Congress won only 50 percent of the vote of these minorities, then it needed to win the support of only 35 percent of the remaining caste Hindu population to net a national vote of 40.7 percent. And if the Congress won 60 percent of the minority vote, then with the support of 35 percent of the remaining electorate the national Congress vote would be 44.5 percent.*

This simple arithmetic goes a long way toward explaining why the Congress won only 34.5 percent in the elections of 1977. With the large-scale defection of the Muslims, scheduled castes, and scheduled tribes from the Congress as a result of the Emergency, a major increase in the vote for the Congress among caste Hindus would have been needed for the party to have won. If the minorities had simply dropped their vote for the Congress to the same levels as that of the vote of the rest of the country—35 percent, to use a hypothetical number—that would account for the 1977 results.

Urban-ruled differences do not figure significantly in the vote for the Congress. In the 1980 parliamentary elections, the Congress won 43.3 percent of the vote in the urban constituencies and 42.6 percent of the vote in rural constituencies. An analysis of voting in state assembly constituencies from 1952 to 1972 shows that with the exception of 1967, the Congress performed slightly better in urban than in rural constituencies (see Table 7.4).

From 1952 to 1967 the Communist parties and the Jana Sangh,

TABLE 7.4
The Vote for the Congress in Urban and Rural Constituencies: All India (1952–1972)
(percent)

	1952	1957	1962	1967	1972
Urban	45.6	46.8	45.3	38.2	48.7
Rural	43.2	45.1	43.4	41.6	46.2

Source: Myron Weiner and John Osgood Field, *Electoral Politics in the Indian States: The Impact of Modernization*, Delhi, Manohar Book Service, 1977, p. 32.

which won a larger portion of India's urban vote than of the rural vote, grew in the cities. In recent years, however, the Communist Party Marxist (CPM) seems to have reversed this trend by growing substantially in the Bengal countryside while losing Calcutta. Similarly, in the Kerala villages the strength of the communists seems to have increased. The Jana Sangh, however, continues to be a primarily urban-based party. Both the radical right and radical left grew not at the expense of the Congress but at the expense of independent candidates and other opposition parties. Also, the struggle, in the main, has not been between the radical right and the radical left but between each radical party and the political center.

In 1977 when many of the opposition parties consolidated into the Janata the conflict in most of the urban constituencies shifted to a contest between the Janata and the Congress, the two parties of the center. The Janata swept the urban constituencies in 1977, winning twenty-five of thirty-nine seats in the nineteen cities with a population of a million or more. In 1980 the results were reversed: the Congress won twenty-five of the thirty-nine constituencies (compared with only seven of the thirty-nine in 1977). The Janata's national vote was only 18.9 percent, but the party won nearly 30 percent of the vote in urban constituencies. Cities remained polarized, no longer between the center and the left or the right, but between the two parties of the center.

The Congress apparently wins more support among the lower income groups in the urban areas (in most cities the squatter areas vote for the Congress rather than for leftist or rightist parties) than among the middle classes. Both the Jana Sangh and the communists seem to do well among the urban middle classes.

As far as the working class is concerned, the picture is mixed, too. India has only a few industrial labor constituencies, and these are split. The communists have a foothold in some: Madurai. Coimbatore,

Alleppey, Calicut, Palghat, and Kottayam in the south, Jamshedpur, some sections of Bombay, Calcutta, Howrah, Asansol, and Dum Dum in the north. The Congress is generally the largest party in the remaining industrial constituencies, including several of the non-Bengali working-class constituencies in and around Calcutta.

The Congress does less well in rural constituencies with few Muslims, scheduled castes, or scheduled tribes and does worst of all in those constituencies of Uttar Pradesh, Haryana, and Bihar with a substantial proportion of middle peasants. In these three states, the Congress won, respectively, only 36 percent, 29 percent, and 36 percent of the vote in 1980. A constituency-by-constituency analysis in Uttar Pradesh for the 1980 elections reveals that wherever the peasant-cultivator class was most numerous, the Congress did poorly.

To generalize from the Uttar Pradesh-Bihar-Haryana data to the rest of the country would be a mistake, however. Among the dominant peasant-cultivator classes elsewhere, the Congress has held its own. In earlier elections, the Congress attracted support from the Reddis in Andhra, from a variety of middle and backward castes in Karnataka, from the Maratha caste in Maharashtra, and from the Patidars in Gujarat. Even in the election of 1977, the Congress did substantially better in these states than in the rest of the country; and in the 1980 elections the Congress won a majority in all four states.

As long as there are prospects of victory, sections of all castes and communities give support to the Congress. With so much patronage available to the winning party, propertied classes are particularly reluctant to turn their backs on a party that has a good chance of winning. Much of the business community, irrespective of its ideological preferences for other parties at various times, has provided the Congress with financial support. Among the dominant agricultural castes in any village, at least one faction almost always backs the Congress candidate. Even in the 1977 sweep against the Congress in the Hindi-speaking region there were few constituencies in which the party failed to get a fifth or more of the vote.

Given the heterogeneity of support for the Congress, how has the party kept internal conflicts in check? The answer to that question today is considerably different from what it was before the Congress split in 1969. Though continuity exists in terms of electoral support and a national leader, in an organizational sense there have been two Congress parties—the party from 1952 to 1969 and the party since 1969. In the 1950s and 1960s much of the power within the Congress was in the hands of state party bosses who ran party machines based on control over patronage. Party factions, sometimes a single caste but more often a multi-caste group, fought for power within the party organization to win nominations for elections to state legislative assemblies and parliament. Local leaders sought to mobilize their supporters to win power within the party organization at the *taluka* and district level. Winners and losers of local party elections would then battle once again for control over the Pradesh (state) Congress committees. Those who lost one round of party elections might try to win another. Some losers would desert the party in elections to the legislative assembly and to parliament but then return to the party to fight once more. Out of this process—inchoate, interminable, and opportunistic—emerged leaders who knew how to build coalitions within the party, to influence the local bureaucracy, to use the patronage of the state to maximize their support, and to bargain with the central authorities for resources. The best of them also knew how to run state governments.

The Congress lost considerable electoral support in the 1967 elections. It was defeated in several states, and fragile coalition governments took power. Mrs. Gandhi had not yet demonstrated that she had the kind of personal popularity her father had or the skill to bring together diverse interests and factions within the party. The old Congress party—the party of patronage, party bosses, multiple power centres, consensual leaders, and ideologically centrist politics—seemed to be coming to an end. When it appeared as if some of the party bosses might try to replace Mrs. Gandhi, she broke with the party leadership and formed her own Congress party. Mrs. Gandhi then launched a leftist campaign against the syndicate or party bosses, against the former maharajas, and against sections of the business community. In the 1971 elections she campaigned to eliminate poverty and won back much of the support, especially in the urban areas, that the Congress had lost in 1967. Mrs. Gandhi correctly sensed that her father's centrist emphasis on development was not sufficient and that an emphasis on income distribution would win greater electoral support.

The Congress party that emerged out of the victorious 1971 campaign was more centralized. Fearful of threats from state party leaders and chief ministers, Mrs. Gandhi sought to prevent new independent centers of power from rising ever again within her party. State party organizations and state governments were made subservient to the center. Democracy within the party declined. Meetings of the All India Congress Committee and the Working Committee, two important organs within the party, became infrequent. Intra-party elections were no longer held, nominations for state assembly seats were controlled by the center, and the Prime Minister chose the chief ministers. Even municipal governments were often superseded, and municipal power shifted into the hands of officials appointed by the state or central governments. Mrs. Gandhi succeeded in reducing political threats to her own power, but the result was that she weakened local and state Congress party organizations and made the state governments weaker and, from 1972 to 1975, less stable.

The growing instability at the state level affected the center. The Prime Minister devoted more time and effort to dealing with political problems in the states. Both inside and outside the party, groups opposed to a particular leader who controlled the state government focused their attacks on the center, for only the center could change the state government. Local protest thus became nationalized. Agitations in Bihar and Gujarat, for example, were attacks not simply against the state governments but against the center. The regime became increasingly unable to cope with the widening protest against the government, and the party itself was torn by dissidence over Mrs. Gandhi's centralizing tendencies. It is in this context that one must understand Mrs. Gandhi's decision to declare a national emergency that gave her the power to arrest not only opposition leaders but also members of her own party. All those remaining independent of the center of power, both in and outside the party, were eliminated. Opponents were jailed, press censorship was imposed, and chief ministers became subservient to the Prime Minister.

The Congress party that won again in 1980 was a highly centralized party with a weak party organization, with state leaders dependent on the center, and with a weak cabinet of which the members had no independent political stature. Many of the functions that the Congress performed before 1969—mobilizing local support, accommodating itself to local factions, providing opportunities for competing political elites, transmitting to state and central governments information about the local scene, and most importantly, managing social conflict—were no longer well-performed by the party. Though Mrs. Gandhi's party controlled two-thirds of parliament and all the major states except West Bengal, Kerala, and Tamil Nadu, and though Mrs. Gandhi had successfully restored the electoral coalition that had so consistently provided the party with its electoral victories, the structure of the party remained weak. Many of the state governments had politically ineffectual chief ministers, and the Prime Minister spent much of her time dealing with political dissension within the states and correspondingly gave little attention to issues of public policy. Paradoxically, in her effort to prevent powerful state leaders from emerging, Mrs. Gandhi had created a party structure that made for unstable state governments, which then required her political attention.

Mrs. Gandhi's legacy to her son, Rajiv, was thus a weak party organization, state party leaders with little popular support whose political power rested upon support from the center, and a party with few figures of national stature. Rajiv Gandhi's overwhelming electoral victory in 1984 gave the appearance, as did Mrs. Gandhi's similar electoral victory nearly five years earlier, that the Congress party and its leaders were in effective control of both the national and state governments. How shallow was the victory was made clear by the subsequent defeat of the Congress party in one after another state election, and the difficulties encountered by the Prime Minister in building a coalition that could effectively govern. Rajiv Gandhi's political weakness is matched only by the divisions among the opposition parties. The fragility of the governing Congress party, the fragmentation of the opposition, and the risks to governance that both imply in a country that remains torn by regional movements, ethnic and religious strife, represent a major long-term threat to the stability of India's democratic political order.

8

The 1971 Elections: India's Changing Party System

The 1971 elections restored the ruling Congress party to the dominant position which the united Congress held in India from 1952 to 1967. The period 1967–71 was very different from the preceding one. It was a period of unstable governments in the states, a precarious government at the center, indecision in government policy, and growing violence in the countryside. The instability, paralysis and violence was the direct consequence of the Congress setback in the 1967 elections, which brought coalition governments into office in half the states and left the Congress with a demoralized narrow majority in the center. The elections of 1967 themselves reflected a growing disillusionment with the Congress government following two years of drought, an unpopular decision to devalue the rupee, and a growing sentiment that state party bosses had provided ineffectual government.

The spectacular rise in the Congress vote is reflected in this comparison of the percentage of votes won by the united Congress in the 1967 parliamentary elections, and Indira Gandhi's ruling Congress in 1971 in the states in which it contested most of the seats. The most impressive increases for the Congress were in Himachal Pradesh (28.7 percent), Delhi (25.7 percent), Mysore (21.8 percent), U.P. (15.5 percent), Maharashtra (15.2 percent), and Assam (11.2 percent). The only state which failed to give the ruling Congress a higher vote than the United Congress received was Gujarat, where the opposition Congress won 39.3 percent of the vote, bringing the combined Congress vote in Gujarat in 1971 up to 84.6 percent as against 46.9 percent

Previously published under a slightly different title in *Asian Survey*, Vol. XI, Number 12, December 1971, pp. 1153–1166.

in 1967. The percentage of votes for the ruling Congress also declined in Kerala, where the Congress chose to contest only six seats as against nineteen in 1967, Tamil Nadu, where only nine seats were contested compared with thirty-nine in 1967, and West Bengal, where the party put up thirty-two candidates in 1971 and forty in 1967.

Why was there such a substantial increase in the Congress vote throughout the country? The question is best left to those who are studying electoral behavior. Our concern here is primarily with the impact of the results on the Indian party system.

National factors played a more important role in the 1971 elections than in any previous election in post-Independence India. For the first time there were two major electoral forces opposed to one another— the ruling Congress (Congress-R) on one side, supported in a few areas by the CPI, the Muslim League, the Praja Socialist Party (PSP), and in Tamil Nadu by the DMK, and on the other side a coalition of the old Congress, the Swatantra, the Jana Sangh and the Samyukta Socialists (SSP). Parliamentary candidates, standing for the first time without the support of contesting state assembly candidates, toured their constituencies more than ever before and gave more attention to national affairs. And in no previous election had virtually all parties— not only the Congress but even its major opponents—given so much attention to a national leader.

Mrs. Gandhi's efforts to get voters to cast their votes for the Congress candidate on the basis of her appeal, as distinct from choosing among parliamentary candidates on the basis of local considerations, had to overcome four handicaps. First of all, India had no national mass media which would ensure the Prime Minister of an instant national audience. All India Radio, which does not reach all the voters, was in any event not used by candidates; newspapers touch only a fraction of the electorate; and television hardly exists outside Delhi.

Secondly, she lacked a party organization in every constituency of the country comparable to the organization of the undivided Congress; nor did she have an army of party workers who could transmit her messages into every village and town. Several state party organizations—those in Mysore, Gujarat, and Tamil Nadu—were mainly with the opposition Congress and the party organizations in U.P. and Bihar were badly split. Moreover, many of her parliamentary candidates stood in constituencies in which the state assembly representatives were in opposition parties.

Thirdly, Mrs. Gandhi lacked a single dramatic national issue, such as the demand for independence or the threat of war, which could unite a large part of the country behind her government. Some of the issues she raised would lose her some voters even as they might gain her the support of others. Her demand for abolishing the privileges of princes, for example, might increase her votes in the cities but it also united the princes against her in Rajasthan and Madhya Pradesh, where, only a year earlier, she had had their support.

Finally, this was a parliamentary, not presidential, election. Outside of her own constituency, Mrs. Gandhi's name did not appear on the ballot. She had to persuade voters that if they wanted to support her, they had to vote for the ruling Congress parliamentary candidate without regard for his personal merits. Her father, in spite of his enormous popularity, often failed to swing the electorate to his party's candidates. Nehru's tours of Kerala, for example, though arousing huge crowds, were notably unsuccessful in winning votes for the Congress in that state.

Elsewhere in the world, national politics has triumphed over parochial politics when one or more of these factors has been at work—a national mass media, a national political party with local organizational roots everywhere, a dramatic national issue or a presidential election. It was the absence of these factors which led so many observers to underestimate the extent of Mrs. Gandhi's electoral appeal.

It was widely assumed that factors other than national issues or the appeal of a national leader would affect electorate behavior. The first assumption was that most Indian voters and local influentials were more concerned with the administration of policies and programs than with policy itself. It was assumed that the distribution of government resources—licenses, permits, credit, fertilizers and seeds, and roads, schools and wells—would primarily influence voters and local leaders. The successful MLA and MP was one who knew how to service his constituency. His position on state and especially national issues seemed to be of little importance to most voters. Secondly, it was widely assumed that party control over village *panchayats*, municipalities, *panchayat samitis*, *zilla parishads*, and quasi-governmental institutions such as sugar cooperatives, banking institutions, seed cooperatives, school boards, etc., were important in winning assembly and parliamentary seats since patronage powers had increasingly devolved to these local institutions.

Thirdly, since Indian villages and towns are socially divided into caste, linguistic, religious, and factional groups which lean to one party or another, or to one faction or another within the major parties, it was widely assumed that the successful district and state party leaders were those skillful in providing rewards to these diverse factions and communities—by giving one local leader a position in the *zilla parishad*, another a position as an MLA and still another a position as a member of parliament. Thus one party or faction of a party might throw its weight behind a parliamentary candidate in return for another faction's support for its assembly candidate.

Finally, in the past, voter loyalties to local leaders seemed to be relatively stable and insofar as local leaders remained loyal to a particular assembly or parliamentary representative, the votes for political parties from one election to another had been relatively constant. Electoral alliances, rather than swings in electorate behavior, accounted for dramatic changes in election results. Even in the 1970 Kerala elections, the number of votes received by each political party did not differ sharply from the results of previous elections, and the enormous shift in assembly seats in Tamil Nadu from the Congress to the DMK in 1967 took place with scarcely any shift in popular votes.

The Congress bosses of the 1960s—Atulya Ghosh, Sukhadia, S.K. Patil, Morarji Desai, Kamaraj, Brahmananda Reddy, Sanjiva Reddy, Nijalingappa, Chavan, Patnaik, C.B. Gupta and Kairon—were men who understood these principles of electorate behavior and on balance were successful in winning assembly and parliamentary seats for their party. For these men, what party workers, MLAs and MPs did for their constituents and how they balanced one interest and ambition against another, was the substance of politics. Party manifestos, government policies, and socialist slogans simply constituted the rhetoric of politics.

Mrs. Gandhi challenged these assumptions. By nationalizing banks, disinheriting the princes, proposing ceilings on rural land holdings and urban property, and publicly challenging big business, she sought to move the electorate toward issues and away from the politics of patronage. By splitting the party—one might say in retrospect by expelling from the party those who did not believe in her kind of politics—she repudiated those who operated under these old assumptions. Her most explicit challenge to these assumptions was to call parliamentary elections separately from state elections. She was, in effect, asking voters to put aside the performance of the state MLAs and even of the individual MPs in serving their constituencies, and to vote instead on the basis of national issues. It was the 1967 election results that virtually forced the Prime Minister to move in this direction. The defeat of prominent members of the old guard in the 1967 elections, the loss of many seats, and the declining position of the Congress in parliament meant that the Congress party could do longer win if it continued to operate as it had in the past. Mrs. Gandhi recognized this, while most members of the old guard did not. Faced with a declining organization, the defection of a substantial part of the electorate, and more effective electoral coalitions on the part of the opposition parties, Mrs. Gandhi searched for a new basis for winning electoral support.

Rajni Kothari has argued, and has produced survey data to support his argument, that a growing number of voters throughout the country were increasingly oriented toward issues even in the 1967 elections. The decline in the Congress vote in 1967 followed a period of drought, rising prices, two wars, the death of two prime ministers, growing corruption, and an unpopular decision to devalue the rupee. In at least the two big states of U.P. and Bihar, schools and colleges were closed and students campaigned in the countryside against the Congress government. At the time, a concern with issues and performance worked against the Congress party. In 1971, it worked against the opposition.

Paradoxically, the opposition parties contributed to Mrs. Gandhi's efforts to turn the electorate toward national issues. By singling out Mrs. Gandhi as their prime target (and without offering any national leader as an alternative), they supported the efforts of Mrs. Gandhi's supporters to make her a national leader. In 1967 Mrs. Gandhi was comparatively unknown. Though she had the dual advantage of name and lineage, she had been Prime Minister for two years during a period of stagnation and indecision. In 1967 leaders of the Congress party could seriously contemplate her replacement. From the summer of 1969 onwards, when she first challenged the party leadership on the Presidential election, until the parliamentary elections in February and March of 1970, her political decisions established her as a national leader capable of asserting her personality and policies. Moreover, she proved to be extraordinarily astute at eliminating her potential opponents by virtually forcing them to take unpopular stands on such issues as bank nationalization and the privy purses. It is striking that in the 1971 elections there were no national opposition leaders, not even Morarji Desai, touring the country to oppose her.

There can be no doubt that some national factor—Mrs. Gandhi's personal popularity, or party identification, or a concern for national issues or some combination of these—did affect almost every constituency, since the rise in the Congress vote took place in virtually all sections of the country. Nor can the swing be attributed simply to the massive support from Muslims and Harijans, since the highest Congress vote was in Mysore and Himachal, two states with a small proportion of both minority groups.

As we shall see, however, there is some evidence to make us qualify the general argument that national issues did affect the electorate. A substantial portion of the electorate did vote for regional parties and independents, and there were six states (apart from Tamil Nadu, West Bengal, and Kerala where the Congress did not contest all the constituencies) in which a majority of voters supported non-Congress candidates—Bihar, Gujarat, Madhya Pradesh, Orissa, Punjab, and U.P. But while scholars can debate the magnitude of the victory and the extent to which national factors were decisive everywhere, in the eyes of most Indian politicians, journalists, and the educated middle class the elections demonstrated that a determined national leader could mobilize a substantial portion of the electorate behind a national program.

One of the most surprising but unnoticed features of the 1971 elections was the electoral performance of the regional parties. In eight of the eighteen states the first or second largest party, in terms of popular vote, was a regional party. In Andhra the second largest party was the Telengana Praja Samiti which won 14.4 percent of the vote, all of it in the Telengana region of the state. In Assam, the All Party Hill Leaders Conference won 10.9 percent of the vote, all in the hill districts. In Haryana, the Vishal Haryana Party won 9 percent. In Orissa, the newly formed Utkal Congress won 22.7 percent and in Uttar Pradesh, the BKD edged out the Jana Sangh as number two with 12.6 percent of the vote. In Punjab, the Akali Dal won a handsome 30.8 percent of the vote.

In two states, the regional parties won a plurality or majority of votes: Tamil Nadu where the DMK won 35.3 percent and tiny Nagaland where the United Front of Nagaland won 60.5 percent. In Jammu and Kashmir, the Jana Sangh was officially number two with 12.6 percent of the vote, but independents supported by the local Plebiscite Front received a higher vote. And in Maharashtra, the Jana Sangh won 5.4 percent, barely keeping ahead of the regional Peasants and Workers party with 5.2 percent. Nationally, the regional parties won 13.2 percent of the vote, a modest rise over the 10.1 percent they received in the 1967 elections. Though the position of individual regional parties declined in parliament, their overall position improved slightly from forty-one seats in 1967 to forty-nine seats in 1971, the increase mainly reflecting the emergence of the Telengana Praja Samiti in Andhra.[1]

Considering these results, it is surprising that there is a widespread impression that the regional parties did poorly in the elections, but there are two reasons, both relevant, for this impression. The first is the failure of several new regional parties to extend their influence into the national parliament: the Shiv Sena, in spite of a spectacular rise in Bombay city in the last few years, was unable to win a single seat; similarly, the BKD, which had won 21 percent of the state vote in the U.P. assembly elections of 1969, won little more than half that vote in the parliamentary elections and was unable to win more than a single seat in parliament; and in West Bengal the Bangla Congress, which won a substantial vote and seats in the 1969 assembly elections, was unable to extend its position into parliament or even maintain its position in the assembly.

The second reason for assuming a decline in the regional parties is that the overwhelming victory of the Congress in the national parliament and its growing position in the states reduced the capacity of the regional parties to play a significant role in bargaining for coalition governments. When no single party held a majority, then the regional parties could exercise an influence which exceeded their representation in the legislatures. In Bihar, for example, the small Jharkhand delegation in the assembly was able to bring down one government by transferring its allegiance, and in Orissa, West Bengal, and U.P. the regional parties played a major role in cabinet making.

If the regional parties held their own and even improved their position, at whose expense did the ruling Congress grow? Four nationally recognized parties—the Jana Sangh, the Swatantra, the SSP and the PSP—together won only 14 percent of the vote in 1971 (only a fraction more, incidentally, than the regional parties), as against 26.1

[1] This included ten TPS, twenty-three DMK, three Kerala Congress, three RSP, two Jharkhand and one each Akali Dal, BKD, Bangla Congress, APHLC, VHP, Forward Bloc, United Goans, and United Front of Nagaland. The Muslim League and the Republican Party of India have been excluded, since they explicitly represent the interests of their communities rather than the regions in which they function.

percent in 1967. The vote for independent candidates also sharply declined from 13.8 percent to 8.6 percent. The two Communist parties more or less held their own—the CPM increased its vote from 4.2 percent to 5.2 percent while the CPI declined slightly from 5.2 percent to 4.8 percent.

It is thus premature to conclude that the regional parties were displaced by national parties or that issue-oriented politics means the end of regional and local parties. Indeed, if the term 'regional' is understood to mean not simply that a party functions exclusively in a particular state or section of the country but rather that it is programmatically concerned primarily with the region in which it functions, then the CPM should logically be added to the list of regional parties. Twenty of its twenty-five seats in parliament came from West Bengal, and while its program was couched in ideological jargon the primary concern of the CPM was in pressing West Bengal's claims upon the central government. Indeed, the hostility of a large part of the Bengali population toward the central government appeared to have arrested the Indira Gandhi tide at the West Bengal border. The ruling Congress vote in West Bengal was 27.7 percent as against the 39.7 percent which the united Congress received in the previous parliamentary election. Even if the 7.1 percent received by the organization Congress is added, the two Congress organizations still failed to equal the vote of the united Congress. As for the CPM, its share of the vote rose from 15.5 percent to 34.5 percent, making it by far the largest party in the state, in parliamentary and assembly seats as well as in percentage of votes. In fact, by virtue of its performance in West Bengal alone, the CPM emerged as the largest single opposition party in parliament.

The persistence of regional parties in an election characterized by a concern for national issues and when parliamentary elections were held independently of state assembly elections, confirmed the hypothesis that a substantial part of the Indian electorate continued to be stirred by regional issues.

But to this generalization two qualifications must be made. The first is that regional sentiments are not confined to a single section of the Indian population, that in many regions these sentiments are not durable, and that the record of regional parties, therefore, tends to be erratic. The demand for linguistic states, for example, gave impetus to such regional parties as the Andhra Mahasabha, the Samyukta Maharashtra Samiti, and the Mahagujarat Parishad, all of which withered away with the reorganization of states. The Telengana Praja Samiti is another such one-issue party that is likely to disappear if a separate Telengana state is formed. Other disaffected regions may also throw up new regional parties demanding greater autonomy or separate statehood. There is a high potential for such movements in the Vidarbha and Marathwada regions of Maharashtra, the Madhya Bharat and Vindhya Pradesh regions of Madhya Pradesh (though the Jana Sangh may take up the cause of independent statehood for these regions), the Rayalaseema region of Andhra if a separate Telengana state is formed, and the Chhota Nagpur region of Bihar (already championed by the Jharkhand party, though its appeal is still primarily limited to the tribal adivasi population in the region).

There are also instances in which one or two districts have thrown up powerful political movements to agitate for autonomy or for their transference to a neighboring state. Belgaum district has produced the Maharashtra Ekikaran Samiti, which advocates transferring the Marathi speaking districts of northern Mysore to Maharashtra; there is a movement in the Mizo hill district of southern Assam demanding autonomy; and the All India Gorkha League continues to be a major party in Darjeeling district.

Most of the local and regional parties have a base in either social or regional economic disparities or in the emergence of new social identities, and most frequently in a combination of these. And since 'identity building' is a continuous process, accelerated by the spread of communication, the expansion of education, and increasing social mobility, one should expect new political movements to arise. The presence of 'outside' migrants, for example, in a region in which a socially mobile local middle class is competing for employment, is a growing source of political conflict. The Shiv Sena in Bombay is the most well-known manifestation of such conflict, but there have also been such anti-migrant political activities in Assam, Mysore and Bihar.

The wreckage of regional and local parties can be found all over the electoral map of India, for as their leaders died, their primary goal was achieved, or their program was taken on by a national party, they have tended to disappear. Only a few regional parties like the DMK and Akali Dal have such deep social and historical roots that they have been able to persist as major forces in their states for an extended period.

The second qualification to our generalization that regional issues have a persistent basis in the Indian party system is that the electorate appears to give less support to regional parties in the parliamentary elections than in the elections for the state assemblies. In the 1967 elections, when parliamentary and assembly elections were held simultaneously, most of the regional parties, including the Kerala Congress, the DMK, the Peasants and Workers party, the Jana Congress in Orissa, and the Bangla Congress, did not win as many votes in the parliamentary as in the assembly constituencies. And in the 1968–1969 mid-term assembly elections in Haryana, Bihar, Nagaland, Punjab, Uttar Pradesh, and West Bengal, the regional parties fared better than they had in the earlier general elections; this was especially so in U.P., Punjab, and West Bengal. The reasons why regional parties perform better in assembly elections are obvious. For one thing, they often contest fewer seats; for another, discriminating voters often see no reason for sending a handful of representatives of a regional party to the national parliament, though they feel the party can usefully represent their interests in the state assembly.

There is thus some reason to expect regional parties to continue to perform better in state assembly than in national elections; whether they will do even better when assembly elections are delinked from national parliamentary elections, as has been the case in the past, remains to be seen.[2]

Though the old Congress (Congress-O) emerged as the largest single opposition party, in terms of percentage of popular votes, it was reduced to little more than a regional party. It survived as the second largest party only in Gujarat, Mysore, and Tamil Nadu and in these states there was a steady loss of support after the elections as many of its rank and file workers and MLAs defected to the ruling Congress. In both Mysore and Gujarat defections were so widespread that the Congress-O state governments collapsed and President's Rule was established pending the calling of new elections. If the Congress-O does survive in any of these states, it is likely to be as a regional party concerned with the interests of the state vis-a-vis the central government.

The Swatantra was virtually wiped out as a national party. In Gujarat much of its support was transferred to the Congress-O and in Orissa to the local Utkal Congress. In Rajasthan, Andhra, and Mysore it appears as if many Swatantra voters switched to the ruling Congress.

[2] For an excellent account of the performance of the regional parties, see Lewis P. Fickett, Jr., 'The Politics of Regionalism in India,' *Pacific Affairs*, XLIV:2, Summer 1971.

It holds eight seats in parliament, mainly from Orissa and Rajasthan where the party continues as a substantial electoral force.

The Jana Sangh lost severely in Delhi and U.P., two of its major strongholds, but managed to withstand the Congress tide in Bihar, Madhya Pradesh, and Rajasthan, where its percentage of votes increased. In the latter two states, however, the Jana Sangh increase was due to the support of the princes rather than to any enduring social base and party organization. In these two states, it is the princes who are strong, not the Jana Sangh, and a change in the political allegiance of the princes would be at the expense of the Jana Sangh.

The Congress-O-Swatantra-Jana Sangh right-of-center electoral coalition proved to be a failure and after the elections there was much recrimination within each of these parties over their electoral strategy. The leadership and rank and file of all three parties were demoralized by their overwhelming defeat, though the Jana Sangh, with its more committed cadre and coherent ideology, has demonstrated its recuperative powers. While it lost all of its six parliamentary seats from Delhi, the party did win in the municipal corporation elections in that city just a few months later. And it was most active in launching a popular campaign for the recognition of Bangladesh.

The support given by CPI to Mrs. Gandhi's Congress did not result in any increase in votes for the CPI, though it held its own in parliamentary seats. Its popular vote declined almost everywhere, particularly in Andhra, Assam, and Maharashtra, while it maintained its position in Kerala and West Bengal. The CPI's dream of joining a coalition government in Delhi was based more on the hope that the ruling Congress would fail to win a clear majority in parliament and would need its support to form a government, than upon any expectation that it would gain substantially in popular support. But the CPI lost the gamble.

Among the national parties which took part in the 1967 elections, only the CPM increased its popular vote in 1971, but as we have already noted, the elections virtually transformed the CPM into a regional party. The CPM vote sharply declined in Andhra and in Tamil Nadu and it is almost non-existent in all other states except Kerala and West Bengal. In Kerala its vote increased slightly from 24.6 percent to 26.2 percent, but because of the alliance patterns it lost most of its MP seats. Almost its entire representation in parliament is now from West Bengal.

The 1971 elections re-established the dominance of the Congress party in the parliamentary seats of urban India. In the 1967 elections, the united Congress won only eighteen of the fifty-two urban parliamentary constituencies.[3] At the time of the dissolution of parliament, the new Congress held only thirteen of these seats, including one each in Hyderabad, Bombay, and Calcutta but none in Delhi, Madras, Ahmedabad, Patna, Baroda, Trivandrum, Gwalior, Pune, Ernakulam, Amritsar, Jaipur, Coimbatore, Madurai, Lucknow, Varanasi, Allahabad, Kanpur, Meerut, Hoogly, Alipur, Jamshedpur, Surat, Tiruchchirappalli, Salem, Bareilly, and Howrah.

The Congress-R recaptured all but one of its urban constituencies and swept the constituencies of Bombay and Delhi. In all, Congress-R won thirty-three of the fifty-two urban constituencies. To put it another way, of the thirty-nine urban seats held by the opposition at the time parliament was dissolved (including the Congress-O seats), the ruling Congress won twenty-one.

TABLE 8.1
Urban Parliamentary Constituencies

	1967	1971
Congress R	18	33
Congress O		2
CPI	4	5
CPM	7	2
Jana Sangh	9	1
Swatantra	2	1
DMK	3	3
SSP	4	0
Other parties	1	2
Independents	4	3
	52	52

The major losers were the Jana Sangh and the SSP. The Jana Sangh lost all six Delhi seats, Bhopal, Amritsar, and Bareilly to Congress-R while the SSP lost its seats in Meerut, Bombay, and Pune to Congress-R and its Trivandrum seat to Krishna Menon, who ran as an independent.

[3] 'Urban' is defined as cities with at least a quarter million population in the 1961 census.

One consequence of the Congress-R sweep in so many urban constituencies was the likelihood of a major campaign by the ruling Congress to win control of the municipal corporations in those cities which were in the hands of opposition parties.

What are the long term consequences of the 1971 parliamentary elections? The first, and most important, is what did not happen. India did not move into an era of coalition politics at the national level, as had been expected after the Congress decline in the 1967 elections and the Congress split of 1969. India's experiences with coalition governments in the states have not been salutary; in U.P., Bihar, Haryana, Punjab, West Bengal, and Kerala, coalition governments have been characterized by frequent party defections, swollen cabinets, politicized and demoralized bureaucracies, paralyzed decision-making, increased personal corruption, and most alarming of all, a growing cynicism among the educated classes toward the parliamentary and electoral process. Had the Congress-R failed to win a clear majority in the national parliament there was a substantial possibility that these patterns of politics would have spread to the center, creating an atmosphere which would have simultaneously nurtured a politics of opportunism and a politics of ideological extremism.

Instead, the atmosphere in India was one of great élan and relief, and even pride that the electorate chose to vote to power a left of center government with a solid majority, opting for, as Morris-Jones aptly put it, 'change and stability' simultaneously. Even those who were critical of the ruling Congress for its association with the Muslim League and the CPI were relieved at the magnitude of the victory, for it eliminated the need for the ruling Congress to depend upon those parties to form a government.

The impact of the parliamentary elections on the party configuration of the states is still being worked out. The first effect of the victory of the ruling Congress at the center was to undermine the position of a number of state governments. Both the Mysore and Gujarat governments collapsed as Congress-O supporters defected to the ruling Congress. Similarly, the non-Congress coalition government in Bihar (the eighth coalition ministry since 1967) resigned. In U.P., the SVD ministry was replaced by a Congress-R-led government. Though old-style Congress dominance of the states was not re-established— Congress remained weak in Orissa, Kerala, and West Bengal, and the DMK dominated Tamil Nadu—the party configuration did increasingly resemble the pattern of the fifties and early sixties.

The elections called a halt to the defections and splits from the governing Congress party. The splintering which occurred shortly after Shastri's death contributed heavily to the Congress defeats in the 1967 elections. The BKD in Bihar and U.P., the Bangla Congress, the Kerala Congress, and the Jana Congress in Orissa, were all splinters from the united Congress party and were led by individuals who for one reason or another were dissatisfied with the party or their position in it. The 1969 split was, of course, the most massive of all, leaving in its wake a splintered Congress in Mysore, Gujarat, Tamil Nadu, Bihar, and U.P.

After the 1969 split, the process of disaggregation came to an end. Paradoxically, the decision of Mrs. Gandhi to build a more homogeneous party not only terminated the exodus but even resulted in new accretions from other parties. In fact one of the major problems confronting the Congress, especially after its electoral victory, was that the party was attracting back many defectors and Congress-O supporters. It was faced with the prospect of again being the catch-all party it was, not only prior to the 1969 split but even prior to the splintering which took place in 1966 and 1967.

Perhaps the most commented upon by-product of the election was a widespread expectation that Mrs. Gandhi's government would perform better than previous governments. The list of what was expected of the new government was large. On almost everyone's list was decreasing unemployment, while others included increasing the efficiency and profitability of the public sector, encouraging the growth of medium size industries, accelerating agricultural growth in the country's dry areas, reducing labor strife, expanding primary education and reforming the universities, improving the family planning program, restoring law and order in West Bengal, and in general reducing disparities between the rich and the poor.

Alas, while expectations rose the capacity of the new government to cope with these problems continued to be small. The Prime Minister was yet to demonstrate her ability to shake up the bureaucracy, make effective demands upon state governments, substantially mobilize new resources for investment and, most fundamentally, convert her political leadership into executive authority.[4]

The most important increment to the Prime Minister's capabilities,

---

[4] The limitations on the central government's capabilities have been effectively spelled out by Susanne Rudolph in 'The Writ from Delhi: the Indian Government's Capabilities after the 1971 Election,' *Asian Survey*, XI:10, October 1971, pp. 958–69.

however, was a greater consensus than ever before on what needed to be done and a greater willingness in the country as a whole to allow the Prime Minister to take the lead—more than at almost any time since the 1950's when Nehru was at the height of his leadership.

The decision to delink parliamentary and state assembly elections predicted important consequences for the development of the Indian party system. If delinking had the effect of contributing to the nationalizing of parliamentary elections, what would the consequences of delinking be for the state assembly elections which would henceforth be held separately? By March 1972, elections were due to be held in Mysore, Andhra, Maharashtra, Gujarat, Rajasthan, Kashmir, Madhya Pradesh, and Assam. Haryana was due to vote again in 1973, Nagaland, Bihar, Punjab, and Uttar Pradesh in 1974, and Kerala in 1975. Only Orissa, West Bengal, and Tamil Nadu remained linked to the parliament election schedule, but since President's Rule was in effect in West Bengal (as well as in Mysore and Gujarat), new elections could be called at any time.

The most tempting theme for opposition parties in the state elections was that the center was not doing enough for the state and that the governing party in the state, particularly if it was the ruling Congress, was failing to put sufficient pressure on the central government. This was the major theme of the CPM in West Bengal and the Utkal Congress in Orissa in the elections, and both did well in popular votes. If opposition parties in the state sensed that the ruling Congress government in the center was losing its popularity, then they would emphasize regional demands for the transfer of more resources from the center to the state, for the expansion of public sector investments in the states, and for the transfer of constitutional powers. If, however, the center remained reasonably popular, then the opposition parties in the assembly elections were more likely to direct their attacks at the performance of the state government. The strategy chosen by political parties in the state elections during the next five years was thus to be shaped by what they interpreted as the popular response to the central government. In this sense, state politics continued to be influenced by national politics in spite of delinking.

The first issue before the new government within a few days after it took office, was its reaction to the civil war in Pakistan. Ironically, foreign affairs played a smaller role in the 1971 elections than in previous elections when parties differed on their attitudes toward China, the Soviet Union, policy toward Kashmir, and issues of foreign aid. These issues were absent, though the hijacking of an Indian plane to Lahore in early February, and its subsequent destruction, led to a brief flareup in the elections.

The events across the border opened a Pandora's box for India, the contents of which could only be dimly perceived. Relations between India's Hindus and Muslims, the internal political complexion of Kashmir (which would go to the polls by early 1972), the position of the CPM and the Naxalites in West Bengal, relations between West Bengal and the central government, political developments in Assam, Meghalaya, Tripura, the Mizo Hills, and the Northeast Frontier Agency, and the political role of the millions of refugees who had come into India, were all affected by the movement to establish an independent Bangladesh.

India's foreign relations had already been dramatically affected. In August India signed a friendship treaty with the Soviet Union which called for consultation in the event that either country was militarily attacked. This treaty was widely interpreted as a deterrent to both the Pakistanis and the Chinese and as an assurance to India that the Soviet Union would continue to provide military assistance in the event of an Indo-Pak war. The Pakistan civil war also strained India's relations with the United States and with Muslim countries and created an atmosphere of unease in the border regions of Nepal, Sikkim, and Bhutan. The internal political situation could hardly have remained unaffected by India's changing international relations.

When the civil war broke out in late March, the initial response of the Government of India was strongly sympathetic to the Bangladesh movement—partly reflecting the emotional feeling Indians had at the disintegration of their hostile neighbor, partly reflecting a sense of vindication that the two-nation theory had failed to keep Pakistan intact, and partly reflecting the calculation that a militarily weak Pakistan enhances India's own military capabilities.

But the initial hope and expectation by India's government that their own economy and political system would not be disrupted by Pakistan's civil war disappeared as millions of East Bengali refugees crossed into West Bengal, Assam, and Meghalaya, and as the cost of supporting them, giving aid to the underground movement, and strengthening the army began to soar. Mrs. Gandhi's program for expanding rural investment to relieve rural unemployment had effectively been shelved and expenditures on development sharply declined. Moreover, as it became apparent that the warfare in East Bengal was likely to be a protracted affair with no immediate end in sight, political pressures on the central government to take more forceful measures against Pakistan increased. The Jana Sangh, with considerable support from other opposition parties, organized mass demonstrations for the recognition of Bangladesh. Within Mrs. Gandhi's government there was an intense debate over the cost and benefits of pursuing the existing course of action, as against a more aggressive posture toward Pakistan.

Hardly a ministry in the central government remained unaffected by the economic and political disruptions in the northeastern part of the subcontinent. The ministries of Home Affairs, Refugees and Rehabilitation, Food and Agriculture, and, of course, Defence and External Affairs gave their primary attention to the Bangladesh crisis, and the burdens on the health services and on the transportation network in the northeast were enormous. Mrs. Gandhi's 1971 campaign slogan, *gharibi hatao* ('eliminate poverty') had become a casualty of the civil war.

9

The 1980 Elections: Continuities and Discontinuities in Indian Politics

Beneath the surface of India's apparently volatile elections and the recent fragmentation of its political parties lie the continuities of both electoral and elite behavior. Many things have changed in India, but one fundamental political fact remains: the elections of 1980 restored the Congress party to the pre-eminent position it held since Independence. Once again, the party had an overwhelming majority in parliament, controlled all but a handful of state governments, and had a national leader who commanded both domestic support and international attention. In retrospect, then, should we view the Emergency, the defeat of Mrs. Gandhi and the Congress party in the election of 1977, and the emergence of an alternative government under the Janata party, as a brief (five year) break in what is otherwise a remarkable pattern of continuity and stability in basic institutions and processes? Or were fundamental tensions revealed that foreshadow still another breakdown in the parliamentary and democratic system? In an effort to answer these questions, we shall first examine the continuities in Indian politics by comparing the elections and the post-election scene of 1980–81 with the election of the last Congress government in 1971, and by comparing both to earlier elections. Then we shall consider some of the discontinuities, particularly by looking at the ways the organizational structure of the Congress party has changed and how these changes have affected the performance of government.

Previously published under a slightly different title in *Asian Survey*, Vol. XXII, No. 4, April 1982, pp. 339–355.

Finally, we shall discuss some of the major politico-economic challenges likely to face Mrs. Gandhi or her successor in the next few years.

Electoral Continuities

How do the election results of 1980 compare with those of 1971?

1. In 1980 the Congress won 351 parliamentary seats with almost 43 percent of the popular vote as compared with 352 seats and nearly 44 percent of the popular vote in 1971.[1] In both instances the electoral coalition was similar. The Congress won the support of the very rich and the very poor, from Brahmins to ex-untouchables, from well-to-do businessmen and government bureaucrats to tribal agricultural laborers and Muslim weavers. In 1980, for example, the Congress won fifty of seventy-nine reserved scheduled caste constituencies and twenty-nine of thirty-seven scheduled tribe constituencies compared with fifty and twenty-six, respectively, in 1971. In 1980 a centrist program won for Mrs. Gandhi and her party not the support of the center, that is, the middle classes and the middle peasantry who were either divided or opposed to the Congress, but rather the extremes of the class structure.

2. The Congress remains the party of choice among India's religious minorities. It did well in the Sikh state of Punjab with 53 percent of the vote in 1980 and 46 percent in 1971. It lost in Kerala with 26 percent of the vote, but in both elections, the Congress did best in constituencies with large numbers of Christians. As far as Muslims are concerned, in 1980, the Congress won a low plurality of seats in constituencies where Muslims form more than 20 percent of the electorate and is the strongest party among Muslims. The strength of the Congress party among the scheduled castes, scheduled tribes, Muslims, Sikhs, and Christians—who together constitute 38 percent of

[1] For an analysis of the 1977 elections, see my *India at the Polls: The Parliamentary Elections of 1977*, Washington, D.C., American Enterprise Institute for Public Policy Research, 1978. For an analysis of the 1980 elections, see my *India at the Polls, 1980: A Study of The Parliamentary Elections*, Washington, D.C. and London, American Enterprise Institute for Public Policy Research.

India's population—remains a major determinant of the electoral victories of the Congress party. The Congress has, so far, done least well in the 'core' majority of Indian society, the caste Hindus.

3. While its victories are based on the rural vote, the Congress position in urban India is also secure. In the cities with a million or more population, the Congress won twenty-five of thirty-nine constituencies in 1980 and twenty-six in 1971, and it did well in the smaller towns.

4. The Congress once again demonstrated in 1980 that it is a *national* party, indeed, in electoral terms India's only national party. It won a majority of parliamentary seats in all major states with the exception of West Bengal and Kerala, improving its position over 1971 when it also failed to win a majority of seats in Gujarat and Tamil Nadu. There is no state in which the Congress was not either the first or second party. In contrast, all other parties were limited to a single state or region. The Janata was the most national of the opposition parties, but in votes polled it was the second largest party in only nine states, with its strength mainly in the north. The Lok Dal was the second largest in Uttar Pradesh and Orissa and the largest party in Haryana. The CPI(M) was the single largest party in West Bengal and Tripura, and the second largest in Kerala. Four other parties, the two Dravida parties, the Jammu and Kashmir National Conference, and the Akali Dal are strong in a single state each. While there is only one truly national party, India actually has many party 'systems', if, by party system, we mean stable patterns of competition among parties. Each state has its own party system, unique ones in the case of Tamil Nadu, Kashmir, and Punjab, and shared ones in the case of some north Indian states.

5. In 1980 the Congress won a majority in all but two of the ten states that held state assembly elections, Tamil Nadu and Kerala, putting the party in control of every major state except these two plus Jammu and Kashmir and West Bengal. Similarly, it swept the state assembly elections in 1972, winning 70 percent of all the assembly seats, following its parliamentary victory a year earlier.

6. The Congress continued to remain weak among the middle peasantry, particularly in northern India, as demonstrated by the electoral performance of the Congress party in Uttar Pradesh,

Haryana, and Bihar where it won only 36 percent, 29 percent, and 36 percent of the vote, respectively. The Lok Dal, the party of the peasant owner-cultivator class, won 29 percent, 34 percent, and 17 percent, respectively, in these states. The Lok Dal did well in this region in 1967 and 1971, but its position in 1980 improved greatly and the corresponding strength of the Congress party within this class declined.

7. The Congress position within the urban middle class, never as secure as it was among the lower income groups in urban areas, was also not as great in 1980 as in 1971. Much of the intelligentsia was opposed to Mrs. Gandhi, and there were indications that the middle class in the largest cities voted against the Congress. In 1980, the Congress lost a majority of seats in the metropolitan cities of Calcutta, Bombay, and Madras, but carried Delhi.

On each of these dimensions—the electoral coalition of the Congress party the position of the Congress among the scheduled castes and tribes, the Muslims, and in the urban areas; its geographic spread; the fragmentation of the opposition; and the position of the Congress in the states—the 1977 election was an exception. In 1977 the Congress dropped to 153 seats in parliament and captured less than 35 percent of the vote. The lowest income groups voted against its candidates. The Congress won only sixteen of seventy-eight scheduled caste constituencies, twelve of thirty-eight scheduled tribe constituencies, and twenty of eighty-one Muslim populated constituencies. In the urban constituencies, the Congress won only seven of thirty-nine seats. It was smashed in the Hindi-speaking states where it won only two of 239 seats, turning the party into a regional party of the south and west. In the state assembly elections of June 1977, the Congress lost all fourteen states, remaining in power only in the two southern states of Karnataka and Andhra. In 1977 the electoral coalition behind the Congress fell apart, a victim of the Emergency and the resulting unity of the opposition parties.

With the formation of a new electoral coalition around the Janata party, India in 1977 had come as close to a two-party system as the country ever had. The Janata won 43 percent of the vote and 298 seats. The Janata and the Congress together won 78 percent of the vote and 83 percent of the seats in parliament. Indeed, the combined two-party vote in 1977 exceeded what it would have been in 1971 had all the constituencies of the Janata then been joined together into a single party.

The breakup of the Janata coalition in 1979 and the victory of Congress (I) in 1980 restored India to its normal political state: one national party and many opposition parties confined to a single region or single state, with almost all of the parties further divided into factions. The 1980 elections and the party splitting that followed produced a veritable parody of the fragmented multi-party system. There were now three Congress parties, two Communist parties, two Janata parties, two Lok Dals, two Dravida parties, two Muslim Leagues, and countless small state parties.

The party names may differ, but once again opposition parties were fragmented as they were in the 1950s and 1960s. And while there are some electoral differences between the position of the Congress and the opposition parties of 1980 and 1971 as compared with the earlier years, it is also striking how much similarity there is. The electoral results for the Congress party from 1952 through 1980 show how stable the vote for the Congress has been, with the exception of the elections of 1977 (see Table 9.1). In the six other parliamentary elections, the Congress has never fallen below 40.7 percent nor risen above 47.8 percent.

TABLE 9.1
Congress Party Results in Six Parliamentary Elections (1952–1980)

Election	Vote (in percent)	Seats Number	Seats Percentage
1952	45.0	357	73
1957	47.8	359	73
1962	44.7	358	73
1967	40.7	283	54
1971	43.7	352	68
1977	34.5	153	28
1980	42.7	351	67

Party and Electoral Changes

Thus far we have focused on the similarities between the election and post-election scene in 1980 and 1971 to emphasize the degree of political continuity. Let us now compare the trends in the seventies and the eighties with those in the first two decades after Independence. Differences in two respects stand out.

The first is the weakness of the local organization of the Congress party and its corollary, the extent of centralization within the party. In the 1950s and 1960s power within the Congress was in the hands of state party bosses who ran traditional party machines based upon control over patronage. This pattern of multiple power centers came to an end with the split in the party in 1969, when Mrs. Gandhi, fearful that the party bosses might try to choose a new national leader, formed her own Congress party. She then launched a populist campaign against 'big business,' the ex-maharajas, and the 'syndicate' (as the Congress party bosses were called), and campaigned to 'abolish poverty.' The result of these popular appeals was that Mrs. Gandhi's Congress won a substantial victory in the 1971 parliamentary elections and the following year, after winning a popular war against Pakistan over Bangladesh, the party further consolidated its position in the state assembly elections. Since it was the state leaders who had challenged Mrs. Gandhi between 1967 and 1969 and whom she defeated when they ran against her candidates in the 1971 and 1972 elections, she was eager to prevent new independent centers of power from ever rising again.

Mrs. Gandhi restructured the party by centralizing it. State leaders, including chief ministers, were no longer allowed to build an independent local base in the countryside or in the party but were appointed (or dismissed) by the Prime Minister. As state party organizations and state governments became increasingly subservient to the center, intraparty democracy within the Congress declined. Meetings of the All India Congress Committee and the Working Committee became infrequent and their political importance reduced. Not only did state governments become less independent, but even municipal governments and village *panchayats* languished as local governments were often superseded and local elections became infrequent. Under these circumstances, the local Congress party atrophied. Mrs. Gandhi reduced the threat to her political power, but in doing so she also weakened the local and state party organizations. The result was that state governments became weaker and less stable between 1972 and 1975, the year she declared an emergency.

Many of the older functions of the Congress party—mobilizing local support, accommodating itself to local factions, providing opportunities for competing political elites, transmitting to state and central governments information about the local scene—dissipated. In place of the party, Mrs. Gandhi turned to other institutions—the government intelligence apparatus, the central reserve police, and various paramilitary institutions. For advice on political affairs, she turned increasingly not to party leaders but to a small band of trusted political advisors, a kitchen cabinet that came to be popularly known (in an invidious way), as the 'caucus'.

While Mrs. Gandhi's position within her own party had never been greater, nor had the party ever been as dependent upon a single leader to sustain its electoral support, Mrs. Gandhi continued to fear the emergence of any independent center of political power. The reason had less to do with political reality than her sense of personal insecurity and vulnerability. The result was that none of the country's well-known national and state leaders remained in the Congress. The Congress became a one-person party (or as one wit put it in 1980 when Sanjay Gandhi was still alive, a one-and-a-half-person party). Some former associates of Mrs. Gandhi in the Congress (U) returned to Mrs. Gandhi's Congress, and her son Rajiv was said to be interested in 'consolidation,' but there was no major movement back, and those who returned would have been leaders without followers.

Mrs. Gandhi's cabinet was made up of political unknowns, and cabinet members knew that if they attempted to build a political base of their own they would be removed. The chief ministers she appointed were also little known, and in several cases she deliberately kept them weak by appointing their opponents to the central cabinet. She avoided holding elections within the party, knowing that elections produce leaders with an independent political base.

It would be interesting to know what proportion of time is spent by various national heads of state on politics apart from programs and policies. Surely, the Indian Prime Minister would be high on such a list. It is not difficult to imagine what kinds of issues absorbed Mrs. Gandhi's attention that year: How should the government deal with the agitation in Assam against illegal migrants from Bangladesh? (How about forming a new government with a Muslim as chief minister?) How should the government respond to the agitation of farmers in Maharashtra and elsewhere for higher procurement prices and lower rates? (How about Rajiv organizing a pro-government rally of peasant cultivators in Delhi?) What should be done about the agitation among students in Gujarat against reservations for scheduled castes in the medical colleges? (How about offering caste Hindus an equivalent number of new seats to compensate for those that are put aside as reservations?) What these issues shared was not only the sharp and often violent social and political cleavages involving language, class, and caste, but also the extent to which the Prime Minister would have to devote her attention to these conflicts without the support and guidance of strong state party leaders. Indeed, in some instances—mostly notably in Maharashtra until the chief minister was forced to resign when a court ruled that he was guilty of charges of corruption—the Prime Minister intervened to keep state government chief executives in office.

No wonder the Prime Minister increasingly turned first to her son Sanjay and then to her son Rajiv. Succession was obviously central, but the Prime Minister also needed a trusted advisor who could help with local and state political issues that were increasingly becoming national.

That leads us to the second way in which contemporary Indian politics differs from the politics of the 1950s and 1960s: the increasing nationalization of electoral politics. One measure of how *national* politics has become is the extent to which the vote for the Congress swings in each state in accordance with the national results. In 1967, when the national Congress vote dropped from 1962, the party declined in twelve states. The national Congress vote went up in 1971, and fourteen states followed the trend. In 1977, when the Congress declined, thirteen states followed suit. Even more striking is the fact that in the 1971, 1977, and 1980 elections, twelve states and one union territory consistently conformed to the national trend, or, to put it another way, created the national trend. These included Karnataka, Maharashtra, Punjab, Himachal Pradesh, Orissa, Delhi, Madhya Pradesh, Rajasthan, Bihar, Uttar Pradesh, Haryana, Jammu and Kashmir, and Assam, and they contain two-thirds of the Indian population. Of the five major remaining 'non-conformist' states, Andhra Pradesh deviated from the national trend only once, while Gujarat, Kerala, Tamil Nadu, Tripura, and West Bengal broke with the national patterns in two, and sometimes all three, elections.

What accounts for the national trend? One factor is exposure to a common communications network that makes it possible for a large part of the electorate to share a common pool of information. Clashes, for example, between the police and Muslims in Uttar Pradesh, between backward castes and Harijans in Bihar, and a split within the Janata party in New Delhi, are quickly known throughout the country. To the extent that some religious, linguistic, caste, economic, and occupational groups share a similar political perspective, what happens in one portion of the community in one part of the country politically affects another portion of the same community elsewhere.

A second factor is shared national economic experiences as a result of the growth of a national market. Rising prices and food shortages are less local than they once were. In the 1980 elections, for example, the high price and shortage of sugar was a national, not local issue. Similarly, shortages of electric power, diesel fuel, and fertilizers have an impact on agriculturalists everywhere. Government policies on dearness allowances, bonuses for industrial labor, and procurement prices for the purchase of agricultural commodities affect classes that are geographically widely dispersed. The more monetized the economy, the more inflation has a national political impact.

Third, the separation of the national parliamentary elections from, the state assembly elections by Mrs. Gandhi in 1971 has had a nationalizing effect. Until that year the two elections were held simultaneously, with the result that factors affecting voting preferences for state assembly elections often influenced voting for national parliament (the reverse, incidentally, of the coat-tail effects in American politics, with national elections shaping local outcomes). This delinking of state and national elections made it possible for candidates to run as representatives of national parties, with national leaders, a national program, and a national campaign. One indication that delinking was an important factor is that even in the elections of 1967, which many observers described as a national election in which inflation, the balance of payments deficit, devaluation, and a widespread disillusionment with the Congress seemed to affect the entire country, the state voting patterns were erratic. While the national vote for the Congress declined from 1962 to 1967, the vote for the party actually increased in the states of Maharashtra, Madhya Pradesh, Rajasthan, Tripura, Haryana, Kerala, and Assam. But with the delinking of the parliamentary and state elections in 1971, most of these states followed the national voting trend in the 1971 parliamentary elections and subsequently.

While there are national electoral swings affecting most of the states, it is important to note that the variations from state to state in the strength of the Congress party were greater under Mrs. Gandhi than under Nehru. In West Bengal, Kerala, and Tamil Nadu, the Congress electoral position was consistently worse, while in Andhra and Karnataka, it was consistently better. Once again we are reminded

TABLE 9.2
Congress Party Vote by State (1962–1980)
(percent)

State	1962	1967	1971	1977	1980
Andhra Pradesh	48.0	46.9	55.8	57.4	56.2
Assam	45.2	45.8	57.0	50.6	—
Bihar	43.9	34.8	40.1	22.9	36.4
Gujarat	49.5	46.9	45.3	46.9	54.8
Haryana	40.3	44.1	52.6	18.0	29.3
Himachal Pradesh	56.7	48.3	77.0	38.6	50.7
Jammu and Kashmir	—	50.5	53.9	16.4	19.3
Karnataka	52.7	49.0	70.8	56.8	56.3
Kerala	34.3	36.2	19.8	29.1	26.3
Madhya Pradesh	39.6	40.8	45.5	32.5	46.5
Maharashtra	30.3	48.3	63.5	47.0	53.3
Manipur	26.0	32.7	30.1	45.3	23.0
Nagaland	—	—	39.5	48.3	—
Orissa	55.5	33.3	38.4	38.2	55.7
Punjab	41.9	37.3	45.9	34.9	52.5
Rajasthan	37.6	33.9	50.3	30.6	42.7
Tamil Nadu	47.4	41.7	12.5	22.3	31.6
Tripura	31.9	58.3	36.3	39.7	22.6
Uttar Pradesh	38.2	33.7	48.0	25.0	35.9
West Bengal	46.8	39.8	27.7	29.4	36.5
Delhi	40.0	38.8	64.5	30.2	50.4
India	44.7	40.7	43.6	34.5	42.7

that India has many different party systems, reflecting the varied social cleavages, class structures, and historical circumstances of each of the states. All they share is a national Congress party. It was the special circumstances of the Emergency—the fear by various state and regional parties that the government was bringing competitive party politics to an end—that temporarily produced a coalition, making many of the state party systems look alike. With the disintegration of the Janata, Indian politics returned to normal.

Policy Directions

Once Mrs. Gandhi was again in control of her party, of two thirds of parliament, and all the major states except West Bengal and Tamil

TABLE 9.3
Shift in Congress Vote by State (1967–1980)
(percentage points)

State	1967–1971	1971–1977	1977–1980
Andhra Pradesh	+8.9	+1.6	−1.2
Assam	+11.2	−6.4	—
Bihar	+5.3	−17.2	+13.5
Gujarat	−1.6	+1.6	+7.9
Haryana	+8.5	−34.6	+11.3
Himachal Pradesh	+28.7	−38.7	+12.1
Jammu and Kashmir	+3.4	−37.5	+2.9
Karnataka	+21.8	−14.0	−0.6
Kerala	−16.4	+9.3	−2.8
Madhya Pradesh	+4.7	−13.0	+14.0
Maharashtra	+15.2	−16.5	+6.3
Manipur	−2.6	+15.2	−22.3
Nagaland	—	+8.8	—
Orissa	+5.1	−0.2	+17.5
Punjab	+8.6	−11.0	+17.6
Rajasthan	+10.4	−19.7	+12.1
Tamil Nadu	−29.2	+9.8	+9.3
Tripura	−22.0	+3.4	−17.1
Uttar Pradesh	+14.3	−23.0	+10.9
West Bengal	−12.1	+1.7	+7.1
Delhi	+25.7	−34.3	+20.2
India	+2.9	−9.1	+8.2

Nadu, how did she use her power? Not well, her critics replied. She appeared to be spending most of her time on political matters and the remainder on hundreds of administrative decisions that cabinet members and officials were reluctant to make on their own. There were some changes here and there—fewer controls over investment and imports, some efforts to expand exports, some efforts to deal with the bottlenecks in coal production, electricity, rail transport, and the ports, and more attention to industry than to agriculture, as compared with the Janata government. Some observers suggested that these changes constituted an important new direction, especially the government's greater receptivity to foreign investment and its reported willingness to reduce government regulations and to provide greater incentives to private investment. But such shifts in policy had been a regular feature of India's planning process and involved no fundamental shift in direction, especially when compared with the kinds of major shifts that have occurred in some other developing countries. India today remains very much an administrative state.

The government also expanded allocations for development. The Indian bureaucracy is superbly equipped, technically and administratively, to do project planning. Few bureaucracies in the third world can equal India's in building a hydroelectric dam or irrigation project, or constructing a fertilizer plant, a MiG factory, or a plutonium reprocessing facility! But the government seemed ill-equipped to effectively coordinate investment decisions (or to allow the market to deal with the resulting bottlenecks), or to chart new courses. Pronouncements from the Prime Minister's office dealt more with the appointment of personnel than with new policies. Though Mrs. Gandhi's government ran the largest development program and the largest public sector in the non-communist world, she remained remarkably unconcerned with questions of economic policy.

There were plenty of issues that could have been addressed by the Prime Minister. In a review of the prevalent Indian economic policy, the *Economist* assailed India for its autarchic development policies that led successive governments to encourage import substitution, favor capital over labor-intensive industrial development, nationalize industry, and oppose foreign investment. The result was slow industrial growth, slow growth in industrial employment (especially since 1965), and protected and inefficient industries that were less productive than their counterparts elsewhere. Since planners emphasized new industrial investment, maintenance was neglected; inefficiencies in coal production and rail transport and poor maintenance in electric power plants kept electric supply below demand and slowed the pace of industrial growth and employment. Agriculture needed more irrigation, electricity, credit, and in some places land redistribution, if the boom affecting the Punjab, Haryana, and other Green Revolution areas was to spread to Bihar and eastern Uttar Pradesh. Failing or 'sick' companies were nationalized, with the result that limited government resources were used to sustain uneconomic enterprises. An Industries Development and Regulations Act required government permission to set up new industrial units or expand existing units, and firms were punished for setting up 'illegal' capacity—a policy that more often served the patronage needs of government than the needs of the economy. And a Monopoly Restrictive Trade Practices Act. intended to halt the spread of monopolies, served to limit the expansion of some of the country's most productive, profitable, and innovative firms.

In short, India's critics—and friends—believed that India had the potential to become a major grain producing and exporting country, that agricultural-led growth would provide an increase in consumer demand that could stimulate industrial productivity, that an influx of foreign investment would bring in new technologies, and that a major reduction, not merely cosmetic changes, in regulations and protection would stimulate more efficient production, but all of this depended upon the pursuit of a different strategy of development and the choice of new policies.

There was no evidence that Mrs. Gandhi, or any cabinet members or high officials, were rethinking fundamentals. Ideological commitments may have been a greater barrier than political constraints, though neither were as important as the simple fact that Mrs. Gandhi was not a policy-oriented leader. In the past when new measures were adopted, the reasons were purely political, for example, the nationalization of banks and the end of the privy purses for ex-maharajas. Mrs. Gandhi had been prepared to relax controls but had shown no inclination to rethink the question of the role of controls in the economy. As several observers noted, she was a leader with attitudes rather than policies, with a point of view rather than a coherent ideology. Politics, personnel, and administrative decisions were what drew her attention, not the larger questions of what new policies should be pursued. It would have taken a major economic crisis, not simply a change in cabinet personnel, to force the government to rethink economic policies.

There are at least three major sets of economic problems that will force the government to make politically difficult decisions in the next few years. The first of these is the growing balance of payments deficit, the result of rising oil prices, slow growth in trade, and growing dependence upon imports not only for petroleum and petroleum products, but also for iron and steel, aluminium, fertilizers, man-made fibers and yarn, paper, and even edible oils. Domestic oil production, though rising, has been able to meet only 40 percent of the country's requirements. Oil accounts for 48 percent of the visible import bill in contrast to 8 percent a decade ago.

The deficit in the balance of payments was nearly $3 billion in 1979–80 and was $5 billion in 1980–81. If the deficit grows and the country's exchange reserves are drawn down, India is likely to experience a foreign exchange deficit as it did in the 1960s, though probably not of the same magnitude. Under these circumstances, policy makers will try to increase exports and reduce imports through import substitution. Dependence upon external agencies for funding— the World Bank for long-term loans, the IMF for short-term relief— will grow. Invariably there will be disputes, particularly if the foreign exchange situation becomes serious enough for international donors to press for devaluation, the end of subsidies, or changes in policies. The question of private foreign investment, relatively dormant for some time, has already been raised, with a decision by the government to encourage investment by OPEC countries under more favorable terms. The need for an assured oil supply, for concessional payment terms, and for barter agreements (oil in return for grain, in the case of the Soviet Union), will be important considerations affecting India's policies in West Asia. Food grain production was 133.5 million tons in 1980–81 and could increase to 160 million tons by the mid-1980s. So one difficult choice for the Government of India will be whether a grain surplus should be used for expanding exports or for a politically popular food-for-work program. As the balance of payments deficit grows, some officials in the central government may want to use food exports for oil or military purchases rather than for rural works programs, while politicians in the states will pressure to continue these programs. Still others will want to use surpluses to keep food prices down. Moreover, should India increase its military purchases, the case for exporting food to pay for imports will be stronger. In the 1970s when India had both a surplus balance of payments and a food reserve, the government did not have to choose between exporting food for oil and arms or using food for rural employment, but it may be forced to make these choices in the 1980s. Only a substantial growth in domestic oil production can relieve the government of politically difficult choices.

The second political economy issue is the disparity between the prices of agricultural commodities and the soaring costs of agricultural production. In the last few years, peasants have become more concerned with the price and availability of agricultural inputs: chemical fertilizers, fuel for pump sets and tractors, electric power, warehouses and marketing facilities, irrigation, and credit. Farmers want procurement prices for produce at a price that will cover the cost of inputs and provide them with a profitable return on investment. As a class they want better terms of trade with the city—that is, agricultural prices that are commensurate with the cost of industrial goods that they buy for their use.

The Lok Dal has been the spokesman for this class in Uttar Pradesh, Bihar, Haryana, and Orissa. Since the elections the middle peasants have also become politically articulate elsewhere. In late 1980 there were peasant demonstrations in Maharashtra, Tamil Nadu, and Karnataka. One interesting feature of these agitations is that they were not organized by political parties but produced their own leaders.

Higher procurement prices are not easily provided by the government because higher food prices generate protests from industrial labor, the urban middle class, and the urban and rural poor. Leftist supporters (and critics) of the government are divided, some discrediting the middle peasantry by labeling them '*kulaks*' and 'capitalist farmers,' while others see in their protest a political potential. For the government all the solutions are painful. The country needs the energies of the middle peasantry, whose productivity is essential if the economy is to expand and exports grow, but the government finds it politically difficult to pass on the higher costs of production to consumers. The decision of the government in mid-1981 to import one-and-a-half million tons of wheat and 200,000 tons of sugar to keep prices down provides a clear indication of its preferences.

It is striking that it is the middle peasantry, not the landless agricultural laborers or poor marginal farmers, who are politically aroused. Outside of West Bengal and Kerala, the poorest agriculturalists have not been politically organized as have the middle peasantry. The prediction that the poor would not benefit from the Green Revolution has proved false, for many small farmers have adopted the new technologies, and more agricultural labor is employed where the new crops are planted. Inequalities may have grown, but absolute incomes for some of the poor have improved.

A third set of issues deals with the growth of middle class unemployment. Unemployment is linked to the high birth rates and declining mortality rates of the 1960s and the slow industrial growth of the 1970s and early 1980s. The high annual population growth rate of the 1970s, 2.2 percent, suggests that the problem will grow worse in the 1990s. But the problem of unemployment should also be seen in the context of expanding enrollments in secondary schools and colleges. The result is a higher educational level among the unemployed. The combined effect of rapid population growth and expanding education has been to create not a middle class, but middle class aspirants in search of white collar jobs.

One safety valve has been the export of educated manpower. Nearly a million Indians have migrated to advanced industrial countries, particularly to the U.K., the United States, Canada, and the Netherlands. Since 1973, another half million Indians, many of them unskilled construction workers, but also clerks, typists, nurses, doctors, managers, shopkeepers, foremen, accountants, skilled machine operators, technicians, and engineers, have found employment in the Middle East, particularly in the Gulf states. Most of the migrants have come from Kerala, Tamil Nadu, Punjab, Goa, Gujarat and Bombay, where education levels are high and there are traditions of emigration.

For the newly educated, among those social classes that have previously not been educated, opportunities for overseas employment are more limited, while the competition for employment within India is more acute. The problem, therefore, of educated unemployment is particularly severe in some of the less developed regions—in Assam, Orissa, the Telengana region of Andhra, and backward sections of Maharashtra, Madhya Pradesh, and Bihar. There is also an unemployment problem among the scheduled castes and scheduled tribes as their educational level has increased, although they are partially helped by the system of reservations. And there is now a growing demand from the sons and daughters of the backward castes, many belonging to the middle peasantry, who have graduated from the secondary schools and colleges, for non-agricultural white collar employment.

The employment demands by the newly educated take a variety of forms: for regional development, industries located in rural areas, and job reservations that can assure their social group a share of positions.[2] The educated unemployed do not, of course, form a single class. As members of particular linguistic communities, castes, and tribes, they turn to their community for political support with the result that demands often take an ethnic form.

The emergence of demands for reservations from the backward castes in Uttar Pradesh and Bihar were manifestations of this phenomenon. There are also signs of growing politicization among the

[2] For a study of the relationship between middle class unemployment and the system of job reservations, see Myron Weiner and Mary Fainsod Katzenstein, *India's Preferential Policies: Migrants, the Middle Classes and Ethnic Equality*, Chicago, University of Chicago Press, 1981.

emerging Muslim middle classes whose demand for the adoption of Urdu as an official language in various states has employment as well as cultural implications. And the backlash *against* reservations for the scheduled castes in Gujarat is an indication that the improvement of the lower castes is now seen as a threat by many members of the middle and upper castes.

In human terms the problem of unemployment among the newly educated is probably less acute than the larger problem of unemployment among the rural poor. But in political terms, it is often more serious since the middle classes are politically more articulate and have a capacity to rally large numbers of people to their cause by appeals to ethnic solidarity.

Conclusion

Mrs. Gandhi's government was thus faced with a series of gaps— between imports and exports, between agricultural prices and the cost of agricultural inputs, and between the rapid expansion of education and the slow growth of employment. Each of these economic issues created political challenges for the government, particularly since policies to deal with the political problems arising from these gaps often created political costs. Giving job reservations to one community, for example, generated political hostility from another; helping peasants hurt consumers; inviting more foreign investment evoked the anger of left nationalists.

The government could, of course, muddle through as governments often do. Several good monsoons that still further increased agricultural productivity would slow the inflation rate and stimulate demand for, and the production of, consumer goods. A more rapid development of offshore oil and an improvement in coal production would ease the energy and foreign exchange situations. If the agitations were confined to a few areas, then ad hoc political solutions could be possible. However, with the expansion of a market economy in agriculture and the growing trade linkages between India and the outside world, the economic problems and the policies the government adopted were often international or national, not regional or local.

If these economic problems grew, if they were accompanied by an increase in agitation, if neither the center nor the states could find political ways of managing these demands, if the level of violence increased, then within the bureaucracy, the government, and the Congress party there would be many to call for authoritarian measures. (The American aphorism, 'when the going gets tough, the tough get going,' seems appropriate.) In the mid-1970s a government led by Mrs. Gandhi failed to muddle through, and took recourse instead in authoritarianism. It was the growing centralization of power within the Congress party from 1972 to 1975 and a corresponding decline in the organization and popularity of the party within the states that set the stage for Mrs. Gandhi's decision to declare an Emergency. The reinstating elections of 1980 produced an even more fragile system of authority than was produced by the elections of 1971 and 1972. The Congress remained organizationally weak, and once again the Prime Minister was reluctant to allow political leaders with independent popular support to emerge in the states or at the center. At no time since Independence had the electoral standing of the governing party been so dependent upon a single person's popularity. The party desperately needed to have in the wings a nationally popular, vote-winning personality—hence, the interest in building up her son, Rajiv.

A combination of intractable economic problems, a fragile institutional structure for the management of political conflict, and a leadership that was not innovative continued to make the Indian political system vulnerable to authoritarianism.

Where will India go in the next few years? Will it shift to the right? To the left? Toward civil conflict or another Emergency? And economically, will it move toward an agricultural boom or a foreign exchange disaster? Can political scientists predict any better than economists, who, in the words of Paul Samuelson, have successfully predicted two of the last four major recessions?

Some lines of development seem more likely than others.

It is inconceivable that a country as poor, ethnically diverse, and politically open as India will not experience some severe economic and/or political crises—perhaps a drought-induced decline in agricultural productivity one year, a worsening of inflation, and political protest movements by peasant proprietors, landless laborers, industrial workers, backward castes, university students, religious minorities, regional malcontents, and other groups not yet heard from. So long as the central leadership prevents the emergence of powerful state leaders, instability in the states seems inevitable, and the center must spend much of its time mending state governments.

Political turmoil in the Hindi states, particularly Uttar Pradesh and Bihar, eroded Mrs. Gandhi's position in 1974–75 and led to the Emergency, and in 1976–77 to her electoral defeat. She kept a close watch on this region, and so will her son.

Corruption by party and government officials has grown, showing no promise of diminishing. This is an ever present problem in a system which generates scarcities through regulation, and whose political classes are able to extract resources from the regulated, either for personal gain or political use. Among the consequences are an erosion in the belief in administrative justice, an increase in conflicts within the Congress party for access to lucrative positions within governments, growing political intervention in the police and administrative structures, and a declining access of tax authorities to much of the country's economic activities.

Voluntary organizations, more developed in India than in most developing countries, partly because of the greater freedom allowed in India's open competitive political system, find that their operations are increasingly limited by a government concerned with their political loyalty. Legal action has been taken by the government against several Gandhian organizations, some of whose leaders are personally sympathetic to opposition parties. Government funding to voluntary organizations, especially those engaged in adult literacy, has been cut. Whether this foreshadows a major government campaign to constrict voluntarism and to discourage the growth of autonomous institutions in the society remains to be seen.

India's most productive classes remain frustrated by the existing set of economic policies and they will press hard on the fringes for change. The middle peasantry, the scientific/engineering community, the new entrepreneurial/management class—all three the product of India's increasingly modernizing economy and the growth of its educational system—are impatient with a leadership preoccupied with politics and a bureaucracy preoccupied with regulations.

There were no signs that this government would be innovative, either in domestic or foreign affairs. Its stance was a reactive one—to wait for a crisis, then try to cope with it. In domestic affairs there were no indications that the government was moving to the 'left' or to the 'right,' whatever these labels meant, for there were no indications of any significant policy movements at all. New policies were likely to be crisis induced or would await major shifts in the distribution of national political power.

IV. Stalemates, Crises and Attempted Reforms

10

India in the Mid-Seventies:
A Political System in Transition

Introduction: A Break from the Past

For nearly twenty-eight years, from 1947 to 1975, India was widely regarded as being among the few newly independent countries that had successfully maintained both a stable and democratic form of government. In June 1975, the Government of India declared a national Emergency, arrested thousands of members of opposition parties, suspended the right of *habeas corpus*, imposed censorship on the press, banned twenty-six political organizations, including militant groups on both the extreme right and the pro-Peking left, declared illegal the holding of public meetings, expelled numerous foreign journalists, and amended the Constitution to limit the power of the courts.

The government justified the Emergency by asserting that the opposition parties—barring the Communist Party of India which supported the government—had been resorting to extra-parliamentary and extra-constitutional methods to force the governing Congress

A lengthier version of this essay was previously published under the title 'Critical Choices for India and America' in Donald C. Hellman, editor, *Southern Asia: The Politics of Poverty and Peace*, Vol. XIII, Lexington Books, D.C. Heath and Company, 1976, pp. 19–78.

For commenting on an earlier draft of this essay and for discussions of various points made here, I am grateful to Jagdish Bhagwati, Paul Brass, Pran Chopra, Donald Hellman, Samuel Huntington, Mary Katzenstein, John Lewis, Joseph Nye, Lucian Pye, Kartikeya Sarabhai, George Verghese, and Nur Yalman. Many of my ideas were further honed at a meeting of Asianists and Washington officials held under the auspices of the Commission on Critical Choices.

party out of office. The government accused Jayaprakash Narayan, a leading opponent of the Prime Minister, of seeking to 'incite' the police and the armed forces to commit acts of 'indiscipline'. The government also blamed the opposition for seeking 'to disrupt the economy' through a nationwide railway strike.

Mrs. Gandhi's domestic critics and most foreign observers concluded that the Prime Minister acted less to meet a national threat than to meet a challenge to her own power. In mid-June 1975, the Allahabad High Court found Mrs. Gandhi guilty of violating the Representation of the People Act in her 1971 election campaign—not, ironically, on the major abuses that are widely practised (such as the illegal collection of 'black' or untaxed money by political parties from companies and individuals), but on a series of relatively minor technical violations of the law. A few days later, the Supreme Court gave her a 'conditional stay' until her appeal could be heard by the full court. The opposition parties, which had just defeated the Congress party in elections for the state assembly in Gujarat, announced that they would launch a campaign to have her resign. Five of the country's leading national newspapers also urged her to step down. On June 26, Mrs. Gandhi struck against the opposition, the press, and dissidents within her own party. Parliament was subsequently called into session to ratify the declaration of Emergency and to amend the electoral law retroactively so that the offenses committed by Mrs. Gandhi would no longer be illegal.

Mrs. Gandhi declared that she was acting within the framework of the law, since the Constitution of India permits the government to declare an emergency when the security of India 'is threatened by internal disturbances.' Moreover, within a few weeks parliament approved the Emergency as required by the Constitution; hence the arrests, restrictions on public assembly, and the press censorship were within the law.

Mrs. Gandhi's critics retorted that she had broken the rules, for never in the twenty-eight years of Indian democracy, not even during the wars with China and Pakistan, had the government clamped down so hard on the opposition or the press or ever arrested dissidents within its own party. Moreover, the manner in which she had proceeded—her decision to request the President of India to sign the declaration of Emergency before discussing the matter with members of the cabinet—suggested that the Prime Minister intended to take a series of measures to create an authoritarian structure that might not win the support of senior officials within her own government.

Within a few months it became clear that Mrs. Gandhi had fundamentally changed the Indian political system. Through a series of parliamentary acts, restrictions on the press were independent of the ordinances declared during the Emergency. The proceedings of both parliament and the courts were censored before appearing in the press, while the press was barred from publishing articles 'likely to excite disaffection against the constitutionally established government,' or to publish 'defamatory' writings against the president, prime minister and other key officials. A number of newspapers published by the opposition were closed by the government, including the Socialist *Janata*, the leftist *Frontier*, the Gandhian *Everyman's Weekly*, and the Jana Sangh Delhi daily, *Motherland*. The government consolidated the wire services, presumably to facilitate control over the collection and dissemination of both domestic and foreign news.

The government issued a series of ordinances empowering officials to arrest individuals without disclosing the grounds for detention or arrest—even before the judiciary. These ordinances were subsequently confirmed by a parliamentary act amending the Maintenance of Internal Security Act (MISA) so that the government would continue to possess the power to detain political prisoners without charges even when the Emergency ended.

The expansion of two institutions during the previous few years substantially facilitated the movement toward an authoritarian regime: the strengthening of central intelligence, and the expansion of centrally-controlled paramilitary forces.

An intelligence gathering unit was created within the Prime Minister's secretariat—the Research and Analysis Wing (RAW)—which provided the Prime Minister with her own independent source of political information. The expansion and consolidation of intelligence gathering facilitated the nationwide arrest of thousands of members of the opposition on the morning of June 26, and helped to keep control over the underground press that had emerged after the declaration of the Emergency.

With the expansion of the Border Security Forces and the Central Reserve Police, the central government acquired paramilitary forces independent of the defense ministry and the state governments. The government was thus able to impose the Emergency without the deployment of the armed forces.

The Prime Minister also made considerable use of India's limited television facilities. The Satellite Instructional Television Experiment (SITE) made possible the spread of television to thousands of villages, with television centers established in Amritsar, Bombay, Calcutta, Delhi, Lucknow and Madras. The Prime Minister appeared on television frequently during the Emergency and there was reason to believe that she was eager to see the dissemination of television receiving units throughout the country. The expansion of television would presumably enhance the government's capacity to influence the cities and countryside without depending on the local units of a weakening Congress party organization.

While it was clear that, temporarily at least, the Emergency meant the suspension of India's democracy, it was less clear what its economic effects would be. Were the economic improvements that accompanied the Emergency the typical initial effects of establishing an atmosphere in which fear motivates more efficiency and there is less corruption, or were there indications that the government was able to end the paralysis that had characterized the Indian political economy for the past decade?

India's fundamental political problem was that the governing elite was unable to move the country, either in the direction of greater economic growth or toward greater equity in income. Each major force in the political system had been carefully poised to protect its own interests. While the cumulative effect of this well-established balance was to provide India with a degree of stability that few other countries in the developing world had experienced, there were also no significant political forces for change. By arresting members of the opposition and dissidents within the Congress, censoring the press, and establishing emergency rule, the government hoped to set into motion forces that would break the deadlock. But neither the opposition, the press, nor even the dissident members of the Congress were responsible for the deadlock—in spite of the government's efforts to cast blame upon them. The opposition had been divided and its voice in both parliament and in the state governments had been limited, especially since the overwhelming Congress electoral victories of 1971 and 1972. And while it was true that the opposition parties had won considerable support from the urban middle class and the organized working class, and had supported strikes among workers in the railways and in other public sector industries, the growth of urban dissidence was probably more the consequence of inflation, declining personal income, and governmental corruption than the organizing skill of the opposition. The press, too, had been vocal, but it reached only a small fraction of the country, and its influence on government was in any event minimal. And the arrested Congress dissidents were largely in the left wing of the party, critical not of Mrs. Gandhi's policies but of her failure to implement them.

The Prime Minister's declared objective was to generate change through imposing a new sense of discipline that would lead the bureaucracy to work more efficiently, stir workers to increase productivity, prod state governments into carrying out land reform policies, eliminate hoarders and black marketeers and thereby bring down the prices of essential commodities, and in general improve the country's self-confidence. Indeed, during the early months of the new political order there was a noticeable improvement in government efficiency. Government workers came to office on time, the rate of inflation (which had been 30 percent per annum) dropped precipitously, food production rose, and industrial production and exports increased.

But how many of these changes could be attributed to the steps taken since the Emergency, as opposed to developments independent of the Emergency (such as the improved monsoon), or to policies that preceded the Emergency (such as anti-inflationary monetary policies initiated in 1974)?

A twenty-point program, which included promises to implement land reform, abolish rural debt, provide assistance to college students, encourage industrial production, end bonded labor, and eliminate corruption in government, was, in the main, welcomed. But it hardly represented any bold new measures to accelerate the country's modernization. A variety of new economic policies did, however, appear to offer incentives to the private sector to expand their investment and make greater use of their underutilized industrial capacity: the ending of compulsory bonuses for industrial workers irrespective of the profits of firms; the de-control of cement, steel, and other commodities; the simplification of regulations and licensing procedures; financial incentives to exporters and a loosening of import restrictions for spare parts and raw materials for industrial use; and reductions on both corporate and individual income taxes. But while these measures suggested that the Indian government was liberalizing its policies toward the business community (a paradoxical move for a government whose foreign policy was tilted toward the Soviet bloc and whose only support from the opposition was from the Communist party), the business community remained uneasy as to the government's long-term intentions.

Did these policies represent a fundamental shift in direction, or were they simply a short-term governmental response to low demand, excessive inventories, and the industrial recession? Would the government again impose restrictions and controls on the private sector, once there was an increase in investment, a more rapid expansion of the private as against the public sector, and an increase in private profits? Moreover, even with these concessions, the pace of industrial recovery (as of early 1976) remained slow.

Authoritarianism also threatened to unleash new forces unwelcomed by the government. The overthrow of Mujibur Rahman, the charismatic President of Bangladesh, by a right-wing military group only months after he had suspended democratic rights in his country, would remind the Indian Prime Minister that a repressive regime stimulates illegal behavior among political dissidents and conspiracies within the government. With the decline of legitimacy implied by the suspension of democratic rights, the Indian military, its tradition of being above politics notwithstanding, would have to be persuaded that the regime was more effective.

The prolongation of the Emergency seemed likely to create new forces. Some civilian critics moved underground; the more militant and organized among these could grow as the Emergency was prolonged. Conspiracies could develop within the governing Congress party, among members of the cabinet, within the Defense and Home ministries, the military, and the police. And if these underground movements and conspiracies grew, government was likely to tighten its exercise of power, convinced that it was even more justified in declaring and maintaining the Emergency. Authoritarianism thus attracts—and creates—new personalities: those with a conspiratorial mentality, as well as those who believe in the necessity of employing coercion against their critics and enemies.

Even if Mrs. Gandhi continued, as she had in the past, to skillfully tread through the mine field that she had by her own actions created, and successfully outmaneuvered her opponents not only within political parties but within the civilian, paramilitary, and military bureaucracies, what kind of legacy would she leave for her successors? While she had demonstrated a capacity to dismantle institutions which appeared to threaten her position in power (first the governing Congress party between 1969 and 1971, and then the opposition, the press, and the judicial system), it was unclear what political institutions, if any, would take their place.

In Mrs. Gandhi's view, these institutions— state Congress organizations with local leaders independent of the center, a hostile opposition, a critical press, and an independent judiciary—had impeded the movement toward a modern, socialist, equalitarian social and economic order. Like so many third world leaders she aspired to create a political order in which policies emanated from among her supporters in the national bureaucracy, were implemented by centrally appointed politicians and bureaucrats whose careers were dependent upon her support, and were backed by popular acclaim. The intermediate political institutions which process demands, stimulate dissent, and constrain government were to be dispensed with by intelligence and police surveillance. Had Mrs. Gandhi's policies unleashed the forces of productivity that are latent within India, then India would have come to resemble that handful of countries in the developing world that can be loosely described as authoritarian modernizing states; but if the government's policies did not unleash these productive forces, then India would have lost its democratic institutions and gained nothing in its place.

Stalemated Modernization: India in the Seventies

Since 1966, in all fields other than agriculture, India's attempts to modernize had been stalemated. Even the dramatic strides that India made in the late 1960s in agriculture had been halted, the casualty of drought and rising fertilizer and petroleum prices. Food production declined from a high of 108 million tons in 1970–71 to about a hundred million tons in 1974. Per capita foodgrain production in 1975, following an excellent monsoon, was still below the 1970 level. Stagnation in industrial development set in around 1965–66, notably in the public sector. And since the country was dependent on public industries to generate funds for other development projects, stagnation in the public sector affected the rest of the economy as well. Industrial growth during the Fourth Five-Year-Plan was only 4 percent annually. There were shortages of steel, power, coal, fertilizers, and food. Real per capita income had been declining since 1971, and in 1974 it was approximately at the same level as 1969–70. In 1974 inflation was running at 30 percent annually. Meanwhile, the population continued to grow at 2.2 percent a year, or more than a million persons per month.

Throughout 1974 and early 1975, there were reports from all over India reflecting the disarray in the economy. Six-and-a-half million tribals in Bihar were said to be near starvation in late 1974—many were trekking to nearby towns in search of food and employment; in West Bengal, the relief minister estimated that fifteen million rural people, especially landless laborers, were 'either starving or living on one meal a day'; in northern India an estimated fifteen thousand persons were reported as having died in a smallpox epidemic in late 1974; in Goalpara district, in Assam, several hundred thousand people were subsisting on wild roots and leaves.

Political and social tensions were mounting. In the city of Madras, local Tamilians launched demonstrations against migrants from the neighboring state of Kerala, who had taken 'their' jobs. In Delhi, ten companies of Border Security Forces were sent to disturbed areas of the old city where shops and houses were burned and dozens injured in communal clashes between Hindus and Muslims. In Patna, the capital city of Bihar, a demonstration of a half million persons marched on the state assembly to protest corruption, high prices, and food shortages. In Gujarat, student-led demonstrations against the state government led to the resignation of the chief minister, the establishment of central government rule over the entire state, and then new elections which brought a non-Congress coalition to power. A national protest movement against the government, led by Jayaprakash Narayan, an aged and ailing Gandhian, became the rallying point for much of the opposition to the government.

In the months prior to Mrs. Gandhi's declaration of a national Emergency, journalists described a political order that seemed incapable of arresting the economic decline. Ved Mehta, an Indian correspondent writing from New Delhi, described the country as a place in which 'fear, corruption and violence' had become a way of life. B.G. Verghese, noted editor of the *Hindustan Times*, wrote that the country was experiencing a 'moral rot,' that 'rising prices, shortages, corruption, adulteration, untaxed "black" money, economic stagnation, empty sloganizing, indecision, and mismanagement have bred cynicism, frustration, indiscipline, anger and violence.'

Few believed that the country was on the brink of revolution. 'Revolution is not round the corner,' wrote Verghese, for 'that too connotes a larger purpose, a central effort, direction. The alternative is riots, a slide to anarchy, the weakening of central authority, a petty warlordism, and external pressures.' And to those who said that things could not go on as they were, Ved Mehta approvingly quoted Galbraith as saying that India is a 'functioning anarchy.' Among both Indian and Western observers there was (and continued to be) a sense of fore-boding: India could either move in the direction of a major political transformation—a political revolution, praetorian takeover, an authori-tarian leaderhip—or, alternatively, slide steadily into greater corrup-tion, disorder, and some form of 'warlordism', decentralized units of authority that resist central control. Few observers saw the political structure as in a state of equilibrium.

While the crisis led some to conclude that 'something must be done' to break out of the stalemate, others, notably Philip Handler, presi-dent of the National Academy of Sciences, expressing a view widely shared by many in the West, concluded that the situation in South Asia was so hopeless that unless the West was prepared to take massive steps it would be more merciful to do nothing while using resources to assist other countries more likely to succeed. Thus, he argued, the humanitarian concept of aiding the neediest should give way to the more hard-headed goal of aiding those who have the bes. chance of survival and growth.

It was in this psychological environment that Mrs. Gandhi chose to arrest the opposition and suspend democratic rights. She blamed the opposition for politically exploiting the rising prices and food shortages which she attributed to external events beyond the control of the government and to the venality of hoarders and blackmarketeers), while the opposition parties naturally blamed the government for the mismanagement of the economy, for corruption, and for administrative ineffectiveness.

In the months before the declaration of Emergency, vocal and organized opposition to the government came from the most modern (some might say, the most privileged) sector of the country—the very groups which had provided Mrs. Gandhi political support in her battle for political power within the Congress party in 1969 and 1970. The Congress Working Committee, in a resolution supporting the decision of the Prime Minister to establish Emergency rule, pointed to the growth of 'organized strikes, go slow movements by government employees, railway employees and industrial employees . . . student agitations and indiscipline,' all urban-centered protest movements.

The establishment of the Emergency brought to an end—for how long it was not certain—strikes, student demonstrations, and protest movements, while there was an immediate improvement in the performance both of the economy and the administration. But the country's long-term problems remained.

Economic Performance in Retrospect

The performance of the Indian economy over the decade 1966–76 was disappointing. True enough, the economic upturn which took place in India after Independence was a marked change from the preceding period of extended stagnation, but India's long-term economic growth over a twenty-five-year period had hovered around 3.5 percent per annum, a little more than 1 percent per capita rise per year. Seen in historic terms, this was no mean accomplishment, not only for India, but even from the perspective of Western industrialized nations during their early years of growth. Nevertheless, it was far below the high growth that developing countries have achieved, far below what India was capable of doing, given both the human and natural resources of the country, and far below planned targets.

Two broad factors account for the low rate of growth: those dealing with India's external relations and a series of 'external' developments which government did not anticipate, and those that were internal, that is, those that were the consequences of choices made by the government of India that resulted in the misuse of India's resources to the detriment of its economic growth.

External Constraints

India experienced a substantial economic upturn in the 1950s: there was a modest expansion in agricultural production after more than fifty years of stagnation and a similar movement forward in industry and the development of infrastructures—hydroelectric power, irrigation, and transport. India's war with China in 1962 was a setback, not only because the war temporarily dislocated the economy, but because India then diverted a considerable proportion of its resources to expanding its army, enlarging its defense industries, and importing military equipment. The economy barely adjusted to these changes when war broke out with Pakistan in 1965. Again, there might have been an upturn had the country not experienced two years of drought that brought down food production, depressed industry, and generated a foreign exchange shortage and an overvalued currency.

In 1969–71, India's agricultural production increased as a consequence of the widespread adoption of new agricultural practices, particularly in the use of fertilizers and new high yielding varieties of grain. For the first time, India established a substantial food reserve. But the Bangladesh crisis in early 1971, the influx of millions of refugees into India, the war with Pakistan, all followed by rising fertilizer and petroleum prices and another two years of bad weather in northern India, arrested the growth of agriculture and forced India to use up its limited food reserves. In 1974, 80 percent of India's annual export earnings were spent on importing food, oil and fertilizers. Nearly a half billion dollars were spent on importing fertilizers. Again, India's economy spiraled downward with food shortages, industrial stagnation, inflation, unemployment, and a dwindling foreign exchange reserve made worse by growing debt repayments and declining aid. Thus, the failures in the performance of the Indian economy could partially be attributed to events largely out of the control of India's policy-makers.

Internal Constraints

How much of India's slow and erratic growth can be attributed to poor economic policy and governmental mismanagement is a matter of some controversy. India's public sector firms had not done well, suffering from (a) shortages of equipment, spare parts, materials, and power, (b) labor problems, and (c) inadequate industrial management. There had been production shortfalls in the two industries which together utilized 45 percent of the public sector investment in the Fourth Five-Year-Plan—steel and fertilizers. There was a high demand for both, and, it was argued, India should have been able to produce both at competitive prices. India had a sufficiently abundant supply both of coal and iron ore to become an exporter of steel, but with severe labor difficulties, power shortages, underproduction in coal, and poor management, steel production continued to remain far short of meeting the demand. As for fertilizer production, existing plants were used at less than 70 percent of capacity. Moreover, in spite of the rapid growth in demand, government had tended to move slowly in licensing new fertilizer plants. In 1972–73, India produced only 1.8 million tons, importing another 1.2 million tons to meet domestic demand.

Nor had the private sector performed well. A cumbersome system of industrial licensing tended to delay private investments, and, since 1969, legislation intended to prevent the growth of monopolies and the concentration of economic power hampered the expansion of larger firms, including firms that proposed to expand fertilizer production.

The import substitution policy pursued by India created protected domestic markets so that private firms did not aggressively seek export markets. Nor were Indian prices competitive with similar manufactured goods produced elsewhere in the world. There had been some efforts to move from an import substitution policy to a more export oriented outlook—by providing export incentives, and by depreciating the rupee in relation to other currencies. Over the previous two years, India's export earnings increased by 30 percent, but mostly as a consequence of higher world prices rather than an increase in export volume.

India's long-term growth rate in agriculture from Independence to the early 70s was 2.7 percent per year. There had been substantial fluctuations—some declining years and a few spectacular years—but the long-term trend continued to be moving slightly ahead of population growth. From 1972 to 1974, water shortages plus shortages of inputs—fertilizers, power for irrigation and mechanization, and improved seeds—pushed production downward. The fertilizer shortage might not have been so great if the government had accepted proposals made by private firms to enlarge fertilizer capacity, if the existing public sector firms were more productive, or if India had purchased larger quantities of fertilizer in the world market in 1973 rather than postponing purchases in the hope that prices would decline.

India's energy crisis, which hampered efforts to expand production both in agriculture and industry, was made worse by falls in hydroelectric power generation—the result of drought, machinery breakdowns, shortages of spare parts, strikes by engineers, and other labor difficulties. According to one estimate, the supply of electric power during the Fourth Five-Year-Plan increased at 6 percent per annum, while the annual demand grew at 11 percent.

The story was much the same in coal production. India has one of the world's largest reserves of coal, but coal continued to remain in short supply. Production targets had not been met, and there were problems in management and organization and a deteriorating labor situation. Moreover, as a consequence of problems in transporting coal by rail, supplies had not been delivered to industries when needed. Failures in coal production and distribution and in the supply of electric power had been major factors in the low level of productivity of India's industrial plants. If India were to have made greater use of its *existing* industrial capacity, there would have been a substantial increase in the availability of goods, a growth in savings, an expansion in government revenues, and an easing of India's domestic resource difficulties.

Domestic resource difficulties intensified in those years; again, both internal and external factors were responsible. The war with Pakistan, the need to care for Bengali refugees and to provide famine-struck Bangladesh with assistance out of India's limited food reserves, were all major setbacks in 1971 and 1972. Thereafter, two years of drought reduced the growth in tax revenues while increasing expenditures for drought relief. There were substantial pay increases to government employees, reflecting the greater capacity of government workers as compared to other sectors of the labor force to present organized demands for raises to meet the rising inflation. One consequence was that an increasingly smaller proportion of government resources was available for development expenditures.

The revenue position of the state and central governments improved in 1975. This was partially the result of inflation, and partially the consequence of a successful campaign to tax 'black' money by promising taxpayers that they would be free of prosecution and could pay lower tax rates if they voluntarily disclosed their untaxed income. For the first time in several years an increased proportion of government resources were available for development expenditures.

The more successful agriculturists whose income had risen remained largely undertaxed. The Indian Constitution precludes central government taxation on agricultural income, a power left exclusively in the hands of state governments controlled by the more prosperous farmers. The result was that state governments neither taxed agricultural income nor imposed 'betterment' levies, substantial irrigation and water use taxes, or other fiscal measures which would have ensured that peasants whose incomes had risen paid a larger share of taxes.

Unlike some low income countries, India's potential for rapid economic growth was high. India has coal reserves of 80 billion tons, while annual production remained less than 80 million tons a year. Some 10 percent of the world's high-grade iron resources are located in India, along with substantial deposits of bauxite, copper, diamonds, manganese, and phosphate. Its hydroelectric potential, especially in northern India, where there are assured runoffs from the Himalayan snows, is considerable and only marginally developed. While there had been substantial efforts to increase the installed capacity of power generating facilities, the achievements were well below targeted objectives. (In the Fourth Five-Year-Plan only half of the planned additions to capacity were actually built.) India's offshore oil deposits also continued to remain largely unutilized, though explorations in the Gulf of Cambay, north of Bombay, were underway. Studies suggested that India may have a substantial offshore petroleum reserve.

Finally, India's greatest productive potential, its enormous agricultural industry, remained one of the largest underdeveloped agricultural landmasses in the world. In the few areas where irrigation had been extended, and seeds, fertilizers, pesticides, and other inputs made available, production rapidly increased. But only 20 percent of India's agricultural land was assured of irrigation, and India's fertilizer consumption in 1972–73 was, as we have noted, only 3 million tons—a more than sixfold increase in a decade (from 477,000 tons in 1962–63)—but no more than Americans used for their lawns and golf courses. Per hectare application of fertilizers in India for 1970–71 was 13 kg, as against 749 for the Netherlands and 580 for New Zealand.

While India's failure to utilize her own resources effectively had been handicapped by external considerations—'external' including acts of nature, as well as wars with Pakistan and China, international price rises in fertilizers, petroleum, and food, and the unfavorable terms of trade for many of India's commodities—much of the responsibility lay with the kinds of policies adopted by the Indian government.

What weight one gives to 'external' rather than 'internal' factors shapes one's perspective of India's long-term economic prospects and the role which could be played through international transfers in accelerating India's development. This controversy also gave rise to a growing interest in exploring the political economy of growth, that is, in examining both the structure of power in the Indian political system and the ideological underpinnings of policies. This also leads us to consider why a country in which the growth rate has been so slow and erratic and income disparities have been increasing, succeeded in maintaining a stable and democratic political structure for so long, and, in turn, in what ways that political system created constraints on economic development. Such an analysis permits us to consider whether the shift toward a stronger center and an authoritarian government might offer the prospects of releasing new forces or generating new policies that could accelerate the country's economic development.

The Political Economy of Development

For many years India provided an extraordinary contrast between its economic failures and its political successes. While the leadership had not been skillful at coping with economic affairs, the tensions that elsewhere in the developing world led to unstable governments, praetorian regimes and civil war, were until 1975 effectively handled by India's political leadership within a democratic framework.

The Management of Ethnic Conflict

Consider, for example, India's success in the management of ethnic conflict since Independence. As is well known, India is a multi-ethnic society and, as in most societies with divergent races, tribes, languages, and religions, its ethnic conflicts have tended to take precedence over class conflicts. India has a dozen major languages, a large Muslim population (it is the third largest Muslim country in the world, and has more Muslims than any country in the Middle East), 35 million tribals and numerous castes.

In the mid-50s India appeared to be threatened by movements for the creation of linguistically homogeneous states. These conflicts took a variety of political forms: demands for secession, demands for autonomous, culturally homogeneous states, and demands for control over education and employment. Hardly a year has passed since Independence that one region or another has not been afflicted with ethnic conflicts—sometimes electorally, but more often in the streets, the bazaars, and in the fields. These conflicts were frequently perceived incorrectly outside India as a sign of the country's impending disintegration. Could a society with such enormous internal differences long endure, or would India join the lengthy list of moribund multi-ethnic empires that litter the history books—such as the Ottoman and Hapsburg empires? And would an authoritarian regime have been better able to manage these ethnic conflicts?

Viewed from a comparative perspective, India has not done badly in the management of ethnic conflict; certainly better than Pakistan's military regime that proved so inept at coping with the claims of the Bengalis, and certainly better than the Nigerians and several other ethnically-torn African states. Indeed, India's national leaders have demonstrated an almost instinctive feeling for when to be responsive and when to use force, and how best to negotiate political settlements that would reduce the level of conflict. Nehru successfully unraveled his way through the linguistic controversies of the 1950s, and while the creation of linguistic states was accompanied by a new set of problems, it successfully dissipated what threatened to be a long drawn-out period of linguistic conflict within more than half the states. Similarly, Mrs. Gandhi managed to resolve some of the tribal conflicts in India's northeast—areas where the Nagas and Mizos were engaged in armed revolts against the government—while elsewhere in India other tribes, though less violent, also demanded greater political autonomy. The Indian government appeared, in the main, to have had better success in coping with the tribes than the other states of southern Asia who have also had difficulties in dealing with the rebellious, militant, independent tribals that dwelt in the hill zones extending from northern Afghanistan, through northern Pakistan, northern India, the hill tracts of Bangladesh, the northern regions of Burma, and farther across Southeast Asia into Laos, Cambodia, and Vietnam.

Order-Maintaining Structures

At least three factors appear to have been particularly crucial in India's success in the management of ethnic conflict. One is related to the peculiarities of its social structure, the other to its political structure, and the third to the organization and use of political intelligence.

India is a highly segmented social system. Each state has its own peculiar ethnic configuration. Conflicts within a state—ethnic or otherwise—do not readily affect most of the other states. The demands of a linguistic or tribal group in one state, either for autonomy or for more services, ordinarily do not affect demand-making in other states, that is, not to the extent it would if the ethnic group resided in many states and the country had a highly developed system of mass communication. For this reason, government can handle one conflict at a time without having to face the kind of massive national problem that was experienced by both Nigeria and Pakistan. The government's handling of conflicts in Assam has had little impact on Kerala or Andhra, and while the government must take precedent into account, it is often free

to choose a solution that seems to be politically appropriate in one region while opting for quite a different solution elsewhere. Thus, the government accepted the demands for statehood by some tribes but not by others, and acceded to the demand for a separate state by the Sikhs in the Punjab, but rejected a similar demand by the Telengana region of Andhra.

The democratic and federal system lent itself well to the management of ethnic conflict. The federal arrangement permitted the central government to provide political autonomy to groups that had territorial contiguity and political cohesion, without jeopardizing the powers of the central government. The democratic system, by making it necessary for party leaders to be responsive to groups with electoral power, made political leaders sensitive to acutely felt concerns. National and state leaders also learned to dissipate demands by coopting the leaders of ethnic communities. By giving posts within the party or government to dissident tribal leaders, Muslims, scheduled castes, and minority leaders in each of the states, the Congress party was also able to attract leaders who could often ensure that their followers would continue to vote for the ruling party, election after election. Thus, by satisfying the desire of leaders of minority communities for sharing power and wealth, the governing party at a relatively low cost has been able to maintain the political loyalty of low income communities.

In assessing the capacity of India's political leadership to cope with ethnic conflicts—or, for that matter, any kind of political conflict including trade union-management conflicts, agrarian conflicts, and party and factional struggles—one should not underestimate the importance of intelligence gathering services or law enforcement institutions. Through the Home Ministry, the central government has been able to keep remarkably well-informed as to what has been happening in any part of this large country. Some of India's most capable administrators have spent a substantial part of their career in the Home Ministry; the Ministry is itself in charge of personnel appointments and transfers for the entire central government, so that it has the first pick of talent within the senior administrative cadre. It is the Home Ministry, working with the Prime Minister, that had responsibility for the management of the states reorganization controversy, for the integration of the princely states into the Indian Union, for the management of the tribal areas, for central government policy toward Kashmir, for intelligence gathering on the frontiers, for decisions concerning the takeover by the central government of unstable states, and for the intelligence and police activities involved in counterinsurgency activities (from the Communist insurgency in Hyderabad in the late forties to the pro-Chinese Naxalite movement in the late sixties and early seventies). Moreover, while the police services are under the control of the state governments, there are central reserve forces and a number of other special police units that are directly under the management of the Home Ministry of the central government. The Indian constitution provides that in the event a state is politically unstable or is unable to maintain law and order, the central government may take control over a state and establish 'President's Rule,' or, in effect, rule by the central administrative services. Since it is the Home Ministry that takes primary responsibility for state governance in the event of President's Rule, Home Ministry officials have a special authority in relationship to state governments not possessed by other central government ministries.

The skill with which the Indian political leadership balanced competing interests and claims, assessed the electoral power of those who made claims, coopted dissidents, and reached out into the countryside for political support has been quite extraordinary. No doubt the capacity—both through the Home Ministry and the Congress party—to acquire political intelligence, the coercive instruments at the government's disposal, and the many resources with which government can reward those who support it and which it can deny to those who do not, are all elements in this skill. Nonetheless, there is an added, not easily defined element of political acumen—a kind of sensitivity to the political marketplace that Nehru, Shastri and, until mid-1975, Prime Minister Gandhi displayed. Should India be governed by an authoritarian regime, its capacity to be responsive to competing claims and to cope *politically* with secessionist movements may well decline, thereby forcing government to rely more heavily than in the past upon its coercive powers.

Mrs. Gandhi's Government

Mrs. Gandhi took office in 1966, a year of drought and famine, when India was dependent upon the United States for food imports. The devaluation of the rupee failed to arrest India's declining share of world trade while it further eroded the popularity of the governing Congress party. The Congress party failed to win a majority of seats in half of the state legislative assemblies, and won only a precarious majority in Parliament in the 1967 elections. There followed an intense conflict between the Prime Minister and the state and national Congress party leaders, a struggle that ended with a split in the Congress party and an electoral triumph for Mrs. Gandhi's Congress in the special national elections of early 1971. This victory was reconfirmed in the state assembly elections in 1972 when Mrs. Gandhi's Congress swept all the states, even West Bengal where the Communists had earlier undermined Congress dominance.

Mrs. Gandhi's emergence as a powerful national leader, in some respects even more powerful than her father, was accompanied by the pursuit of a populist set of policies. She abolished the special privileges of the former princes, nationalized the country's major banks, passed a Monopolies Act to regulate the activities of some 800 large firms, and nationalized the wholesale trade in wheat. Simultaneous to her attacks on the wealthier strata, Mrs. Gandhi promised to adopt measures to provide greater wealth and income to the lowest 40 percent through land redistribution, the extension of credit, irrigation and seeds to dry areas thus far not affected by the Green Revolution, and public works to increase rural employment to agricultural laborers. But little of this program was adopted, partly because of the resource bind of the central government, and partly because the state governments did not support many of her proposals.

At the risk of vastly oversimplifying India's complex politics, one can say that two groups within the states limited what Mrs. Gandhi's government could do: the land-owning peasant proprietors and the middle class with its dominant position in the state bureaucracies. The peasant proprietors were eager to prevent the passage of land reform legislation that would transfer land from the larger landowners to agricultural laborers and tenants, and when state governments imposed ceilings on land-holdings, landowners were typically able to find ways to evade the implementation of the legislation. The peasantry was also concerned with preventing state governments from imposing agricultural income taxes upon them, and they were able, through their influence on the state governments, to oppose proposals to transfer such taxes to the central government. Agriculture thus remained the least taxed sector of the Indian economy.

The middle classes wanted an expansion of the public sector because of the employment opportunities they believed such an expansion would provide while members of the bureaucracy continued to press for higher wages, though this was accompanied by deficit financing and the growth of non-plan expenditures. At the insistence of the middle class, the government invested heavily in higher education (to the proportionate neglect of primary and secondary school education), provided low rent housing for government officers in urban areas, and kept urban taxes low.

A third group, the business community, was much abused by government as a source of corruption and as an opponent of many of Mrs. Gandhi's policies (such as the nationalization of the grain trade), but it was, in fact, much more limited by government than it imposed limits upon government. The business community was forced to work closely with the bureaucracy in order to obtain contracts and licenses— to open or expand a plant, to import machinery or spare parts, even to purchase raw materials for production. The degree of dependence upon the government was illustrated by a study conducted by the Planning Commission which reported that on the average it took 460 days to obtain a license to import capital goods. The study also estimated that it took nearly four years for an Indian businessman to run the gamut of government regulations to start a business. The businessman may eventually earn a high profit—given India's protected market and protected prices—but the opportunity costs to the economy from delays are staggering.

In this highly regulated environment the businessman had to work closely with both the local bureaucracy and the governing party, corrupting the one while also providing financial support for the electoral campaigns of the other. The political leadership might have been ideologically critical of the business class, but the party and the bureaucracy, especially at the state level, found the relationship profitable. Between the business community and the government there was thus a symbiotic relationship.

Paradoxically, the strengthening of Mrs. Gandhi's authority in the center was accompanied by declining stability in the states. Between 1965 and 1973, twenty-two state governments collapsed and were taken over by the central government through President's Rule, while in the previous sixteen years, these emergency powers were utilized only ten times. In a substantial number of instances, President's Rule was established because of internal factional conflicts within the governing Congress party. In Uttar Pradesh, factional conflicts following a police mutiny against the state government in 1973 resulted in the resignation of the chief minister, while in Andhra regional conflicts

within the state took such a violent turn that the central government sent in the military and suspended the state government. In 1974, factional conflicts in Gujarat, combined with charges of corruption and governmental mismanagement, resulted in the resignation of the chief minister, the establishment of President's Rule, and new elections, which brought a non-Congress government to power.

Few of the states had political leaders powerful enough to keep party factionalism under control, as was the case when Nehru and Shastri were Prime Ministers. Mrs. Gandhi's assertion of national leadership was made possible, not through the consensus of state leaders, but through her success in eroding the political position of many of the state leaders. But by politically eliminating those who threatened her, she also removed from positions of influence the very men who, for so many years, were able to maintain leadership in the states. The state leaders who replaced these men were largely chosen by, and were therefore beholden to, Mrs. Gandhi. This may have strengthened her national position, but these leaders were often politically impotent in dealing with conflicts within their own areas.

Of the three major social groups at the state level, neither the peasants, nor the bureaucracy, nor the business community were necessarily damaged by the breakdown of state governments and the establishment of central government rule, for their interests were likely to be respected by the central government. Superficially, the instability of state governments would appear to be a political problem, but in fact there was a careful balancing of forces that continued even when a state government was unstable. It was, however, a balancing of forces that tended to impede rather than facilitate social change.

The business community was able to make its profits, create untaxed wealth, and protect itself against stringent taxation, but it had not been free enough to play an expansive role in the economy. The bureaucracy had not demonstrated that it could run the public sector profitably or productively, but it could impose restrictions on the expansion of the private sector, limit the investment of the larger industrial houses, and, with the support of the left, threaten to nationalize industries. The peasant proprietors, at least those who lived in areas with assured irrigation, demonstrated their ability to substantially raise agricultural productivity, but they were politically able to resist efforts to impose an agricultural income tax. It was this balance of forces that created limits on India's capacity to tax, to raise the rate of savings, expand investment, and thereby substantially increase economic growth. And it was this same balance of forces that limited the capacity of government to achieve a more equitable distribution of wealth and income.

Economic failure was not, in itself, likely to lead to a major restructuring of Indian economic policy. The government was committed, rhetorically at least, to a policy of economic growth, equity in income, self-reliance, and socialism. 'Socialism'—by which is meant a large public sector, heavy state control, and regulation of the private sector—was not viewed by the Indian leadership as the *means* for achieving the goals of growth, equity and self-reliance, but was itself a goal of policy. The country's intelligentsia (for ideological reasons), the political leadership (for reasons of patronage), and the bureaucracy (for reasons of self-interest), were committed to an extension of state power into the economy and tended to be critical of moves to expand opportunities for private investment.

Political Order with Economic Stagnation

The non-Congress opposition parties pointed to their victory in the Gujarat state assembly elections of June 1975 as an indication that the Congress had nationally lost its mandate. Though there had been a substantial increase in political protest in India's urban areas throughout 1975, it was nonetheless striking how successful the regime had actually been in maintaining political support in the face of a declining economy, substantial unemployment, a high rate of inflation, food shortages, and corruption at high levels. But if the Indian political system had been stable in spite of the low growth rate, it could also be argued that the policies that were conducive to maintaining stability also contributed to the low growth rates and to the low levels of equity.

What precipitated Prime Minister Gandhi's decision to suspend the democratic process was her defeat, not by the electorate or her own party, but by the Allahabad High Court when it ruled that she had violated the election law and had to relinquish her seat in Parliament, and hence her position as Prime Minister. Though her appeal was pending before the Supreme Court, the opposition parties, led by Jayaprakash Narayan, declared that they would launch a national movement for her resignation. The agitation was evidently intended to build up popular support for the non-Congress parties and to strengthen their organizations in preparation for the forthcoming national elections, but Mrs. Gandhi chose to interpret their actions as a move to bring her and her government down even before the elections. She pointed to statements by opposition leaders calling upon the army and the bureaucracy not to obey 'illegal' acts of government as a call for subversion and rebellion. Whether the army or the bureaucracy would have actually disobeyed government orders is uncertain, but what is clear, however, is how successful India's national leadership had been in maintaining the support of the military and the bureaucracy, along with their own Congress party, and the importance of these three institutions in maintaining a durable central government.

The military had been well-nurtured by the government, especially after the military defeat by the Chinese in 1962. Until then, India spent less on defense than almost any major country; but since 1962, there had been a massive expansion of the army and navy and the development of defense industries. Moreover, the government readily deployed the military for internal security when neither the state government nor the central reserve police seemed adequate to meet threats of internal disorder. In the years just preceding, the central government used the army to curb violence in the Brahmaputra valley of Assam, in the Naga and Mizo hills, and in the Telengana region of Andhra. The readiness of the regime to utilize the military had not, as elsewhere, politicized the military, but apparently had ensured the regime of the military's support.

In spite of the efforts by the Indian government to recruit more broadly and from a wider range of castes, ethnic groups, and regions into the Indian army, the army still drew heavily from what were once characterized as the 'martial' races, and many soldiers belonged to military families whose fathers and grandfathers had also served. As Stephen Cohen in his study of the Indian army points out, electoral politics enabled representatives of these martial classes—the Sikhs, Jats, Rajputs and Dogras—to resist broadening the recruitment into the army. But since 1965, there has been a considerably wider recruitment into the officer corps, leading to more multi-caste, multi-regional and multi-ethnic units.

While the Indian army, like the Pakistan army of the 1950s and early sixties, emphasized its non-political outlook, the military remained out of politics largely because of its acceptance of Indian political authority as legitimate and its recognition that the Indian government has by and large been successful in maintaining a strong center, deterring secessionist movements, and sustaining law and order. But the officer corps was imbued with a strong technocratic sense, and, like a substantial part of India's educated classes, would have liked to see a stronger center, a corruption-free leadership, and a more efficient administration. Each of these factors was likely to be weighed against their disposition not to intervene in political affairs, particularly if the legitimacy of civilian authority should be undermined by a governmental decision to suspend the electoral process.

The morale of the military, greatly weakened by its defeat by the Chinese in the 1962 war, was restored by the military accomplishments of the 1965 war with Pakistan, and again, with the overwhelming Indian military victory in the 1971 war over Bangladesh. With its national outlook, its professionalism and concern for efficiency and its generally high self-regard, the military was a potent force behind the government—but a potentially dangerous one, should it have turned against the government.

The expansion of paramilitary forces, especially the Border Security Force and the Central Reserve Police, was intended to reduce the dependence of the central government on the regular Indian army. But while expenditures on these police forces reportedly doubled between 1969 and 1971, the army continued to play the major role in the maintenance of internal law and order, not only in Kashmir and in the states of northeastern India, but also elsewhere in the country. On one occasion, army units were used to disarm a rebellious Provincial Armed Constabulary in the north Indian state of U.P., when police units sided with the students, then demanded pay increases. The clash, the first of its kind since Independence, raised the spectre of future conflict between the army and paramilitary police forces. How the military was likely to respond to a decline in the legitimacy of the Prime Minister, to an expansion in the use of paramilitary forces, or to its own use in coping with domestic disturbances, were questions of considerable importance for the government.

While the Prime Minister justified the declaration of Emergency on the grounds that the opposition had sought to instigate rebellion within the army and police, it was the improvement in the performance of the administration that was most often cited by government to support its claim that the country had benefited from the Emergency. According to the government, there was a marked decline in administrative corruption, officers reported to work on time and remained at their desks throughout the day, trains and airplanes departed and arrived on schedule, and there were no more strikes in the public sector. Moreover, the government claimed that many of its programs—

land reform, the distribution of housing sites to the landless, anti-smuggling and anti-hoarding programs, improved tax collection—were all being implemented by the administrative services.

The powers of the civil bureaucracy markedly increased under the Emergency. Indeed, the decline in the power of members of Parliament, the state legislators, and local Congress officials meant a corresponding increase in the powers of the civil service. The senior civil servants had a freer hand in dealing with recalcitrant or inefficient junior officers who, in the past, had been able to turn to elected officials or party leaders to protect themselves against senior officers. One result was that after the Emergency was declared the government was able to dismiss many civil servants, mostly through retirement.

How far the government was able to implement the twenty-point program was a matter of conjecture, but one point was noteworthy: the twenty-point program was itself the program of the bureaucracy, especially of members of the Prime Minister's own secretariat and selected officers within key ministries of the central government.

Probably no group in India was as supportive of the Prime Minister and of the Emergency as the country's bureaucrats. For one thing, the civil service continued to be well-nurtured by both central and state governments, which provided officers with low-rent housing, special low-interest loans, educational facilities for their children, cost of living allowances, and tenure of employment. For another, as we have noted, the Emergency diminished the power of those who were elected and increased the autonomy of government officials. Resentful of 'too much politics' and 'interference,' senior bureaucrats were then free to carry out their favorite programs.

One such program was a campaign, launched by officials of the Delhi Development Authority, to clear Delhi of its unauthorized dwellings. An estimated 43,000 dwellings containing a quarter million residents were moved from the city. In the past, slum clearance programs aimed at removing squatters were opposed by municipal councilors, who defended their voters against proposals by administrators to clear unsightly slums to improve the appearance of the city. With the suspension of the Delhi Municipal Corporation by the government, the officials were able to carry out their program. The government claimed that the uprooted residents were all adequately re-located on the outskirts of the city, but the critics remained skeptical, especially since the censor barred one newspaper from continuing its series of articles on the re-location program, and questions raised by opposition members of Parliament on the subject were banned by press censors.

For nearly three decades the Congress party was the third part of this institutional triumvirate which formed the basis for the stability and authority of the Indian political system. To those who joined, the party offered a share of power, the status, and sometimes the financial gain that went with holding political office. An historian of eighteenth and early nineteenth century agrarian India once described India's land system as one based upon reciprocity and redistribution, a system in which those who had access to the wealth of the land shared portions of that wealth with others on the basis of services provided to them in turn. A similar pattern of exchange prevails in the contemporary political system. Those who wield power and wealth within government share that power and wealth with circles of supporters. It has been an open system which has permitted previously non-participant social classes, castes, tribes, and linguistic groups to demand and then receive a share of power. But in a system of severe scarcity, sharing has often been with the leadership of potentially dissident groups rather than with the rank and file. The cooptation of elites is a comparatively inexpensive way of sharing power.

What can be most readily shared are the resources of government—jobs, social programs, educational funds, etc. What is protected are those interests vital to each portion of the coalition. Hence, the absence of effective land reform and the low incidence of agrarian taxation can be understood by noting the political influence of the peasant proprietor classes; the inadequate managerial performance in the public sector can be understood by considering the way in which the administrative sectors have taken over the public sector and the desire of the bureaucratic management to preserve bureaucratic procedures (seniority in preference to merit, regularization of procedures rather than innovations and risk-taking, price fixing to avoid competition, and performance criteria that excludes profit-taking and market performance).

Thus, India has had a stable coalition which could govern the country, but which could not accelerate economic growth or distribute income effectively. The coalition was not necessarily threatened by poor economic performance so long as its relative status and income remained secure. What has been important to India's dominant social-economic groups is the share of status and wealth which they acquired, not absolute growth. Moreover, during a period of economic stagnation and decline, the regime has been particularly careful to preserve the position of its supporters; hence during inflation, pay raises for the bureaucracy have been a high priority; during food shortages, special efforts were made to provide food at fixed prices to government employees; the wealthier peasants have had first claims on fertilizers and irrigation; educational targets for primary schools could not be met, but expenditures on higher education for the middle classes continued to rise; unemployment grew, but state governments gave employment preferences to 'local' members of the middle classes (as opposed to migrants from other regions). The system by no means satisfied all its supporters—the level of discontent and cynicism even among those social classes that supported the regime had been very high and was growing—but yet there was no large-scale shift to more radical alternatives.

Moreover, those who govern and, to a large extent, even those in opposition to government, share many assumptions concerning the nature of the social, economic and political order. For one thing, there are few educated Indians who believe that India is likely to enter a period of accelerated growth. It is this acceptance of a steady state economy or slow growth that places a premium on finding ways to share what is available more equitably, rather than on undertaking measures to accelerate the pace of economic change. Another shared viewpoint is a deep belief, almost religious in its dimensions, that a well-ordered society is one in which individuals perform their duties and avoid conflict. In a good society, educated Indians believe, each social group is entitled to some 'appropriate' proportionate share of both goods and status: equity, not equality, is the moral foundation of such a social order. While the concept of equality suggests that everyone is to have equal access to opportunities (implying thereby a competitive system) or equality of condition (implying the absence of hierarchy), equity suggests that each social group should have some socially-defined share. Thus, those who are downtrodden (scheduled castes, tribes, minorities) are entitled to a larger share of 'seats' in colleges and universities, a larger share of appointments in government service, and reserved 'tickets' for election to public office.

Another expression of this viewpoint is in the regulation of monopolies by the Indian government. While in the United States monopoly regulations are adopted by government with the intention of freeing the marketplace for greater competition, in India such legislation is intended to protect smaller businesses by ensuring them a share of the market. Similarly, government prefers to license small firms to produce textiles, fertilizers and automobiles, rather than license large firms where economies of scale might prevail, and then it fixes prices so that one firm does not drive out another.

Competition within the work situation is also discouraged. Merit promotions are not wholly absent within the administrative system, but, ordinarily, those who are employed are rarely dismissed, promotions are routinized, and there are few opportunities to move from one level of the administrative system (for example, from non-gazetted to gazetted positions) to another, since the education system certifies (in the way caste traditionally did) the place one can rightfully expect within the job market.

In the midst of India's turmoil and conflict, violent upheavals, and electoral struggles, one cannot but be struck by the extraordinary regularity of the Indian social order, the durability of India's institutions, the social conservatism of its leadership, and the consensual character of its belief systems.

Conclusion

While in its rhetoric the government could have shifted to the left, within the government there were strong pressures for a more conservative economic policy. Many in the government recognized the dangerous parallels between the problems of the mid-seventies and those experienced by the government in 1967: both were periods of agricultural stagnation, industrial slowdown, high inflation, and a time of cyclical decline for the Congress party. In 1967, as in the mid-seventies, the opposition parties were strongly motivated to build electoral coalitions to prevent the Congress from winning seats with a plurality. In both periods, the opposition sought to undermine the position of the Congress with the urban electorate, especially the middle class bureaucrats, the intelligentsia, and the labor unions.

Keeping the lid on inflation, improving the food supply, increasing urban employment—in short, some marked improvement in the economy particularly as it affected urban India—were critical if the government was to avoid a recurrence of the turmoil of early 1975. For this reason many members of the government, especially within the Prime Minister's secretariat, pressed for increased expenditures for agriculture (including irrigation), greater incentives for the private sectors, the non-enforcement of the Monopolies Act, a loosening of import restrictions, providing greater incentives to exporters, even encouraging foreign investment. This group, while accepting the existing socialist rhetoric, would rely more heavily on the marketplace and would be less doctrinaire about the role of domestic or foreign private investors. While maintaining a low profile politically, they would seek increased World Bank and International Development Agency (IDA) support, noting that only an improved economy could halt the decline of the Congress party and the strengthening of the Communist party, or greater authoritarian moves by the government in an effort to avoid both.

'Judging by all objective indicators,' declared Finance Minister C. Subramaniam in a speech to Parliament a few weeks after the Emergency was declared, 'the Indian economy is now poised for a major phase of rapid economic expansion.' He went on to predict a doubling of the industrial growth rate to 5 or 6 percent per year, a rise in food production to 114 million tons, a 20 percent increase in power generation, a rise in coal production by ten million tons, a 40 percent growth in fertilizer production, and a growth of saleable steel from 4.9 to 5.7 million tons within a year. In an equally optimistic statement, the Petroleum and Chemicals Minister, K.D. Malaviya, reported that the country would be self-sufficient in oil within five years, as a result of current offshore and onshore explorations and development (*Overseas Hindustan Times*, August 14, 1975).

Outsiders remained unimpressed, for such optimistic predictions had been made before. In a political economy marked by elaborate bureaucratic regulations, hostility to the business community, anxiety over foreign investment, an inefficient public sector, influential landlords, and corruption within both the administration and government, would the expansion of the powers of the Prime Minister be enough to change the country's direction?

11

Rajiv Gandhi:
A Mid-Term Assessment

Introduction

To the acclaim of India's middle class and much of the world's media, Rajiv Gandhi in his first year as Prime Minister set forth a new agenda for India: to embark on a new economic policy that would accelerate India's industrialization and economic modernization, to reconcile the concerns of India's restive linguistic, religious, and tribal communities with the need for national integration, to improve relations with India's regional neighbors, and to restructure the governing Congress party. By his third year in office, the economic reforms, though accompanied by signs of economic growth, were faltering, conflicts among ethnic communities showed no signs of abating, India's relations with its neighbors had deteriorated, and party reform had fallen by the wayside. Worst yet for a political leader, the governing Congress party, which had triumphed in parliamentary elections in December 1984 and state assembly elections a few months later, had lost assembly elections in eight states—Assam, Andhra, Karnataka, Kerala, Haryana, Mizoram, Punjab, and West Bengal—and had maintained a foothold in state elections in Jammu and Kashmir only by allying itself with a popular regional leader. Rajiv Gandhi's hold on his own party, on the bureaucracy, on the middle class that had initially embraced him, and on the electorate, had plummeted, his own future and that of his party for the parliamentary elections in 1989 were now clouded, and the agenda he had set for the nation seemed to be getting nowhere.

An earlier version of this paper appeared in Marshall M. Bouton, ed., *India Briefing 1987*, published by Westview Press for the Asia Society, New York, 1987.

To what extent this rapid political descent was the result of Rajiv Gandhi's failure to demonstrate leadership skills, or whether the Indian situation and system makes leadership initiative increasingly difficult and uncertain, are central issues in assessing whether a political recovery is possible and more broadly, whether major reforms in the near future are likely. To answer these questions, we need to examine how Rajiv Gandhi became Prime Minister, how he set about seeking to carry through his agenda, what were the challenges to his leadership, and what qualities he brought to bear to deal with these challenges.

The Path to Power

The story of Rajiv Gandhi's rise to power is too well-known to recount in any detail here. Suffice it to say that prior to June 1980 Rajiv Gandhi was not a political figure. The eldest son of Prime Minister Indira Gandhi, and older brother to Sanjay Gandhi, Rajiv Gandhi led a quiet, private life as a pilot for Indian Airlines. His major ambition, it was said, was to pass the examinations that would enable him to fly 747s. Though both brothers, with their families, lived in the private residence of the Prime Minister, it was Sanjay Gandhi who regarded himself, and was regarded by others, as the heir apparent to the office of prime ministership. With Sanjay's death in a daredevil plane crash in June 1980, the Congress leaders pressed Rajiv to step into his brother's political shoes. For nearly a year he resisted entering politics, supported, it is said, by his Italian wife Sonia. He 'helped' his mother, but remained out of public life. With some of Sanjay's supporters pressing Sanjay's wife, Menaka, to stand for his seat for Parliament, Rajiv came under growing pressure from opponents of Sanjay's faction to stand on the Congress ticket. In June 1981, Rajiv ran for Sanjay's vacant parliamentary seat; with his victory, he was widely regarded as the most likely successor to Mrs. Gandhi as leader of the Congress party and as her successor as prime minister.

The dynastic character of the succession process was a consequence of the transformation of the Congress party after the split of 1969, when the Congress (I) emerged as the victorious heir of the old Indian National Congress that had dominated the country's politics for most of the twentieth century. After having successfully defeated the leading Congressmen in the country in a struggle for national power, Mrs.

Gandhi created a new Congress organization that was personalized and centralized, where there would be no danger that independent provincial party leaders could threaten her position. No internal elections for party officers were held. State party leaders and Congress chief ministers were not elected by local rank and file, but were chosen by the Prime Minister. Loyalty, not local support, became the basis for party leadership at the state level. This new pattern of party organization—so different from the federal/electoral structure of the old Congress—had two consequences for national governance. One was that since state Congress leaders were appointed by and therefore dependent upon the center, they had no independent capacity to deal with local political conflicts, with the result that conflicts within states necessitated intervention by the central leadership. The second consequence was that since the state Congress parties could no longer produce politicians of local popular standing, the Prime Minister's cabinet soon consisted of politicians without a political base of their own. No one could threaten the Prime Minister, but there was also no one in a position to be her successor. In the 1970s a few senior Congress politicians remained with Mrs. Gandhi, but even these drifted away when the Emergency was ended and Mrs. Gandhi, her son Sanjay, and the Congress party were rebuked by the electorate in the parliamentary elections of 1977.

The Congress (I) that was returned to power in 1980 was the party, as one wag put it, of one-and-a-half leaders. Sanjay was the chosen successor simply because there was no alternative leader, and the rank and file of the party and the members of Parliament consisted of careerists and loyalists—loyalists not to the party but to its leader. With Sanjay's death, Mrs. Gandhi and the party needed Rajiv Gandhi.

For a little over three years Rajiv Gandhi was tutored by his mother. In February 1983 Indira Gandhi appointed Rajiv secretary of the Congress (I). As party secretary his style was hardly different from that of his mother. Under his mother's guidance he sought to bring down the handful of opposition party state governments. By providing support to dissident elements, he attempted to undermine the Janata government in Karnataka, the Telugu Desam government in Andhra, the Sikkim Sangram Parishad government in Sikkim, and the National Conference government of Farooq Abdullah in Kashmir. It was also reported that Rajiv encouraged Jarnail Singh Bhindranwale, the militant Sikh priest whose call for the creation of an independent Sikh state, Khalistan, was dividing the Akali Dal. Rajiv's major political contribution as Congress party secretary was thus to support the

Prime Minister's efforts to weaken those opposition parties that had strong local support in the states. Nonetheless, Rajiv retained a reputation for personal integrity. He was not tainted by any financial scandals, nor was he regarded as an aggressive and domineering person, as was his younger brother. His close friends were not politicians but classmates from the Doon School, an elite private school located in the hill-station of Dehra Dun. They were private businessmen, managers in multinational corporations, advertising executives, people with managerial and (like himself), technical training. (Rajiv studied engineering at the University of Cambridge, though he did not earn a degree).

Within hours of Mrs. Gandhi's assassination on October 31, 1984, the Congress leadership chose Rajiv Gandhi, then age 40, as her successor. On November 12 he was unanimously named president of the Congress (I), and the following day he announced that parliamentary elections would be held in late December. While *gharibi hatao* ('abolish poverty') was Mrs. Gandhi's theme in the parliamentary elections of 1971, 'restore democracy' was the election theme of the victorious Janata party in 1977, and 'elect a government that works' was Mrs. Gandhi's theme in 1980, Rajiv's theme was 'national unity', a slogan translated by many Hindu nationalists into *desh bachao* ('save the motherland'). In the campaign that ensued, Rajiv warned that the country was in danger, that national unity was threatened not only by the Sikh militants and the Akali Dal, but by the opposition parties which, he asserted, had endorsed the secessionist Anandpur Sahib resolution of the Akali Dal. (The opposition parties, it should be noted, had not endorsed the resolution, nor was the resolution secessionist.) Rajiv thus tarred the opposition with the brush of anti-nationalism. His much-quoted comment that 'when the tree falls the ground will tremble' seemed to provide a justification for the Hindu attacks against Sikhs in New Delhi in the days following his mother's assassination.

The Congress (I) was re-elected with a record 401 seats out of the 515 for which polling took place—the largest parliamentary victory in India's history. In the months following his victory, Rajiv Gandhi seemed to do everything right, winning support from the press, the business community, the Congress party workers, and even, grudgingly, from opposition leaders who were earlier offended by his campaign tactics. He took on the two major political problems left unsolved by his mother: Sikh militancy in Punjab, and the agitation in Assam against illegal migrants from Bangladesh. He signed 'accords' with the leaders of the two movements. In Punjab the Prime Minister agreed to transfer Chandigarh, the joint capital of Punjab and Haryana, to the exclusive control of Punjab in return for the transfer of a number of Hindi-speaking villages to Haryana. That, along with a commitment to adjudicate the dispute over the sharing of river waters between Punjab and Haryana, and the rehabilitation of Sikhs who had been discharged from the military after the government's attack against the Golden Temple, led the Akali Dal to renounce the demand for Khalistan and agree to take part in new state elections.

In Assam an agreement was reached to close the international borders, to grant citizenship to those who illegally entered the state before 1967, to delete from the electoral rolls those who had entered between 1967 and 1971, and to expel those who entered after March 1971. The Assam leadership in return agreed to end their agitation and to take part in state elections. For appearing to bring about a settlement on these two issues where his mother had failed, Rajiv Gandhi was hailed by the press, by his own party, and even by most opposition leaders for his healing skills. When the two states elected opposition parties which then became responsible for restoring order within the states, Rajiv was praised for putting the needs of the country over those of his own party.

Rajiv was also admired for his new economic policies. Within months after taking office, the Prime Minister announced new policies to accelerate India's slow industrial growth—liberalizing imports, providing new incentives for exports, permitting the import of technologies, encouraging foreign investment through joint ventures, reducing taxes, and de-regulating the economy so as to make it more competitive. Liberally-oriented economists and administrators were placed in charge of the Planning Commission, the Finance Ministry, and in other key economic positions.

Rajiv also promised to restructure the Congress (I), to hold party elections for the first time in fifteen years, and to encourage a new younger leadership to take responsibility in the states and in the central government. He appointed a number of young MPs as junior ministers. An Anti-Defection Bill was introduced to discourage elected members of Parliament and state assemblies from threatening to bring down governments in order to improve their own chances of becoming ministers. At the Congress party's centenary celebration in 1985 he criticized the party for its corruption, for its self-seeking leadership, and for its failure to attract new talent. The Prime Minister's style was decidedly anti-political and managerial. He spoke of making the Indian government 'work faster' and in an uncharacteristic rhetorical flourish, promised to lead India into the twenty-first century.

Rajiv Gandhi's new approach, and his willingness to take a fresh look at old problems, aroused the hopes of India's large middle class and received enthusiastic support from India's business community and from the press. His youthfulness, his managerial style, his modern attitude toward technology as manifested by his eagerness to expand India's computer industry, his reputation for personal integrity ('Mr Clean'), and his contempt for old-style politicians pleased India's large modern urban middle class who had become disheartened by the slow pace of change, the rising tide of violence, the inefficiency of government, and the absence of political leadership. Expectations were so high that in early 1986 Rajiv Gandhi warned an interviewer with the influential magazine *India Today* that 'the euphoria has to stop.'

It did. Rajiv Gandhi's second year as Prime Minister was marked by disillusionment. His effort to work with the moderate Sikh leadership in the Akali Dal against the militants, did not bring an end to terrorism. The Punjab accord itself was not implemented as a result of a controversy over the territorial transfer from Haryana to Punjab in return for Chandigarh. There was also much criticism in Punjab of the government's failure to take action against individuals accused of killing Sikhs during the Delhi riots following Mrs. Gandhi's assassination. Terrorist attacks were resumed in Punjab, followed by retaliation against innocent Sikhs in Delhi by Hindu militants. In Assam, state government leaders expressed their anger at what they regarded as the failure of the central government to remove illegal migrants. By the end of 1986 there were threats of renewed agitations against the central government. In both Assam and Punjab it was clear that Rajiv could not rely upon his subordinates or upon local leaders for follow-up actions to implement the agreements.

Elsewhere in the country, violence erupted among a number of linguistic, caste, and religious communities. In Gujarat and in Andhra, 'backward' castes demanded reservations comparable to those given to the ex-untouchables for admission into colleges and into government employment and were opposed by the upper or 'forward' castes; in Gujarat, there were communal clashes between Hindus and Muslims; in northern West Bengal a militant party of Nepalis demanded a separate state of Gorkhaland; in Goa a demand was raised for the creation of a Konkani-speaking state; in Tripura militant tribals clashed with Bengalis; and throughout northern India Muslims agitated against two court decisions—one to subject Muslim divorcees to the civil law of alimony rather than to Muslim law, and another to give Hindus repossession of a shrine regarded by Muslims as a mosque.

Not only had the Prime Minister not fared well in reducing the level of violence in the country, but, noted his critics, his new economic policy was faltering. Deficit financing increased, the trade deficit worsened, exports failed to grow, many industries were threatened by import liberalization, there was a drop in the output of capital goods industries, and industrial growth was slower than anticipated. The business community itself was divided in its assessment of the new policy, and with few exceptions the country's economists were critical.

The Prime Minister, initially praised for his openness, was now criticized for his lack of accessibility. While he appeared daily on national television, giving the appearance of accessibility, the reality was that he rarely met with senior Congress politicians, cabinet positions were frequently reshuffled, signifying his lack of confidence in his own party, and for advice he fell back upon a small number of bureaucrats and personal friends. The result was that all too often the Prime Minister made hasty and politically unwise decisions or issued statements that were politically inept. A decision in early 1986, for example, to sharply increase petroleum and kerosene prices—at a time when international prices were declining—simultaneously antagonized the middle classes and the poor. After a sharp popular reaction, and opposition from senior figures in the Congress party, the Prime Minister hastily reversed the decision.

Some of the criticism of Rajiv Gandhi can be regarded as the inevitable aftermath of a period of excessive euphoria and unrealistic expectations. But some of the criticism represented greater articulateness on the part of Rajiv Gandhi's leftist critics opposed to economic liberalization, and rightist critics opposed to his accommodative attitude toward linguistic and religious demands. Both sets of critics are advocates of a stronger state—the former to manage the economy and to give the government a stronger role over the private sector, and the latter to strengthen state authority against what Indian nationalists call 'fissiparous' forces. To the critics of both the left and right, the Indian state is under siege and the Prime Minister has either failed to meet the challenge or, worse, pursued policies that weaken the Indian state.

Rajiv Gandhi and the Crisis of the Indian State

Rajiv Gandhi assumed the office of Prime Minister at a time when the capacity of the Indian state to perform three tasks had seriously eroded: to maintain law and order in a sharply divided society; to play a positive role in facilitating economic growth in an economy with a high saving rate, skilled managerial and technical personnel, and promising entrepreneurial talent; and to cope with an uncertain international security environment.

Indira Gandhi's assassination was part of a larger pattern of growing violence directed by various groups against one another and against the Indian state. Many of the policies adopted earlier by the Indian government for managing social conflict that had worked reasonably well in the past no longer worked, and the coercive institutions of the state—the police, the paramilitary, the intelligence services, and the military—were themselves weakened. The pace of industrial growth, low from the mid sixties till the late seventies—especially when compared with the dynamic economies of East Asia—picked up after 1980, but the state sector remained a drag on the economy. Power and transport, both public sector industries, had failed to keep pace with the needs of the economy. Public sector steel was inefficient and overpriced. The state-run capital goods industry was not competitive and its high cost reduced the efficiency of the consumer goods sector.

India's security environment had also deteriorated. Pakistan's acquisition of military equipment from the United States, the possibility that Pakistan was developing nuclear capabilities, the continued border dispute with China, the strained relationship with Sri Lanka over that country's ethnic conflicts, and the presence of Soviet forces in Afghanistan, all presented new security challenges to the Indian government. Moreover, India's relationship with her neighbors now spilled over into India's domestic politics. The ethnic conflict in Sri Lanka affected India's own Tamil population and the central government's relationship with Tamil Nadu. The decision of the Government of India to grant statehood to the union territory of Arunachal Pradesh was denounced by the People's Republic of China, since the territory was disputed. The Indian government charged the government of Pakistan with abetting Sikh terrorists and found itself faced with illegal migrants from Bangladesh in Assam, refugees from the Chittagong Hill Tracts, and armed tribals in Tripura using Bangladesh as their sanctuary.

Then there was the crisis of the Congress party. Though the Congress won an overwhelming majority in the parliamentary elections in late 1984, the party itself remained organizationally weak in the states. In 1985 the Congress lost the state assembly elections in the Punjab to the Akali Dal, in Assam to the Ahom Gana Parishad, in Sikkim to the Sikkim Sangram Parishad, in Karnataka to the Janata party, and in Andhra Pradesh to the Telugu Desam. Since the Congress had been defeated earlier in West Bengal and Tamil Nadu, by the end of 1985 the party was largely in control only in the states of central and northern India: Bihar, Gujarat, Haryana, Himachal Pradesh, Madhya Pradesh, Maharashtra, Orissa, Rajasthan, and Uttar Pradesh. In the assembly elections in early 1987, a Congress-coalition government in Kerala was defeated, and the Congress failed to defeat the governing CPM government in West Bengal. The Congress had become the party of the Hindi heartland and its nearby neighbors, while the opposition parties were in control of most of the states in the geographic periphery. Moreover, a mid-1987 defeat in Haryana by the Lok Dal cast a dark shadow over the Congress position in the Hindi region.

A review of Rajiv Gandhi's attempts to deal with the problems of internal order, rejuvenate the economy, shape the country's foreign policy, and restructure the party not only provides us with an opportunity to assess his personal leadership, but it also enables us to consider the kinds of constraints upon the Prime Minister and the pressures he faces to accommodate to the realities of the Indian state, the polity, and society.

Confronting Violent Social Conflict

Not since the mid-fifties has any Prime Minister of India been faced with such geographically diverse and acutely violent social conflicts as those faced by Rajiv Gandhi: the Sikhs in Punjab, conflicts in the tribal areas of Mizoram, Tripura and elsewhere in the northeast, caste conflicts in Andhra and Gujarat, language conflicts in Goa and Tamil Nadu, unrest in Assam, demands by Nepalis in north Bengal, and Hindu-Muslim clashes in Uttar Pradesh and in other states of northern India. If similar social conflicts were managed more effectively in the 1950s, it was because Prime Minister Jawaharlal Nehru could rely upon several well-regarded national and regional Congress party leaders to serve as mediators, the police were more disciplined and less politicized, and conflicts within states and between the states and the central government could often be accommodated within the Congress party itself. In addition, conflicts were farther away from the borders, and thus were less affected by the policies of neighboring states, and arms for militants were not so readily available.

Central government policies have largely been reactive: to wait until the movements develop, to allow ethnic conflicts to grow, and then to accommodate them. Rajiv was left with a legacy of several ethnic conflicts, especially in Punjab, Assam, and Mizoram, while several new conflicts erupted shortly after he became Prime Minister. He has, in the main, taken an accommodative stance, with mixed results.

The 'accord' signed in 1985 by Rajiv Gandhi and the Sikh leader Sant Harchand Singh Longowal (who was subsequently assassinated) failed to end violence in Punjab. Throughout 1986 Sikh terrorist attacks against government officials, Hindus, and moderate Sikhs continued. Assassination attempts against both the head of the police and the chief minister failed, but the former chief of the Indian Army was slain. Random attacks against Hindus led to counter-attacks against Sikhs in Delhi, further embittering the Sikh community. For some time the Prime Minister continued to support the Akali Dal government, though the Akali Dal was divided and opponents of Chief Minister Surjit Singh Barnala won control of the Sikh Gurdwara Committees, some of which were known to finance the terrorists. The Prime Minister subsequently concluded that the state should be placed under the direct rule of the center so as to enable the police to take a firmer position in dealing with the militants. But by the end of 1987 the problem seemed no closer to solution. Terrorist violence continued, directed as much against Sikh moderates as against Hindus, while the dispute over Chandigarh remained unresolved. Large sections of the Sikh community remained alienated, many Hindus were angry at the central government for its failure to re-establish order, and Rajiv's stature as a political problem-solver declined.

The violence in India's northeast—in Assam, Tripura, north Bengal, and along the borders of the Chittagong Hill Tracts—though unrelated to Punjab, is also in states where terrorists can readily seek sanctuary across an international border and where it is difficult for the government to control the flow of arms. Rajiv successfully negotiated a settlement with the rebels in the northeastern tribal state of Mizoram, statehood was granted, elections were held, and Laldenga, leader of the Mizo insurgency, was made Chief Minister. In north Bengal the conflict centers around the demand by Nepali migrants for a state of their own, Gorkhaland, independent of West Bengal. Though the movement is armed the Prime Minister declared that it was not 'anti-national.' He charged that the neglect of the area by the state government had fueled the Gorkhaland agitation, a statement regarded as an attempt to erode support for the CPM government of West Bengal before the forthcoming state assembly elections. In a speech in Darjeeling, the Prime Minister subsequently declared his opposition to the creation of a separate state of Gorkhaland. He also asserted, probably incorrectly, that the India-Nepal treaty of 1950 prohibited the Indian government from granting citizenship to Nepalis who entered India after the treaty was signed. The obvious conclusion is that large numbers of non-citizen Nepalis could have no voice in the politics of the state—a conclusion that seemed likely to further fuel the agitation. The Prime Minister also expressed his opposition to the breakup of the Indian states into smaller units and said that it had been a mistake to reorganize the Indians states along linguistic lines in the 1950s. It was not clear whether the Prime Minister was enunciating a new national policy intended to warn linguistic, tribal, and sub-regional groups that claims for statehood within the Indian union would henceforth be rejected, or whether this was a casual remark, intended to reinforce his opposition to the claim for Gorkhaland.

Another major social conflict erupted in 1986 in the state of Andhra. Violence broke out after the state government extended reservations for college admissions and jobs in the state government to the backward castes. A cycle of agitations broke out, first by upper caste students who protested the reservations, then by the backward castes after the Chief Minister, forced by the courts, gave in. Because the agitation on reservations was a problem for the opposition state government, the Prime Minister chose to remain aloof from the controversy, though a year earlier a similar dispute in Gujarat had led him to replace the Congress Chief Minister who had initiated reservations for the backward castes. At that time the Prime Minister had suggested that a national policy was needed on the backward caste reservation issue. However thus far none has been suggested.

In the case of reservations what was at issue was whether the state should ensure to all economically and socially subordinate groups a position in the modern sector, especially in higher education and in state employment, proportionate to their numerical place in society. A dispute also arose between Hindus and Muslims on whether there should be a uniform personal law, guided by some conception of justice and equity, that would be applicable to all religious communities irrespective of their traditions of personal law. In this dispute, precipitated by a court case involving a Muslim woman seeking alimony from her husband in accordance with secular rather than religious law, the Prime Minister chose to support legislation enabling the Muslim community to follow its religious law with respect to marriage, divorce and other personal matters. In his effort to retain Muslim political support the Prime Minister encountered opposition from the women's movement, from the secular middle classes, and from many Hindus.

The Indian government's policies toward demands by caste, linguistic, religious, and tribal groups has generally been guided by the notion that within limits the state should be accommodative. India is, of course, more than a country; it is a civilization with a variety of religions, tribes, languages, and a complex hierarchical caste system. Identities are fluid, shaped in part by birth, but often by political circumstances, by acts of government, and by forces of social change such as education, migration, and economic competition. Indians tend to regard society as autonomous of the state, and they adhere to the view that the state should not seek to remake identities but rather should create state structures and policies that suit the variegated identities that make up India. The creation of reservations, the formation of linguistic states, the use of the mother tongue in education, and the recognition of community personal law, are all expressions of this view.

But many of the policies adopted earlier to accommodate ethnic demands no longer mitigate social conflict. Resentment at reservations has grown. A large middle class is uncomfortable with the notion of religious personal law. State governments are now unwilling to allow themselves to be fragmented by tribal, linguistic and sub-regional demands and the Prime Minister himself, as we have noted, fears that by acceding to the demands of the Nepalis and other groups there would be no end to the process of state formation.

Moreover, what has also made ethnic conflict more unmanageable in recent years is that the claims of one community are now increasingly resisted by others, making it difficult for government to accommodate demands by mobilized groups without taking into account the

reactions of other mobilized groups. To transfer the capital city of Chandigarh to the Punjab, for example, without some territorial concession to Haryana, is a political risk for the governing Congress party. The further partitioning of states is unpopular, though there are some who argue that India might be better off with a larger number of smaller states.

In response to growing and often violent group identity demands, Rajiv Gandhi has taken a piecemeal approach: to deal with each demand on its own, to be accommodative to group claims where possible, to postpone action when contending groups make conflicting claims, to use the police and paramilitary forces, rather than the military, and to rely upon advisors within the Prime Minister's secretariat rather than upon state and local political leaders. There is no conceptual framework to his approach, nor does there appear to be any attention to the broader policy issues raised in the individual agitations. The issues, for example, of whether states should be made smaller or existing boundaries kept intact, whether group reservations for specified tribes and castes should be reconsidered, whether there should be a uniform code for personal law, and how the laws of citizenship should be applied to migrants from Bangladesh and Nepal, have received little attention. The result is that the Prime Minister's statements often lack consistency and it is difficult for groups and individuals to anticipate what the center's policy response to their claims will be—a situation conducive to extreme demands and popular agitations.

Party Reform and Cabinet Politics

Rajiv's distaste for politics and politicians was articulated in a remarkable speech commemorating the centenary of the Congress party in Bombay in December 1985. Sounding more like a leader of the opposition than of the Congress, he denounced the Congress 'power brokers,' as he called them, 'who dispense patronage to convert a mass movement into a feudal oligarchy' and the Congress party bosses 'who thrive on the slogans of caste and religion.' Rajiv promised to reform the party and to bring in a new breed of politicians. He appointed his close political associate, Arjun Singh, as the party vice-president, along with several new party general secretaries who were charged with the mission of reorganizing the party. New members were to be recruited into the party, scrutiny committees were to be appointed to verify party membership lists, and elections for local Congress committees—the first since 1969—were promised. In an effort to maintain contact between the party and the electorate, the party's mass organizations—the Youth Congress, the Mahila (Women's) Congress, and the Seva Dal (Service Society)—were to be strengthened.

Nearly three years later, little had been accomplished. The mass organizations remained ineffective. Party elections were postponed after Rajiv Gandhi's advisors warned that bogus memberships would enable the very power brokers to win elections whom the Prime Minister hoped to check. Though the Prime Minister said he welcomed criticism within the party, Pranab Mukherjee, onetime Finance Minister and a leader of an Indira Gandhi dissident faction within the Congress, was expelled, while the All India Congress (I) Committee's octogenarian Working President, Kamalapati Tripathi, was forced to step down after he expressed sympathy for the dissidents. V.P. Singh, his Finance and then Defense Minister, and Arun Nehru, Minister for Internal Security, were forced out of the government and then from the party.

In the absence of independent leaders within the party, Rajiv continued to maintain centralized control. He seemed to be the only significant voice that mattered in the selection of Congress candidates for the Rajya Sabha elections. Rajiv's preferences, rather than those of state assemblies and state Congress leaders, determined the choice of chief ministers in a number of key states. Presidents of the Pradesh Congress Committees were changed frequently by the Prime Minister or his lieutenants. But the newer politicians appointed by the Prime Minister were unable to use the traditional patronage machine, since local party bosses retained their influence within the bureaucracy. Nor did the chief ministers, even those appointed by Rajiv, have easy access to the Prime Minister.

In short, Rajiv has not succeeded in creating a new party leadership, while at the same time the older party workers are disgruntled. Congress leaders in the states remain weak because of their dependence upon the center and are, therefore, highly vulnerable to revolts from dissident factions within the party. Moreover, the failure thus far of Rajiv Gandhi to translate his victory in the parliamentary elections of 1984 and the state assembly victories in early 1985 into electoral victories in state elections thereafter, reduces his capacity to cope with dissident Congress factions in the state organizations.

Cabinet appointees have not fared well at the hands of the Prime Minister. There were major cabinet reshuffles in 1985, two major cabinet reshuffles in 1986, and still others in 1987. The influential P.V. Narasimha Rao, the Home Minister, was demoted to the new Human Resources Development Ministry. Three different ministers in succession were appointed to run External Affairs. Arun Nehru, a relative of the Prime Minister and widely regarded as one of the most powerful figures in the government, was dropped as Minister for Internal Security and, as we have noted, subsequently forced out of the government. Arjun Singh was removed as vice president of the Congress (I) and given the portfolio of Minister of Communications. And in early 1987 Rajiv abruptly transferred Raja Vishwanath Pratap Singh, the powerful Finance Minister and architect of the liberalization program, to the Defense Ministry, reportedly because he had zealously cracked down on income tax evaders (though some critics thought the Prime Minister also wanted to remove a potential political rival). Later in the year, V.P. Singh was removed from the government and he, along with Arun Nehru, joined the opposition.

These repeated changes in key portfolios meant that effective power, especially in Home and External Affairs, has been in the hands of bureaucrats and a handful of personal advisors. The Prime Minister has been unable to find political leaders upon whom he can rely, either at the state or cabinet level. Consequently, day to day decisions are largely in the hands of secretaries of ministries and officials within the Prime Minister's own secretariat.

Rajiv made a considerable effort to bring back into the Congress 'non-loyalists' who had deserted Indira Gandhi after the Emergency. In 1986 he successfully persuaded Sharad Pawar, the leader of a Congress opposition group in Maharashtra, to join the Congress (I), and in Kashmir he forged a legislative coalition and electoral alliance with Farooq Abdullah, head of the National Conference in Jammu and Kashmir. While some observers expressed the hope that both men would play a part in rebuilding the Congress, it was more likely that the Prime Minister was primarily concerned with having their support for the Congress parties in Maharashtra and in Kashmir.

Publicists for the Prime Minister sought to give the impression that he is accessible, and that he confers frequently with party leaders, but most observers believe that Rajiv Gandhi's confidants are few in number, that they are confined to a few friends and high government officials, and that no major Congress party leaders or chief ministers are part of his inner circle. In an effort to give the appearance of accessibility, the Prime Minister has re-established the traditional *durbar*, a morning meeting with citizens who make complaints, request favors, or, in the traditional manner, seek the *darshan*, or blessings, of the Prime Minister by being in his presence. The Prime Minister, under close guard because of threats to his life, makes occasional excursions to the countryside or to state capitals, where he often announces that he has allocated sums of money for drought and famine relief. The style is majesterial and the impression is given on Doordarshan, the government controlled television, that the Prime Minister, in his personal capacity, has generously distributed resources to aid the distressed and needy. In a similar vein the Prime Minister sometimes travels to a state capital with a retinue of cabinet members and officials so that decisions can be made on the spot.

Critics of the Prime Minister say that his approach is that of an outsider. His roots are not in the party and he remains contemptuous of most politicians, including members of his own party. He is only at ease with a handful of old friends, those he knew before he became Prime Minister, and who have become ministers, members of parliament, and party officials only since he himself entered politics.

Rajiv's impatience with politicians has been extended to the bureaucracy as well. Secretaries of ministries are reportedly chastized in the presence of others, though traditionally Prime Ministers have treated senior civil servants with considerable respect. A particularly egregious episode occurred in early 1987 when the Prime Minister in a casual comment at a news conference dismissed the well-regarded Foreign Secretary, A.P. Venkateswaran, without prior notice. In a rare response, the Indian Foreign Service Association criticized the Prime Minister, charging that his action had undermined the morale of the entire service. The effect of the incident was to further isolate the Prime Minister and to undermine his support from within the government.

The Foreign Policy of Rajiv Gandhi

In 1985 when Rajiv Gandhi spoke of improving relations with China, the United States, and Pakistan, critics warned that he would endanger India's traditional close ties with the Soviet Union. Although he had some support for his new foreign policy thrusts from within the Ministry of External Affairs (especially from those who sought to give priority to an improvement in India's relations with its neighbors), there was clearly little support for any fundamental strategic re-alignments. By 1986 it was clear that in the area of foreign policy Rajiv had decided to adhere closely to the policies of his predecessors, that he was persuaded by his foreign policy advisors that the military relationship between Pakistan and the United States precluded any significant change in relationship with either country, that defusing China's antagonism toward India by border concessions was politic-ally too risky, and that on balance the close relationship with the Soviet Union was a beneficial one for India.

Rajiv Gandhi spent a great deal of time in 1986 on trips abroad, meeting with foreign leaders and making pronouncements on foreign affairs. He went to Sweden for Olof Palme's funeral in March, the frontline states bordering South Africa in May, Mauritius in July, the Commonwealth meeting in England in August, a six-nation meeting on nuclear disarmament in Ixtapa, Mexico, also in August, the Non Aligned Movement (NAM) summit at Harare, Zimbabwe, in Sep-tember, and Indonesia, Australia, New Zealand, and Thailand in October. As chairman of the NAM the Prime Minister projected India—and himself—as a leading supporter of the anti-apartheid struggle in South Africa and as an advocate of sanctions. He also actively supported proposals for superpower nuclear disarmament, a moratorium on nuclear testing, a test ban verification, an end to the U.S. strategic defence initiative, the dismantling of the U.S. bases at Diego Garcia, and making the Indian Ocean 'a zone of peace.'

The Prime Minister welcomed a number of foreign leaders to India, but no visit received greater acclaim or was accompanied by more euphoria than that of Soviet leader Gorbachev in November 1986. There were extensive closed discussions between the two leaders, a joint statement which indicated a similar outlook by them on inter-national issues, a commitment by the Soviet Union to provide more than $1.5 billion in credit, an agreement to significantly expand Indo-

Soviet trade, and a Soviet offer to build a space center in India. In return Rajiv Gandhi endorsed the Soviet position on arms control and disarmament at the Reykjavik summit, and reconfirmed the 1971 Indo-Soviet treaty of Peace and Friendship. The meeting highlighted the fact that the Soviet Union continues to be regarded by Indian leaders as India's only significant reliable friend and that the Soviet leader accords Rajiv the status of a world leader. These ties were further reconfirmed on a return visit by Rajiv Gandhi to Moscow to commemorate the opening of the Festival of India in the Soviet Union.

Thus the Prime Minister reiterated continuity in two elements of Indian foreign policy: India's close association with the Soviet Union, and its role as a leader of the non-aligned movement. What was played down was Rajiv's earlier hopes to improve relations with India's regional neighbors, with China, and with the United States.

The thaw that had begun in relations with Pakistan in 1985 was reversed in 1986. The major problems, from India's point of view, were alleged Pakistani support to Sikh extremists, indications of progress in Pakistan toward acquisition of nuclear weapons capability, the prospect that Pakistan would purchase airborne warning and control systems (AWACs), in addition to F 16s, from the United States, and purported Pakistan support for the Sri Lankan government's efforts to use military force against the Tamils. The handling by Pakistan of a highjacked Pan American plane carrying large numbers of Indians, led Rajiv Gandhi to sharply criticize the Pakistan government. A number of proposals raised in 1985—President Zia's offer of a no-war pact and Rajiv's counter proposal of a friendship pact—floundered in 1986.

Although a memorandum of understanding concerning the transfer of technology was signed by the United States and India, and the U.S. government agreed to sell India engines and possibly other technology for light combat aircraft and a supercomputer, and there was a significant increase in the number of joint ventures between Indian and American businessmen, any improvement in U.S.-Indian relations could, at best, be described as marginal. The Indian government repeated its concern at the flow of arms to Pakistan, pressed the United States to take more forceful measures to halt Pakistan's nuclear program, continued to be publicly passive on the Soviet presence in Afghanistan, and criticized the United States for its attack against Libya.

Attempts to improve relations with the People's Republic of China were also stalemated. Rajiv Gandhi issued a strong statement opposing any border concessions to China and reacted sharply to the Chinese criticism of the Indian government's decision to declare the disputed union territory of Arunachal Pradesh a state. The appointment of A.P. Venkateswaran, former Ambassador to the PRC and a hardliner on the disputed border question, as Foreign Secretary, was a further demonstration to the Chinese that India had no intention of conceding any of the disputed territory, including territory occupied by the Chinese since 1962. (The subsequent dismissal of the Foreign Secretary was unrelated to his views on China; indeed, there were reports that once he became foreign secretary he was eager to take steps to improve relations with China.) A few foreign policy analysts in India suggested that India needed to rethink its policies toward China, taking into account the possibility either of an improvement in Soviet-Chinese relations, or a settlement between the Soviet Union and Pakistan over Afghanistan. However there was no indication that the Indian government was preparing for any major policy change.

Few foreign policy issues occupied the Prime Minister's attention more in 1986 and especially in 1987 than the crisis in Sri Lanka, as India sought to bring about a resolution of the conflict between the Sri Lankan Tamils and the Sinhalese-dominated Sri Lankan government. India pressed the Sri Lankan government to seek a political solution in the form of some kind of devolution of authority to the Tamils, while at the same time urging the Tamil militants to give up their claim for Eelam, or an independent state. In 1986 the Indian government alleged that the Sri Lankan government was seeking a military solution, and threatened to withdraw India's 'good offices'—with the implication that Indian-armed Tamils working out of Tamil Nadu would escalate their attacks against the Sri Lankan government. The Sri Lankan government subsequently came up with new proposals, including a willingness to create a Tamil province in the north and several provinces (one with a Tamil majority) in the east. Rajiv Gandhi was himself deeply involved in these matters and indicated that if an agreement could be reached between the government of Sri Lanka and the Tamils, the government of India would undertake to ensure its implementation—implying that India would withdraw its support from the militants if they opposed a reasonable settlement.

Failing to reach a settlement, the Sri Lankan government renewed its military attacks against the Tamil militants, but in mid-1987 the Indian government airlifted supplies to besieged Tamil civilians. In July 1987 President Jayawardene, in a stunning reversal of policy, announced major concessions to the Tamils—short of an independent state—and invited the Indian government to send in the army to northern and eastern Sri Lanka to enforce the agreement. The Sri Lankan government had evidently concluded that India's support for the Tamils precluded a military solution, and that the burden of disarming the principal Tamil separatist group, the Liberation Tigers of Tamil Eelam, had best be placed upon the Indian government. An estimated 20,000 Indian troops were sent to Sri Lanka. While the Indian government had anticipated that the Tamil Tigers would voluntarily relinquish their arms, the militants instead turned their fire against the Indians, attacked Tamils who had endorsed the agreement, and sought to force Sinhalese living in the disputed eastern province to flee.

The Indian government now had little choice but to fight the Liberation Tigers and to remain until it had succeeded. What had initially appeared therefore as a triumphant expression of India's regional power and of Rajiv's willingness to exercise it now appeared to be a successful maneuver by the Sri Lankan government to place the burden of dealing with the secessionists upon India. Though criticism of the Prime Minister within Tamil Nadu was muted, especially as Indian soldiers, many of whom are Tamils, were killed by Tamil militants, a prolonged military engagement threatened to undermine his support within Tamil Nadu, as it had already done within the Tamil areas of Sri Lanka. Moreover, the Indian government, having committed itself to enforcing the agreement, was now in no position to walk away from the conflict. Prolonged conflict with the Tamil separatists, disquiet within Tamil Nadu, criticism by Tamil moderates and by Sinhalese for failing to restore order, continued unease by India's neighbors at the use of India's army to deal with the internal affairs of another country, and an image of ineffectiveness, may all lie ahead. Moreover, under the agreement Sri Lanka has reserved the right to demand the withdrawal of Indian forces at any time, and India would find it difficult to reject such a request. A quick military victory and early withdrawal would enhance the Prime Minister's and India's stature, but neither seem likely.

Rajiv Gandhi, the Indian State and the New Economic Policy

It was in economic policy, especially industrial policy, that Rajiv Gandhi in 1985 promised a totally new perspective. To some Indians the new policy represented a continuation of Indira Gandhi's policies, commencing in 1980, to liberalize imports, to others, Rajiv seemed to offer a new view of the role of the state in the economy. To his sympathizers the Prime Minister was trying to come to grips with an industrial structure that had become rigid and inflexible as a consequence of its protection from the competition of the international market and more broadly, from the failure to use market signals to make decisions for the more efficient use of capital resources. The system of industrial licensing gave an assured domestic market to producers, while import controls eliminated the threat of competition from foreign sellers. The public sector was absolved from performing efficiently by a doctrine that emphasized that they had 'social goals,' rather than profit-making, as their objective. Rajiv's new strategy— liberalized imports, greater reliance on market signals, and liberalized rules of entry and expansion, all implied a new recognition that the state should no longer shield industry, public or private, from competition. The Prime Minister did not explicitly articulate the new policy in any systematic fashion, though the specific actions he, his Finance Minister, and the Planning Commission took were consistent with this view.

During Rajiv Gandhi's first year in office the critics of the new policy were relatively quiet, for there was considerable enthusiasm from the business community, the press, much of the middle class, and the international aid community. By 1986 there were many critics. His opponents included a large portion of the economic community committed to socialism and self-reliance, Indian businessmen in protected sectors of the economy, managers of public sector firms, especially those engaged in the production of high-cost capital goods, union leaders in firms in danger of bankruptcy as a result of competition from importers, and most of the bureaucracy engaged in the enforcement of a variety of regulations that gave the bureaucracy the opportunity to extract rents from businessmen seeking licenses. There was also opposition from sections of the Prime Minister's party, loyalists to socialist doctrines who are also financial co-beneficiaries of the system of bureaucratic controls. The academic community was generally critical, reflecting its socialist orientation, but also reflecting the traditional hostility of India's educated classes to the *banias*, the traditional *dhoti*-wearing merchants, or to the new safari-suited manager. And there was opposition from the entire left, charging the Prime Minister with being too concerned with technological modernization aimed at catching up with the developed world, rather than pursuing programs that would cope with the needs of India's poor.

Supporters of the PM's strategy were also critical, but from an entirely different perspective. They were concerned that in practice much of the liberalization had been eroded by the bureaucracy. Though many import items had been placed on Open General License (OGL) and therefore did not require government approval, new tariffs had been imposed on many of these items. Heavy budget deficits were a threat to the new policies, made worse by a $2 billion increase in wages for government employees, major increases in non-plan expenditures, large increases in defense expenditures, and by the Prime Minister's practice of doling out money to some of the states for political reasons. Raids on prominent businessmen, launched by the Finance Minister, presumably with the approval of the Prime Minister, alarmed the business community. But most disturbing to some sections of the business community was that the bureaucracy had delayed implementing many of the Prime Minister's proposals for de-regulation, and had found new ways to prevent the de-control of the private sector. The number of clearances has only been marginally reduced and the bureaucracy continues to have extraordinary discretionary powers that are used to protect some sections of the business community while limiting others. Clearances still take months, even years, and new investments by Indian businessmen and by foreign investors move slowly. Particularly notorious has been the Chief Controller of Imports and Exports in New Delhi, an office that can and has effectively undercut many of the Prime Minister's liberalization policies. Moreover, many foreign collaborations approved by the government never move into production, and a host of obstacles impede the implementation of approved projects. Supporters of the Prime Minister's overall strategy also fear that the decline in foreign exchange reserves, the slow pace with which exports are growing, and protests from India's capital goods sector may lead the government to further slow the process of liberalization.

It was not clear which group would have the greater influence on the Prime Minister. Though he seemed personally committed to continued liberalization, his capacity to make the bureaucracy implement his policies seem limited. A century earlier British officials had complained that their policies were undermined by lower level Indian officials who had learned to use bureaucratic rules to sabotage policies that did not suit their interests or those outside the bureaucracy with whom they were aligned. Without good staff work, effective support from cabinet members, and strong intervention by the Prime Minister himself, many of the proposed reforms have languished, effectively sabotaged by bureaucrats, public sector managers, and private businessmen who fear the competition that comes with liberalization and the loss of state protection. In India, even more so than elsewhere, the politics of policy making is often less critical than the politics of policy implementation: those who are too weak to affect the former can often decisively influence the latter.

The dismissal of V.P. Singh as Finance Minister, following his aggressive campaign against tax evasion by the business community, revealed that some sections of the business community were unwilling to pay the price of tax enforcement. With the dismissal of the Finance Minister, and the absence of any indication that the new policies were being vigorously implemented, it was increasingly evident that the Prime Minister's efforts to liberalize, to expand trade, and to make the Indian economy more competitive at home and abroad were moving slowly, if at all. The one bright spot was that in 1986–87 industrial growth had increased to 7.5 percent, well above the average growth rate of the seventies.

Conclusion: Is India an Immobilized Democratic/Bureaucratic State?

Midway through Rajiv Gandhi's term as Prime Minister, any assessment should begin with a recognition that Rajiv has substantially improved the tone of Indian political life. He may not have the enthusiastic loyal supporters of his predecessor, but nor does he have the bitter enemies. He is not a divisive person—what he has done and said since he became Prime Minister has not thus far sharply divided the country. He is admired for his reasonableness, his absence of deviousness, and his willingness to meet with critics. Recent reports of Swiss accounts held by the brother of one of his closest friends, and reports of illegal payments by a Swedish arms manufacturer to unnamed Indian officials, have cast a shadow on his reputation for personal honesty. But it should be noted that as yet no evidence has been produced to implicate the Prime Minister.

In spite of the violence throughout the country, the Prime Minister has been cautious in the use of the coercive powers of the state. He has not been a passive leader: he has put forth a set of goals that have won considerable popular approval and in his first year in office he was reasonably innovative in suggesting new policies.

And yet, halfway through his five-year term as Prime Minister, Rajiv Gandhi has clearly faltered in each of his major initiatives. His accommodative approach to the demands of religious minorities and to the anxieties of linguistic and tribal communities has not resulted in an abatement of violence and conflict. His commitment to economic liberalization—a codeword for policies intended to reduce controls and to facilitate foreign trade—has been stymied by a coalition of public sector managers, government bureaucrats, and business executives in protected sectors of the economy. His goal of restructuring the Congress party to make it more democratic and to attract younger people has been held back by his own fear that the 'power brokers' would wrest the party from his control. And his desire to improve relations with India's regional neighbors, with China, and with the United States has made little progress, constrained partly by the actions of others, partly by the Indian foreign policy establishment, and partly by domestic political considerations.

Powerful interests within the state bureaucracy and public sector enterprises, a foreign policy establishment that remains cautious and reactive, the inheritance of a weak party organization, and the international environment have thus combined to frustrate a young and politically inexperienced Prime Minister at every turn. His first months in office were a period of enunciating new directions, a heady time both for himself and for the country as a whole. The country, certainly the middle class, the business community and the media, were pleased to have a new Prime Minister who was self-confident, open and innovative. His overall perspective that the state, once regarded as a locomotive of change, had itself become an impediment to change, won a sympathetic hearing from much of the new middle classes. But in his second year in office Rajiv Gandhi was confronted with the hard reality of implementing the new policies. At critical stages he faltered: he hesitated to implement the Punjab accord; he failed to follow up his economic reforms by actually removing power from the hands of bureaucrats; he cancelled the Congress party elections; he did not pursue the option of policy changes toward Pakistan and China. Deeply frustrated, he snaps at civil servants, publicly quarrels with the President of India, becomes flip and unnecessarily combative in answering questions in Parliament, and is dismissive of both bureaucrats and politicians. And like Mrs. Gandhi he and his backers have sought to explain away failures by reference to a 'foreign hand' that sought to destabilize India—a charge that strained relations with the United States and which was mocked by the press and by his opponents. And increasingly he has been blaming the press for his loss of popular support.

Major policy changes invariably create opposition. A political leader initiating new policies needs to build a team with which he can work, and he needs to forge a new coalition from among those who will gain from the new policies. Rajiv mistakenly assumed that his electoral mandate was sufficient for carrying out reforms, forgetting that Mrs. Gandhi's mandate in 1971 and 1972 was followed by political disarray and the declaration of an Emergency in 1975, and that the Janata landslide of 1977 was followed two years later by the fall of the government. The Congress party as presently constituted is too weak and support too fragile for Rajiv Gandhi to be confident that his electoral victories in 1984 mean assured support. Rajiv has not won over the old Congress politicians nor attracted new politicians to his party; he has not built support within the bureaucracy; nor has he been able to elicit popular support for himself. He is no longer a leader more concerned with policy innovation or with aggressively implementing policies than with maintaining his own political position. During the first half of his term in office observers were asking whether he would be able to carry out the reforms he had promised; the question for the remainder of his term is how will the Prime Minister deal with a situation in which his personal political stock is declining, where there is dissension within his own party, and where his party's electoral prospects for the 1989 parliamentary and state assembly elections have fallen. His primary political concerns will be to keep the opposition from uniting while minimizing factional feuding and defections from his own party.

For a brief historical moment there was an opportunity for significant change. That moment appears to have passed.

12

Maintaining India's Democratic Institutions

I

In 1947 the British relinquished power in India, leaving behind a
parliament, a federal structure, an independent judiciary, a nationally
recruited bureaucracy, electoral procedures, a free press, and independent political parties. Today, these institutions and procedures of
governance remain intact—bruised and modified, but intact. Many of
these institutions were assailed and temporarily suspended during the
Emergency, but once again they are functioning. It was neither a
revolutionary upheaval from the masses nor the overthrow of the
government by the opposition that led to the suspension of many of
these institutions in 1975, but the Prime Minister and her closest
advisors who wanted a more 'committed' bureaucracy, a more pliant
judiciary, a more 'responsible' press, a more centralized control, a
quiescent opposition, and an end, at least for a while, of the electoral
process. Indeed, it was the electorate that turned Mrs. Gandhi out in
the elections of 1977, forcing an end to the Emergency, and to which
the present critics of Mrs. Gandhi now turn to seek support for the
preservation of those institutions that are the legacy of a colonial era.
Whatever may happen in the future, the question remains: how does
one explain why India's institutional structure has persisted, and what
does the Indian experience tell us about the adequacy of·theories

This essay first appeared in Peter Lyons and James Manor, eds., *Transfer and
Transformation: Political Institutions in the New Commonwealth, Essays in Honour of
W.H. Morris-Jones*, Leicester University Press, 1983.

propounded to explain the conditions for the preservation of a democratic system?

II

By almost any theory, India in 1947 appeared to be among the least likely country to sustain democratic institutions. At least four theories setting forth the conditions for democracy seemed particularly appropriate for predicting the demise of democratic institutions in India.

The first was a theory of political culture. India's hierarchical social structure, traditions of acquiescence to authority, the expectations of those in authority that deference and obedience would be forthcoming, and the preference for consensus appeared to be an unsuitable political culture and social structure for democratic institutions. In the terminology of Gabriel Almond and Sidney Verba in their classic study, *The Civic Culture*,[1] India's political culture could best be described as a 'parochial subject' political culture, in the process of becoming a 'parochial participant' culture, but it was still far from being the 'civic culture' that democracy required. Another version of the political culture theory was developed by Harry Eckstein, concerned with explaining the variations of political systems within Europe, but which was nonetheless relevant to developing countries. Eckstein argued that congruence in authority patterns as between the institutions of the state and society determined whether a country could or could not sustain stable democratic institutions and procedures. According to Eckstein, it was the congruence of authority patterns in the British family, school, and voluntary institutions with those of the polity which accounted for that system's stability, and it was its incongruence in the case of Weimar Germany that accounted for its breakdown.[2] By analogy, the traditions of hierarchy and authority in India made the soil inappropriate for democratic institutions.

A second theory postulated that social cleavages within India, between Hindus and Muslims, among castes, and especially among linguistic groups, threatened not only democratic institutions but the

---

[1] Gabriel Almond and Sidney Verba, *The Civic Culture*, Princeton, NJ, Princeton University Press, 1963.

[2] Harry Eckstein, *Division and Cohesion in Democracy: A Study of Norway*, Princeton, NJ, Princeton University Press, 1966.